PATRICK DAVIES

THE
GREAT AMERICAN
DELUSION

*The Myths Deceiving America
and Putting the West at Risk*

CARAVAN BOOKS

CARAVAN BOOKS

Published by Caravan Books, 2020

ISBN: 978-1-8382512-0-8

patrickjdavies.com

For mum and dad

Contents

Preface

This book is the result of more than 30 years getting to know America, from my first experiences travelling to the country at the heart of the Cold War when Ronald Reagan and Margaret Thatcher were in power on either side of the Atlantic, to witnessing up close Donald Trump's election as President and the tumultuous first year of his administration.

Most recently, I lived in Washington DC for five years from 2013 as the UK's Deputy Ambassador to the United States. It was a period that included the last years of the Obama administration, the explosive leaks by Edward Snowden from the National Security Agency, the never-ending nightmare of the Syria civil war, Russia's annexation of Crimea and its brutal intervention in Ukraine, the rise of the Islamic State and a growing global cyber threat with Russia blatantly interfering in US and other elections. The same period saw previously unimaginable political upheaval on both sides of the Atlantic. The EU referendum in Britain in 2016 catapulted the country into a morass of political and economic uncertainty. In the US, the election the same year of a property tycoon and reality TV host as president did much the same but with even greater potential impact on the rest of the world.

But my first experience of the US was many years earlier when I won an English Speaking Union student exchange scholarship to America in 1987. Under the ESU programme, I spent a semester at a small, private high school in Pebble Beach, California – a world away from my state comprehensive school in northern England. It was a hugely positive and life-changing experience that almost certainly set me on a path towards an international career. I took classes in American history and literature, was immersed in US culture with a Californian twist and even ended up hosting my own weekly show on the school's FM radio station playing a mix of British and American music to several thousand listeners from Big Sur to Santa Cruz. I travelled widely too, getting my first taste of many parts of the country.

Once in the British Foreign Service, I worked extensively with Americans over more than 20 years. During my first overseas posting to Morocco in the mid 1990s, I joined forces with US colleagues in a concerted push to try to resolve the Western Sahara conflict – one of the UN's longest running peacekeeping missions. Former US Secretary of State, James Baker, was heavily engaged trying to find a way out of years of impasse between Morocco and the Algeria-backed Sahraouian population. As diplomats and allies, we were doing everything we could to support his efforts against significant resistance from Morocco, backed by France. I travelled regularly with my US, German and UN counterparts to the Moroccan-occupied territories of Western Sahara and UN-supported refugee camps in the POLISARIO-controlled desert of southern Algeria. I saw first-hand the hard work, creativity and commitment of American officials trying to bring an end to a conflict that had blighted the lives of tens of thousands of people over two decades.

When back in London in the early 2000s, I was Private Secretary (Deputy Chief of Staff) to two Foreign Secretaries – Robin Cook and then Jack Straw. I was one of the officials in the room during their regular meetings with their US counterparts, Madeleine Albright and

Colin Powell. And I was the guy who often wrote the records of their multiple phone calls at all hours of the day. When I met Colin Powell again in Washington in 2013, it felt remarkably familiar even though it had been ten years since I was listening in to his calls with Jack Straw in the run up to the second Iraq War in 2003.

In my last London-based role before moving to the US to be Deputy Ambassador, I travelled regularly to Washington DC as head of the Foreign Office's Near East and North Africa Department to coordinate the international response to the unfolding crisis in Syria. In partnership with the US we were trying to work out how to bind Russia into a peace process to stop the fighting. We spent many hours constructing sanctions that might get enough international support to be widely implemented and therefore increase the pressure on the Syrian government to come to the negotiating table. We weren't successful. Russia instead chose to step in and support the Assad regime as it went about brutally suppressing dissent. The country quickly descended into a long and deadly civil war. But the experience reinforced my view of the US as a huge force for good in the world, even if it didn't always succeed or get things right.

The only time in my career when I did not work directly with American diplomats was while posted to Iran in 2009-10. The US, understandably, had not had a presence in Tehran since shortly after the Islamic Revolution in 1979 when student supporters of Ayatollah Khomeini stormed the American Embassy and took 53 hostages. The ensuing diplomatic crisis had the world on tenterhooks for more than a year until the Americans were released in January 1981. Thirty years later, the US was still the "Great Satan" to the Iranian Regime and its leaders routinely spouted vitriol about America as the enemy of the Iranian people. So, having an embassy in the Iranian capital and direct diplomatic relations was not an option for the US. Many pro-regime Iranians liked to claim that the British were the brains behind American brawn and a serious threat too. But we were only the "Little Satan" to the Ayatollahs of the Islamic Republic and so we tried to maintain an embassy in the country whenever possible. It was often touch and go with regime-sponsored, petrol-bomb wielding demonstrators regularly outside our gates. But we stayed when we could.

Even being in Tehran did not stop my working with Americans altogether. I simply shared my insights and experiences with US colleagues when I travelled outside the country. The British government wanted its closest ally to have as accurate a picture of developments in Iran as possible. There was always an insatiable appetite in Washington for information from inside the country, particularly as Green Movement demonstrators turned out in their tens of thousands to protest against President Ahmadinejad's stolen re-election in June 2009 and were violently suppressed by a brutal regime fearing a new revolution. We knew too that we could rely on the US to do everything it could to help if things went wrong for our embassy. That is what close allies do.

Amongst all these experiences of working with Americans at home and abroad, I have travelled to almost every corner of the US over more than three decades. As British Deputy Ambassador, when one of my roles was running the UK government's network of offices around the country, I regularly visited our consulates in eight cities from Boston in the north east to Los Angeles in the south west. As a student, I made coast-to-coast trips on Trailways and Greyhound busses during the long university summer holidays. As an adult, I have travelled extensively to the US' vibrant cities and incredible national parks from Maine to New Mexico, Washington state to Florida and almost everything in between. All in all, I have been to more than 40 US states, met Americans from all walks of life and had untold experiences that have shaped my views of the US and its role in the world.

America has been a tremendously important part of my adult life, personally and professionally. It is in my blood unlike almost anywhere else. In many ways, I feel as strongly invested in the country and its future success as I do in my own. It is from this starting point that I decided to write. I was driven by a deep affection for the US. But having got to know the country over several decades and then taking a front row seat on an American political rollercoaster for 5 years, I was left with a deep and growing sense of unease that it risks going off the rails with profound consequences for America itself and for the rest of us.

Some might question why I have not written about the UK as the country grapples with its own identity crisis. Like the US, Britain is increasingly divided and faces its own major political, economic and social challenges. Brexit risks poisoning British politics for decades to come and making the country poorer and more inward looking. Even worse, this now comes on top of the severe economic shock of the coronavirus pandemic. But, the fact is, if the UK were to lose its way, the global impact would be limited. Britain itself may well be severely weakened by Brexit, but the effect on others in the West is unlikely to be significant. The same cannot be said for America. If it is unable to emerge quickly from the crisis that is gripping the country, the impact on the rest of the world will be profound. America still has the economic wealth, military might and soft power to shape the future direction of global events. The UK alone does not.

Above all, I want to see America get back on track so the special relationship between the UK and US which has been so important to our security and prosperity can continue to thrive. But even more importantly, I want to see America maintain its vital role as a beacon of successful, liberal democracy which is critical to the future success of the US itself and to the Western system as a whole. No one in the West, least of all Americans themselves, should want the US to fail.

Introduction

All countries have national myths. They are part of the folklore of every nation and are usually described in inspiring stories or simple sound bites which aim to define a country's national identity and to establish a clear set of values and beliefs for its people.

Over the last few decades, Britain's national myths have included that the UK was a largely benevolent colonial power which brought civilisation, democracy and greater prosperity to many parts of the world – the goddess Britannia as the great provider and protector[1]. It didn't seem to matter that the myth simply airbrushed out the oppression, subjugation and violence of empire. A more recent, and arguably more enduring, British national myth is of a plucky and unbending nation standing alone against Germany in 1940 after most of Europe had fallen to Hitler's war machine[2]. According to the myth, Britain's courage and stubborn resolve allowed the world to re-group and ultimately defeat Nazi tyranny. But the myth adeptly brushes over the role of Britain's huge empire in the UK staying afloat in the early years of the war and the later contributions of the US, Russia and many other nations to Hitler's ultimate defeat.

For France, its national myths centre around the cultural legacy of its language, food and literature. Resistance to foreign influence is an essential part of French national myths too. It's the Gauls heroically fighting the Roman invasion in the 1st century BC as epitomised in the hugely popular Asterix comic books, and it's the French Resistance selflessly challenging Nazi occupation during World War Two eventually leading to France's liberation and de Gaulle's Fifth Republic. In the case of Germany, the east and west developed new, separate national myths in the aftermath of Hitler's defeat. For West Germany they centred around the economic miracle of the country's rapid re-emergence as an industrial power based on hard work, extreme efficiency and good policy. In the DDR, the myths evoked socialist cohesion and the heroism of anti-fascism. After reunification in 1990, the myths had to be adapted again.

In other words, national myths try to capture what it means to be a citizen of any nation in simple, memorable and aspirational terms, often drawing on a perceived golden period of that country's history. They aim to instil a sense of national pride and to encourage certain behaviours that will reinforce feelings of citizenship and nationhood. So, there's nothing necessarily wrong with national myths. They can give people a sense of belonging to a wider community – a common or shared identity. And they can provide a reassuring feeling of permanence or stability in a world that is rapidly changing.

But national myths come with serious risks. By their nature they are an oversimplification of the past, or a rose-tinted view of historical events. They can also be divisive as a country changes and new immigrant communities aren't wrapped up in the traditional mythology that defines a country's citizenship. The myths can easily be manipulated by nationalists to create tension between different groups and neighbouring states. And as countries change, national myths can, in their romanticising of history, conceal serious weaknesses in society – weaknesses which, if not addressed, could undermine the very positive characteristics of the nations the myths describe. Countries fail to challenge or to update their national myths at their peril.

America, like all other nations, has its fair share of national myths. Most are well known. There's the US as a beacon of Western democracy and freedom to which other nations aspire. Then there's the successful melting pot of American society fuelled by waves of immigration. There's the unique opportunity of the American Dream and the US' world-beating capitalist market economy built on the back of dogged hard work and innovation. There's the clear separation of church and state as established by the Founding Fathers. And there's the right to bear arms as a fundamental part of being American, keeping the country safe. Then there are other American national myths about how the country's vibrant media combined with an almost absolute right to the freedom of speech underpins its democracy; how America's model of limited government is the best form of government for economic success; how its healthcare continues to lead the world; and how the greatest threat to the US comes from outside the country in the form of international terrorism.

These national myths about what the US is and what it means to be American are alive and well across the country. They are taken as fact by many Americans and are routinely reinforced by politicians, religious leaders and the media. During election campaigns, candidates for office draw unashamedly on America's national myths to set out how they alone will defend their country's unique strengths once in power or how they will return the US to some golden era when its exceptionalism was unquestioned. When in office, American politicians turn again to the country's national myths to claim how their policies have been successful in making the country even stronger or to win support for reforms which, they argue, will secure America's continued pre-eminence. It is pretty much impossible for anyone in the US to avoid America's exceptionalism narrative drawn from its national myths. It permeates almost everything. The myths are firmly embedded in every part of US society including its popular culture. Country music songs blend romantic nostalgia and rugged patriotism. Disney cartoon heroes defy the odds and improve their lives through honesty, hard work and determination – the animated American Dream. The national myths are a mainstay of US sport too.

Only in America is a 'World Series' a competition just amongst its national teams.

But despite the pervasiveness of US mythology, it is impossible to conclude that the myths genuinely reflect US society in the early part of the 21st century. After five years living and working in the country, it is clear that US national myths are no longer true for large numbers of Americans or, at the very least, are seriously fraying at the edges. The US is facing growing international competition for its claimed exceptionalism too, as established nations innovate and emerging powers strengthen their institutions and become more prosperous and influential on the global stage. In other words, the US' stubborn attachment to its national myths is both concealing serious problems at home and underestimating growing challenges from abroad. It's a heady but dangerous mix.

The US appears particularly prone to myth blindness. The belief in American exceptionalism – that the US has some unique purpose to lead the world as the exemplary free nation – remains strong. In some ways this is perfectly understandable. Few external factors drive Americans to challenge this view. While the US retains its position as the world's superpower and biggest global economy, America's mythological exceptionalism appears to be confirmed by the country's continued preeminent status, whatever the problems at home. The continental scale of the US arguably insulates America from challenge too. Americans are typically less immediately affected by what is happening in the rest of world, much of which is just a long way away across the Atlantic or Pacific oceans. And so, Americans don't routinely compare themselves with others and the myths endure, however flawed.

Perhaps more surprisingly, the belief in American exceptionalism has been largely unwavering over the last few years despite considerable political and economic upheaval. Most Americans would acknowledge a crisis in US politics. Indeed, the airways are filled with highly partisan analysis of the causes of social and economic problems in the US, who is to blame (usually the other party) and how they can be fixed. But few Americans would diagnose a deeper crisis in the US way of life. The national myths persist despite the growing evidence against them.

In the bleak early months of World War Two, Winston Churchill worked tirelessly and sometimes deviously to convince the US to join the war, to help save Europe and protect the freedoms and values of Western democracy from succumbing to Nazi oppression[3]. He deployed various techniques to persuade President Roosevelt to take America into the war against the views of the majority of the American public who did not want to get embroiled in another European conflict after the horrors of the Great War. Churchill wrote frequent personal letters to the President making the case for US intervention and wooed US envoys sent to Britain with exceptional audiences with King George and banquets at Downing Street and his official country residence, Chequers[4]. His quest was eventually successful, aided by the Japanese invasion of Pearl Harbor which brought America into the war late in 1941. What followed was an unprecedented mobilisation of American human capital and industry that helped turn the tide of the war, leading the Allies to victory in 1945.

Nearly 80 years later, the West needs America to mobilise again. But this time the request is not for the US to intervene directly or militarily somewhere in the world in a fight against a fascist or communist enemy to secure the future of Western democracy. Rather it is a call for America to take a hard, dispassionate look at itself, to acknowledge the growing weaknesses in the American system as the US matures as a nation and as competition from other states grows stronger. In essence, it is a call to fight the enemy within, for America to *fix itself* so it can continue to thrive. Only by addressing the growing systemic problems concealed by its national myths will the US be able to maintain its political stability, secure its continued economic success and retain its position as the world's leading superpower. And only then will America continue to be seen as a beacon for others aspiring for democratic freedoms and values which is so essential for the future of the Western system.

No other single country can play the role of 'defender of the West' despite the sometimes lofty claims from the European Union and other individual nations. Only the US has the scale, power and resources to secure the future of the Western system, to influence the course of history by the power of its example, backed by its economic strength and military might. Even the US cannot do this alone as great powers emerge in China and India; it needs to work ever more closely with allies in Europe, Africa and Asia. But whether we like it or not (and many in Europe don't), the future prosperity and the longevity of the West once again depend substantially on the US.

Given the unprecedented political turmoil surrounding the Trump presidency, it would be all too easy to focus on the many specific crises and scandals over the last few years and blame the Trump administration for all America's problems. But the stubborn adherence to America's national myths hides more fundamental flaws that can't be blamed on a single presidency or a single political party. The roots of America's growing political, economic and social problems are wider and more profound than party politics. The issue is not Trump or Obama, Bill Clinton or George W Bush, nor even the Republicans or the Democrats. It goes to the heart of what America is and how America was founded. It begs the question whether the US Constitution that frames the American system remains entirely fit for purpose in a very different world from that of the Founding Fathers. And it demands us to ask whether the US will be able to continue to adapt to a rapidly changing world.

Even before the Trump presidency, the US was struggling through a period of crisis and inertia, fuelled by increasingly destructive partisan politics, growing divisions between different communities across the country and a widening gap between rich and poor. Public faith in politicians and government was at an all-time low well before Donald Trump moved into the White House on Pennsylvania Avenue[5]. Alexis de Tocqueville, the French diplomat and historian who produced the seminal analysis of the US in the 19th century, Democracy in America, said that *"the greatness of America lies not in being more enlightened than any other nation, but rather in her ability to repair her faults"⁶*. The question is whether America is losing the ability to repair itself, blinded by myths of its own exceptionalism. Even when problems are eventually diagnosed – and there are many Americans who see them – entrenched partisanship and the ensuing political gridlock then delays or even scuppers the US' ability to adapt and change. The political crisis in the US arguably makes the myths more attractive too, as people hold onto them even more tightly to retain some hope and stability in an unpredictable and unnerving world. The risk of a negative cycle is real.

Time is no longer on the West's side as the world changes ever more quickly. With emerging powers rising rapidly around the globe, some of whom do not share Western beliefs and values, it is more important than ever to have a strong and successful beacon of Western democracy in the guise of the US. Dictators are increasingly challenging the very essence of Western society too. So, the call for America to *fix itself* today is arguably as urgent as Churchill's appeal for the US to join World War Two as Britain struggled to see off a Nazi invasion in the Battle of Britain. The consequences for the West of the US failing to repair its faults and re-emerging stronger would be grave, even if less immediate.

No one in the West can afford the US to weaken or decline more quickly than it might in the normal course of history. The loss of the US as a strong symbol and defender of Western democracy would have global implications that the West's enemies would quickly seek to exploit. Tensions would grow as malevolent powers would seek to expand their areas of influence and control. The global economy would be hit by falling confidence in America's economic future. And democracy itself would begin to lose its attraction for countries in transition aspiring for a better future.

Britain as America's closest ally would arguably have more to lose than most if the US were to get it wrong. The UK remains closely intertwined with the US politically, economically and culturally. Britain and America's shared history and more recent post-war alliance have created a unique relationship that means the UK is more intimately tied to the success or failure of the US than most other countries. The US and UK armed forces and security agencies work hand in glove to keep Britain, America and their allies safe[7]. British and American businesses have collectively invested more than $1 trillion in each other's economies. More than one million jobs in both the US and UK are the result of investment from the other nation[8]. US and UK academics and researchers collaborate extensively in all fields to make advances to benefit our societies – from science and technology to medicine and the arts and humanities[9]. Both separately and together, Brits and Americans have won more Nobel Prizes than anyone else[10].

The future success of the US is critical to the UK. Despite being in the EU for more than 40 years, the economic and political trends in the UK tend to track the US more closely than Britain's partners in Europe. And as the UK embarks on its own political experiment of leaving the EU, Britain will rely even more heavily on its relationship with America than before. The impact on the UK of a failing or even weakening US would be profound.

In the chapters ahead, I will draw on my experience of the US and additional supporting data to examine America's principal national myths in turn from an outside perspective. I will consider how far the myths now reflect life in the US almost two hundred and fifty years after the country was founded. Where the myths conceal flaws in the US system, I will look at how America could change to secure its continued prosperity and its position as the leading superpower and essential bulwark of Western democracy.

I will argue that the US has reached a point of maturity in its development as a nation that calls for a new approach. Just as private companies have to change as they grow from start-ups to more established businesses and as their environment and competitors change, the US needs to adapt to continue to prosper and even survive in a rapidly changing world. This is not currently happening, or if it is, it is taking place at a glacial pace which leaves the US vulnerable to being overtaken by rapidly emerging powers or global events. And so finally I will consider whether Americans will be able to come together to achieve the reforms necessary to fix the systemic weaknesses concealed by their national myths, or whether growing divisions in US society will put essential change beyond reach before it is too late.

My intention is not to criticise or judge the US in the way that some European commentators like to do with more than a little 'Old World', cultural arrogance. From all my experience of the country, I have come to understand and appreciate America's huge strengths: from its drive and innovation to its remarkable work ethic; from its generosity and openness to all comers to its unbending self-belief that anything is possible combined with an impressive ability to rebound from failure. My intention is rather is to show where the US, from the perspective of a dispassionate outsider and huge advocate for the country, is not always what its national myths would have Americans believe.

Britain like the US can have a tendency to trumpet its own exceptionalism. How else could a small island nation have established a great empire and dominated the world for more than 200 years from the 17th century? But this tendency has not always served Britain well. The self-harming 2016 vote to leave the EU on the back of a romantic notion of Britain's past greatness is but the latest example. I hope the US can avoid going down this same damaging path, both for its own sake and for the West as a whole.

My aim is also to try to help readers understand the current upheaval in the US and what led to the Trump phenomenon. Both have their roots in many Americans feeling left behind or – in other words – the promise of US myths not being fulfilled. I hope I might encourage more debate about America's place in the 21st Century, how best to preserve the essential elements of US society and culture that have propelled the country to the top of the tree, but also how to tackle the growing challenges America is facing which, if not addressed, could derail the US with serious consequences for America and the Western world. Many Americans are increasingly concerned about the future of their country. I hope they will continue to mobilise and work with others to drive change before it is too late.

I don't profess to have unique insights into the US. My conclusions are drawn from my particular experiences in the country which while extensive are not limitless. The closeness of the relationship between Britain and America, our shared history and culture, does give Britons a distinct perspective. We have both the benefit of distance to be able to observe the US more objectively than any national can of his or her own country, but also a deeper familiarity with America than arguably any other country. In many ways, the US is family for the UK. We are personally invested in the country and its success in ways we are not for most other countries. I can only hope that what follows will give some interesting insights and perspectives on what is happening in the US and contribute to the growing debate about how to secure America's future success.

In many ways, America itself – not rising global powers or re-emboldened old empires – is the greatest current threat to the future of the West. Although China and Russia should not be ignored, they do not yet amount to an existential threat to the Western system. It is the deep fault lines emerging in the US – in its politics, society and economy as Americans cling ever more inexplicably to their national myths – which could undermine the very fabric of the country if left unchecked. The potential consequences for the US itself and the West as a whole are grave. And yet many fail to see where the US is heading. It is the Great American Delusion.

Part One

THE MYTHS

"Honesty is the first chapter in the book wisdom".
Thomas Jefferson, 1819[1]

Chapter One

A Model Democracy

Myth number 1 – The US is the most advanced democracy in the world and a beacon for others aspiring to greater freedom.

M any British diplomats arrive in America unwittingly unprepared for the differences between the UK and US democratic systems. I certainly did when I took up my posting to Washington DC, although I never imagined that would be case. I'd spent a good deal of time in the country over the years and almost all my Foreign Office career working closely with American diplomats and other officials. So, I genuinely thought I had a pretty good understanding of how the US worked. It quickly turned out that none of my experiences over almost 30 years had really prepared me for living and working in the US at the centre of American politics and democracy in the nation's capital. The closeness of the UK/US relationship, our shared history and language, tends to lull Brits into a false sense of security. We think we know the US. But the differences can be profound and surprising.

I knew that checks and balances were purposely built into the US Constitution to prevent the tyranny of absolute monarchy from which

America had sought its independence in 1776 – the separation of powers is at the heart of the American model of government. In that sense, the US presidential system was going to be somewhat different from the UK's parliamentary democracy. At the same time, the US was built on British foundations. The US Constitution and Bill of Rights drew inspiration from historic British documents like the Magna Carta. With this history, many American institutions look and feel just like those in Britain, from government agencies to the US court system. So, I expected much to be familiar. I had also seen iconic films like All the President's Men charting Nixon's ignominious downfall over the Watergate scandal and classic TV shows like the West Wing depicting the frenetic daily life of officials in the White House. When put together with my own experiences of America, I genuinely believed the US democratic system wasn't going to be too different from my own. I did expect there to be more money and razzmatazz thrown in having closely followed the great spectacle of a number of US presidential elections. But I rather naively assumed that wouldn't really change the fundamentals.

Arriving at the British Embassy in May 2013, I quickly came face to face with reality. I began to understand the extent of the differences between the UK and US once steeped in the day to day world of Washington politics and by learning on the job how best to get British views across to US government agencies and members of Congress on Capitol Hill. Witnessing first hand a Presidential election playing out over two years was also an essential primer in the Wild West of American politics. And travelling around the country was critical to understanding the balance of power between the state and federal governments and how they interacted. What I learned soon raised questions about just how democratic America really is despite the mythology around the US being the most successful Western democracy and a beacon for those aspiring towards greater political freedom.

The biggest shock was just how far money influences American politics and particularly its elections and quite how much cash is involved. I knew, of course, that there was considerably more money in the US political system than in the UK. That much was obvious. But I hadn't realised quite how much more and what that really meant. The amounts involved are astonishing and the impact more than a little disturbing. Just one Senate race can cost significantly more than a UK general election. In 2015, British political parties and candidates spent £60 million ($78 million) on the parliamentary election which saw David Cameron and his Conservative Party elected with an outright majority after five years of coalition government[1]. In 2016, candidates alone in the Florida Senate race spent almost $60 million. When outside expenditure is included, the total reached $110 million (£85 million). In other words, 40% more money was spent on one election in one US state than on a national UK election[2].

Total spending on the 2016 presidential election reached almost $2.4 billion – 31 times more than the UK general election in a country only five times bigger in terms of population. When the 2016 Senate and Congressional races are added in, the total cost of electing the President and Congress was more than $6.4 billion[3]. The figures aren't directly comparable of course because of the differences between the US and UK presidential and parliamentary systems. But they are quite startling all the same. In essence, the US spends 82 times more than the UK to get an elected head of government and legislature. And that's without taking into account the fact that the US

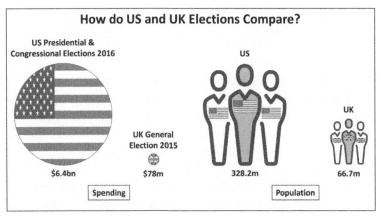

Source: Center for Responsive Politics, UK Electoral Commission, UK Office of National Statistics, US Census Bureau; Icon by svgrepo.com

votes more frequently, with the House of Representatives re-elected every two years and the President every four, compared to every five years for all members of the House of Commons and the Prime Minister in the UK.

Just after the November 2014 midterm elections, when all members of the House of Representatives and a third of the Senate had been up for re-election, I met an experienced member of Congress on Capitol Hill to talk about the ongoing Iran nuclear negotiations and the Syria crisis. At the end of the conversation, I turned to the recent elections.

"You must be happy that the midterms are over," I said. "As you can now stop fundraising for a while and get down to the real business of legislating."

The congressman smiled at me rather like a caring, older relative to an innocent child.

"I started cold calling for donations the day after the midterms," he replied with more than a hint of resignation. "The next elections are only two years away and there is a huge amount of money to raise if I want to stay in office. I am already working the phones several hours a day and attending a number of fundraising events each week."

A little later, the congressman's Chief of Staff expressed privately his frustration about just how much time his boss had to spend on fundraising rather than delivering for his district.

"If you can't raise more than a million dollars, or $3000 every working day," he said, "you won't get elected to the House. So the fundraising never stops".

He paused and reflected on what he had said.

"But if you don't get elected, you can't pursue your agenda. So it's a price members of Congress have to pay, even if they do have to spend half their time in office raising money rather than working on what they were elected to do. That's just how US politics works right now. And it's even worse in the Senate."

It was a sobering encounter. How could America have arrived at a point where elected representatives are so distracted from their core business by the need to raise money? It didn't reflect well on US democracy.

But candidate and party fundraising and spending are not even the whole story of the vast amounts of money in US politics, or even the most disturbing. In many elections, outside expenditure is now increasingly important and can outstrip spending by candidates and their parties by a factor of three or four in particularly tight races. Big companies, business associations, unions, single issue lobby organisations like the National Rifle Association and wealthy individuals plough huge amounts of money into US elections to try to sway voters towards the candidates they believe will most protect their interests.

During the 2016 presidential election more than $1.6 billion was spent by outside groups[4]. The US Supreme Court's decision in Citizen's United vs. the Federal Election Commission in January 2010 essentially paved the way for limitless spending on elections by corporations, non-profits and unions as long as they did not contribute *directly* to any candidates[5]. The Supreme Court argued that limiting expenditure was contrary to the right to free speech as enshrined in the First Amendment to the US Constitution. A federal appeal court ruling just two months later – Speechnow.org vs. Federal Election Commission – allowed individuals to make limitless election contributions too, as long as it was indirectly[6]. And so, super PACs (super Political Action Committees) were born that could raise and spend huge sums of money to support a particular candidate or issue, as long as they did not coordinate formally with candidate campaigns. More money than ever started to flow into US politics.

In the midst of the presidential election primaries in early 2016, I travelled to Las Vegas to watch Republican presidential candidates on the stump vying for Nevada's votes. After witnessing Marco Rubio whip up support in a tent on the outskirts of the city promising a 'New American Century' and raging against the Iran nuclear deal, I went to see billionaire casino magnate and major Republican Party donor, Sheldon Adelson, in his office in the Venetian Hotel and Casino at the heart of the Las Vegas strip.

Adelson is one of the wealthiest men in the world with a net worth of more than \$30 billion[7]. His Venetian resort comes complete with replicas of Venice's St Marks Campanile, Palazzo Ducale and the Rialto Bridge. It's a vast complex boasting more than 4000 luxurious hotel rooms, a huge casino under Renaissance-themed frescoed ceilings, an international conference centre, a glitzy shopping arcade, more than 20 high-end restaurants, a number of nightclubs, a theatre and – as it's Vegas – a river complete with gondola rides.

Adelson's office was in a plush, but fairly modest suite of rooms off the main gaming hall of the casino protected by a single, unsmiling security guard. When I was ushered in, the octogenarian tycoon was alone. He was sitting in a luxurious tan leather executive chair at the end of a long, polished mahogany boardroom table and tucking into the last mouthfuls of his lunch. I sank into the deep cream carpet as I walked across the room to meet him. The wood panelled wall behind the conference table was covered with more than forty framed magazine covers featuring Adelson himself. A younger Adelson was grinning down from editions of Forbes and Fortune. The wall opposite was full of photographs of Adelson's family. Hanging from the ceiling, like some impressive aviation museum display, were large scale models of numerous jet aircraft.

After introducing myself, I commented on the model planes to break the ice, assuming Adelson was an aviation enthusiast. From a quick scan of the aircraft, I'd noticed that Adelson didn't have a double-decker Airbus A380 in his collection, although he did have models of other large commercial jets including a Boeing 747.

"You should get an A380," I said, pointing at the ceiling. "It's an impressive feat of engineering and a great plane to fly in."

Adelson replied without a moment's hesitation. "Oh, I don't need one of those," he said, pointing casually to another of his model jets. "I can fly without refuelling to my Marina Bay Sands resort in Singapore on my A340. The A380 wouldn't be any good. I would need to make a stopover".

It was only then that I realised Adelson wasn't just a plane buff. The aircraft hanging from his office ceiling were actually models of his personal collection of private jets. At that moment, I knew I had entered an entirely different world; the world of the unimaginably rich.

Adelson was softly spoken, but with a razor focus. I wanted to find out whether he would be contributing to the 2016 election and which candidate he was likely to back. When we finally dived onto politics, Adelson was clearly undecided on whether to invest in the 2016 election. He wasn't particularly impressed by any of the Republican Party candidates. His wife quite liked Marco Rubio, but Adelson himself wasn't sure. He pondered Ted Cruz, but with little passion. He admitted that Donald Trump was feting him. But he wasn't convinced the New York property tycoon was the right man for the job. He was scathing about Trump's unsuccessful dabbling in the casino business in Atlantic City and his lack of understanding of international affairs.

In the end, Adelson said he would back whichever candidate would most support Israel, would defend its position as a Jewish state and recognise Jerusalem as Israel's eternal capital. He described how his father, a Lithuanian Jew, had been forced to flee 1930s Europe ultimately to emigrate to the US after a short period in Wales where he had met Adelson's mother. He was close to Benyamin Netanyahu and the Israeli right and did not support negotiating with the Palestinians or a two state solution. According to Adelson, the Palestinians were terrorists and could not be trusted. President Obama's policy towards Israel had been "shameful".

As I left Adelson's office, one of his secretaries whispered to me that Donald Trump had just telephoned again – he was clearly persistent. It was also an approach that ultimately worked. Adelson and his Israel-born wife eventually donated a whopping $82.6 million to supporting Donald Trump and Republicans vying for election to the House and Senate in 2016 – three times more than any other billionaire donor[8]. Adelson's cash undoubtedly bought a change to longstanding US policy too; the Trump administration recognised Jerusalem as Israel's capital in December 2017 and ordered the US embassy to move from Tel Aviv, despite widespread concern amongst

America's closest allies about the impact on regional security and a long-stalled peace process[9]. Under President Trump, US policy towards Israel's nemesis – Iran – grew ever more hawkish too. In the US political system, money talks.

Adelson is not alone amongst the super-rich in spending large amounts of money to influence election outcomes and future policy. Dozens of US billionaires contributed to the 2016 election. Nor are mega individual and corporate donors limited to the Republican side. Michael Bloomberg and George Soros donated more than $20 million each in 2016 to support Hillary Clinton's campaign and other Democrats down the ballot in House and Senate races[10]. But the majority of outside money tends to be spent supporting the conservative cause. In 2016, 55 percent went towards backing Republicans or fighting Democrats; in 2012, when Barack Obama was elected for a second term, that figure reached 67 percent[11].

The effects of all this money on US elections are pretty alarming, and particularly in a country branded as a vibrant, model democracy.

Biggest Billionaire Political Donors, 2016 US Election Cycle

Donor	Business	Democrats	Republicans	Total
Tom & Kathryn Steyer	Hedge Funds	$91m		$91m
Sheldon & Miriam Adelson	Casinos	$40,000	$82.56m	$82.6m
Donald Sussman	Paloma Funds/Asset Management	$41.8m		$41.8m
Fred Eychaner	Newsweb Corp	$37.8m		$37.8m
Dustin & Cari Moskovitz	Facebook co-founder	$27m		$27m
James & Marilyn Simons	Renaissance Tech/ Hedge Funds	$26.78m	$25,000	$26.8m
Paul Singer	Elliot Management/ Hedge Funds		$26.1m	$26.1m
Robert & Diana Mercer	Renaissance Tech/ Hedge Funds		$25.6m	$25.6m
Richard & Elizabeth Uihlein	Uline, Shipping & Packing Materials		$23.9m	$23.9m
Michael Bloomberg	Bloomberg LP	$23.78m	$22,000	$23.8m
James & Mary Pritzker	Pritzker Group	$22.3m		$22.3m
George Soros	Quantum Fund/ Hedge Funds	$22.1m		$22.1m

Source: Center for Responsive Politics, OpenSecrets.org

Brutal TV advertisements funded by wealthy super PACs target the candidates personally and their policies, stoking up fear on particularly emotive touchstone issues like gun rights, religious freedom, tax, immigration and crime often with little reference to fact. In one 2016 gem, an Iranian nuclear attack on America was implied as the likely result of electing candidates deemed as being weak on Iran, despite the fact that the Iranians did not have nuclear weapons (and still don't) and Barack Obama's 2015 nuclear deal had made it much harder for Tehran to get them[12].

Independent organisations and some of the media do try to fact check the adverts. But there is almost no formal oversight, and certainly no process that can react quickly enough to blunt the impact of the deceit and fearmongering of the political commercials which spread quickly around the internet as soon as they are released. Outright lies from supporters of both sides are not uncommon, although half-truths, exaggeration or over-simplification of complex issues are much more widespread. The impact is the same – distorting the electorate's views on candidates and their parties and making it more difficult for voters to make a sensible, rational choice.

From one perspective, this is the definition of democracy – everyone can get involved and have their say. But the vast majority of Americans don't, because they can't afford to. And so the field is left open to Wall Street and other big industry interests, sometimes flaky billionaires, wealthy single issue advocacy organisations and religious groups. The more money you have to spend, the more you can influence US election outcomes and future policy. In an even more sinister development, a growing proportion of US election spending is now 'dark money' where the sources of the contributions don't even have to be revealed under US election law[13]. In other words, Americans don't always know who is trying to buy influence in their elections.

It doesn't feel very democratic in the true sense of the word, particularly when fact is usually the first victim in the febrile atmosphere of US elections. Spending by non-party campaigners in a UK general election is, by way of contrast, strictly limited to a maximum of £450,000 ($585,000) nationwide, with no more than £9750 ($12,675) to be spent in a single constituency[14]. In the 2015 general election, a total of £1.8 million ($2.34 million) was spent by third parties including unions and special interest groups – a tiny fraction of the amount spent in the US[15].

The money in US politics doesn't stop flowing once elections are over either. At the embassy we would sometimes work in parallel with British businesses and their well-paid lobby organisations when federal or state legislation was under discussion that could have a negative impact on UK economic interests. One piece of proposed legislation in July 2017 would have hit British oil and gas companies to the tune of hundreds of millions of dollars if it had been passed by Congress unamended. The impact on the companies was largely unintentional, the result of hastily drafted technical language in Congress' desire quickly to impose new sanctions on Russia after revelations of Kremlin interference in the 2016 presidential election. But getting changes to the draft legislation was not going to be straightforward with lawmakers intent on taking action in a matter of days before their summer break. Congress not only wanted to send a clear signal to Moscow that there were serious consequences for its actions, but also to fire a shot across President Trump's bow. Many members, including Republicans, feared the president might be soft on Russia if left to his own devices.

With expert help, I set about understanding the offending technical language in the draft legislation. I got to grips with why it was problematic and what alternative terms could be used to have the desired sanctions effect, which the UK fully supported, while avoiding the unintended consequences that would be damaging to British business. Armed with this newly acquired expertise, I made a series of calls to senior players on Capitol Hill to highlight the problems the legislation would create for UK companies and to propose alternative language which should achieve Congress' aims without collateral damage. The British energy giants' lobbyists and the companies themselves did much more detailed and persistent work on the Hill to try to get the draft legislation changed. They also spoke to US government departments who would interpret the legislation once passed and provide 'implementation guidance' to US and foreign companies. My role from the embassy was to highlight the UK government's interest in the legislation given the impact it could have on the British economy and jobs.

After a couple of intense rounds of lobbying, Congress did eventually change the language just before the bill was passed. The negative implications for the UK were largely avoided thanks to the lobbyists' work and our own interventions. It had been touch and go at times, and the oil and gas companies did not get everything they wanted. But it was a good lesson in how lobbying works in the US and how effectively it can influence policy.

Lobbying and advocacy is essential in any democracy to allow individuals and organisations to get their views across to their elected representatives. But the scale and power of the US lobby industry is extraordinary. Almost \$3.5 billion was spent on lobbying in Washington alone in 2019, with the most active industries – health, finance and telecommunications/media – spending around \$0.5 billion each[16]. Significant amounts of money are spent at the state and local level too. Lobbyists build influence to deliver for their corporate clients by throwing fundraisers for elected officials who have a constant need to bring in money to get re-elected, by encouraging their clients to donate to candidates and campaigns, and by offering highly paid jobs to members of Congress and their aides for when they leave office. With issues becoming ever more complex, expert lobbyists are also increasingly drafting legislation or contributions to bills themselves and touting them on the Hill on behalf of corporate clients. As members of Congress simply can't be experts on all the issues they have to cover, the lobbyists' proposals are often taken up whether or not they reflect the greater good[17].

At the embassy I was fairly regularly solicited by Washington lobbying companies wanting to offer their services to the British government for a fee. The offers spiked after the EU referendum in the UK and the 2016 presidential election when political developments on both side of the Atlantic added an unusual level of unpredictability to the UK/US relationship. I sensed surprise when I told the companies that we did not employ lobbyists; we relied on our own contacts and access on Capitol Hill and in the federal government to get UK views across. But other smaller embassies with fewer staff resources and without the benefits of the Special Relationship did hire lobbyists as they battled to come to terms with a new, atypical US government.

In essence, the issue is not the lobbying itself in the US, but the fact that only those with significant sums of money to spend can get their voices heard. There is no doubt that money buys access, influence and results in the US in a way that would be considered unpalatable and even corrupt in many other Western democracies. Unless the system is changed, Congress risks ceasing to be the collective voice of the people of the US, but rather the legislative arm of corporations and wealthy interest groups. Members of Congress undoubtedly seek election for laudable reasons – to serve their country and to try to address the challenges being faced by their constituents. But the political system, fuelled by eye-watering sums of money, creates an environment where those who have most to spend increasingly call the shots.

Regular, large scale demonstrations across the US only serve to reinforce this point. The weekend after President Trump's inauguration in January 2017, between three and five million people demonstrated in more than 400 cities across the US in the Women's March. Feelings were running high that the US might slip back on its commitment to women's rights and other civil and human rights issues under President Trump. Many colleagues at the embassy and our consulates around the country felt strongly about the issues and wanted to take part to express their support for the cause. I had to make clear that diplomatic staff could not participate which was not well received. Many British colleagues felt the issues were too important for their views to be constrained by diplomatic niceties. I understood that. But the event was overtly political. The official website of the Women's March clearly castigated the new US president; his election was the driving force behind the movement.

And foreign diplomats have to remain politically neutral in their host country to be able to do their jobs, however strongly they feel about specific issues. Marching was simply not an option.

At the same time, one of the most important roles of a diplomat is to try to understand what is happening in their host country – to observe events and provide analysis and recommendations to their own government. So I travelled into central Washington on the day of the Women's March to get a sense of the scale of the protest, the issues being raised and whether there were any pro-Trump counter-demonstrations of note. The sights and sounds quickly transported me back to the early days of the Green Movement in Iran in June 2009 when I witnessed hundreds of thousands of people of all ages marching peacefully in Tehran to express their anger at a stolen presidential election. Between 800,000 and 1.2 million people turned out to march in Washington. A huge sea of people had overflowed the planned route of the demonstration and spread into many streets from Capitol Hill to the White House[18]. Marchers in flamboyant costumes and armed with witty placards – many lambasting the president – were calling for everything from more women's rights to healthcare for all, from immigration reform to LGBTQ rights. I saw just one float of vocal, Pro-Trump demonstrators angrily trying to disrupt the march. They were flanked by dozens of policemen to keep them apart from the marchers who were engulfing them on all sides.

The Women's March was an impressive mobilisation of people passionate about their cause. I was glad too that, unlike Iran in 2009, the demonstrations weren't violently attacked. The right to peaceful protest remains strong in the US. But here's the rub. Despite millions of US voters taking to the streets across their country, almost nothing has changed on the issues for which they were marching. Exactly the same can be said about gun control. Large protests and an impassioned, nationwide campaign by young Americans following yet another mass shooting at a Florida school in 2018 failed to change US policy. But spending a few million dollars during an election campaign can overturn longstanding US policy on not recognising Jerusalem as Israel's capital until there is a peace deal between the

Israelis and Palestinians. And paying lobbyists to advocate for a particular industry interest reaps dividends in seeing off regulation and oversight whether or not that is in the wider interests of the American people.

The UK and other Western countries are far from immune from some of the less than democratic consequences of corporate lobbying or the sense that voters have limited influence over their elected representatives. The UK's parliamentary democracy is arguably a little less susceptible to US style lobbying. The political parties tend to have pretty tight control over their members of parliament through the whips system when it comes to voting on most issues. But that just means corporations and wealthy interest groups deploy slightly different tactics to advance their interests. It's less about helping elected officials raise money. Getting direct access to ministers is more important as UK governments set the legislative agenda to a much greater degree than a US administration. Just like in the US, the revolving door – the offer of highly paid jobs for government ministers, members of parliament and their advisers when they step down – is disturbingly commonplace[19]. The whole system is much more opaque than in the US too despite efforts at greater transparency through the creation of a lobbying register in 2015[20]. But the amounts of money involved don't reach anywhere near US levels, where corporate lobbying has become almost the lifeblood of the American political system. Without corporate money, few Americans other than the super-rich could afford to fund an election campaign.

The role of money in US politics is also compounded by the length of American election campaigns. The longer the campaign, the more money candidates and parties need to raise to run their election operations, and the more those with money can buy influence. UK news reporting tends to suggest that political campaigning never really stops in the US. Before living in the US, I thought this was probably exaggerated by the British media's obsession with all things American, particularly the 'Special Relationship', and the need to make copy. A week rarely seems to go by without a UK newspaper offering an assessment of whether the British/American relationship is cooler or warmer, or who might be lining themselves up for a run at the presidency and what they could mean for the UK.

It turned out that this was not just another British media obsession. I arrived in the US in spring 2013, less than four months after the beginning of President Obama's second term. Even so, the US media had already shifted their focus to who would run in 2016 and what their platforms might be, only to be distracted temporarily if there was a major crisis like the Snowden leaks or the Assad regime's use of chemical weapons in Syria. Candidates were already putting feelers out for a possible run for the presidency and, of course, beginning to raise money. The most likely result of this, to me at least, was growing public fatigue of politics, leaving the field ever more open to those with an agenda and large amounts of dollars to spend.

The massive impact of money in US politics must now raise very serious questions about just how democratic the American system really is. But it's not the only thing to worry about when assessing America's leading democracy myth. Who gets to vote in the US, where their votes are counted and how ballots are ultimately tallied up to determine the results all influence American election outcomes. It's a disturbing picture, particularly when both the Democratic and Republican Parties are not at all averse to pursuing patently undemocratic actions simply to increase their chances of winning.

In the run up to the 2014 midterms, I invited the CNN bureau chief and self-confessed election nerd to speak to British Consuls General – the heads of our offices around the US – who were visiting Washington for their annual conference. What the bureau chief had to say was shocking. He started by showing us a long, thin snake-like shape printed on a plain sheet of paper and asked us what we thought it might be. In this British audience, no one knew. The bureau chief explained that it was the 12th Congressional District in North Carolina. It had been drawn by the Republican-controlled state legislature and purposefully hugged the I-85 interstate corridor to capture as many minority voters – largely African Americans – in one voting district as possible. The aim was simple – to wrap up likely Democratic Party supporters in one place, reducing the chance that

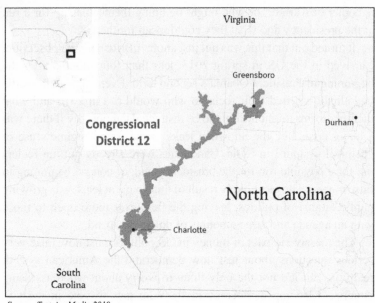

Source: Tortoise Media 2019

any other districts could be turned 'blue' and so ensuring Republican control of the state. The bureau chief then presented another shape – this one more like a twisted praying mantis. It was the 3rd Congressional District in Maryland drawn by the state's Democrat-dominated state legislature to concentrate likely Republican Party voters in one constituency[21]. It was blatant gerrymandering and by both parties.

The shape of a congressional district is not the whole story of course. All sorts of factors including geographical features like mountains and rivers affect the drawing of sensible electoral boundaries. But as I learned more, I was taken aback by the extent of gerrymandering in many states across the US. It begged the question how it could ever have been sensible to allow state legislatures to determine changes to both state legislative and congressional district boundaries. The ruling party then controls a process that should, in any reasonably functioning democracy, be independently determined to prevent political manipulation. But that is not the way the system works in the US.

In the UK, four independent and impartial boundary commissions covering England, Wales, Scotland and Northern Ireland have responsibility for reviewing constituency boundaries every five years and making recommendations for changes to take account of demographic changes. The recommendations of the boundary commissions go through a period of public consultation and further review if any additional changes are proposed before being submitted to both houses of parliament for confirmation. Political parties undoubtedly manoeuvre during the review process to try to temper the impact of any proposed changes on their electoral prospects. But the government cannot amend the recommendations of the boundary commissions before they are put to a vote in parliament. The ruling party therefore has no real ability to influence the overall outcome other than to block a vote entirely[22]. In Canada[23] and Australia[24], redistricting is also carried out by independent commissions. Anyone with partisan connections is automatically excluded from the process to avoid decisions being politicised.

The whole issue of gerrymandering in the US is now rightly before the Supreme Court to determine a way forward. North Carolina's 12th

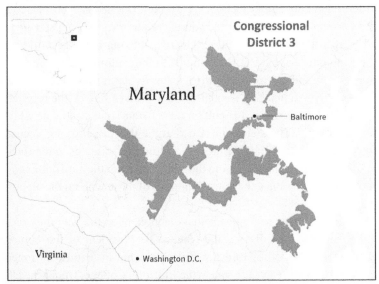

Source: Tortoise Media 2019

district was redrawn after a Supreme Court ruling in 2017 that the boundary amounted to illegal, racially motivated gerrymandering[25]. But in June 2019, the Court refused to rule on redistricting in North Carolina and Maryland more broadly, arguing that partisan redistricting was a political, not judicial matter. The court split 5-4 on partisan lines, with the liberal judges dissenting[26]. The decision leaves numerous districts across the country gerrymandered, which will undoubtedly distort the results of many future Congressional races. It could also embolden state-level legislators to pursue yet more partisan redistricting when boundaries are next formally reviewed after the 2020 US census.

If that weren't enough of a threat to US democracy, not all Americans entitled to vote get the chance to cast their ballot. In recent years, a growing number of largely Republican-controlled US states have introduced legislation making it more difficult for Americans to vote, with many of the measures having a disproportionate impact on minority communities. Florida bars ex-offenders from voting unless they get a pardon from the Governor of the state which is very slow in coming. Estimates suggest this affects around 1.5 million potential voters, about one third of whom are African Americans. North Dakota has introduced a full residential address requirement for registering to vote when thousands of Native Americans living on reservations in the state only have a PO Box Number. Ohio automatically removes voters from the electoral role if they don't vote in two elections and fail to reply to a postcard to confirm they want to stay on the register. Other US states make it difficult for out-of-state students to vote while at university[27]. The states concerned argue the measures are needed to prevent election fraud. But with few proven cases of voter fraud across the US, it's hard to avoid the conclusion that they are politically motivated[28]; to reduce the voting numbers of those who might support the opposition.

When it comes to a presidential election, even the way the votes are finally counted distorts the result. The President of the United States is not elected by direct, popular vote, but instead by a limited number of electors in each state – the Electoral College. Under the US

Constitution, each state is allocated electors equivalent to the number of representatives it has in Congress[29]. So, Ohio which has 16 members in the House of Representatives based on its population and two senators, gets 18 electors; California, which has 53 members in the House and two senators, gets 55. To secure the presidency a candidate must win a majority of the electors nationwide, or at least 270 out of 538 votes.

The system of electors was enshrined in the Constitution by the Founding Fathers as a compromise between choosing the president by direct popular vote or by Congress. The effect is a hybrid system that is somewhat biased towards less populous parts of the country. As each state has two senators irrespective of their population size, small states get a minimum of three electors – corresponding to at least one member of the House and two senators. As a result, four percent of the US population in small states get 8% of the electoral college votes. More significantly, the electoral college system has a propensity to exaggerate results. In all but two states, whoever wins the popular vote in a presidential election is given <u>all</u> the electors; the electors are not allocated proportionately in relation to each candidate's share of the vote[30]. If a candidate loses a state by a fraction of a percentage point or just a few hundred votes, all the electors are still given to their opponent. States which consistently vote for one party can therefore be largely bypassed in presidential election campaigns. In California's case, all its 55 electoral college votes can be counted confidently for the Democratic Party candidate without any real campaigning; similarly Texas' 38 electoral college votes will go to the Republican Party candidate. The selection of the US president is therefore determined by a handful of swing states and sometimes by a very small number of votes. Each individual ballot in every other state is effectively meaningless, whether the vote in the state is close or a landslide.

On the evening of 8 November 2016, I watched the presidential election results coming in at the Washington Post's sleek new headquarters, funded by a large cash injection from Amazon billionaire Jeff Bezos a couple of years earlier. At the beginning of the evening, there was a positive buzz around the place. Flamboyantly costumed waiters and waitresses were circulating with sparkling Californian wine and canapés from some of Washington's best restaurants. As polls were closing around the country, all pollsters, including Donald Trump's own team from the British company Cambridge Analytica, were predicting a Clinton win. And so this largely Democratic Party supporting city was quietly confident. Few of the guests – the great and the good of the Washington political establishment – were showing any interest in the results coming in via CNN or Fox News beamed onto huge screens on every wall of the Washington Post offices. The electoral college system pretty much guaranteed the results in most states.

I found myself distracted by the Florida results as they started to trickle in mid evening. Donald Trump was showing an early lead in this key swing state after a small percentage of the votes had been counted. I remember asking a Republican pollster what she thought Trump's early lead meant. The pollster told me confidently that the first results came from rural areas of the state which tended to lean Republican. But once the results from urban centres started to come in, Clinton would take the lead.

I wasn't entirely convinced. The memory of the EU referendum in the UK just 5 months earlier when pro-Brexit campaigners had conceded defeat on the basis of exit polls only to go onto win by a slim margin was still seared into my brain. Something appeared to be happening. As the percentage of the votes counted in Florida increased over a couple of hours, Trump was maintaining his lead. The guests at the Washington Post party started to watch the results a little more closely. But they still didn't appear to be overly concerned – all the experts continued to predict a Clinton victory. With 29 electoral college votes, a Trump win in Florida would make a Clinton route to the White House more difficult but not impossible.

When Trump sealed victory in Florida around 11pm, securing all the state's 29 electoral college votes, the mood of the party quickly changed. Quiet confidence was replaced by growing anxiety as Washingtonians rushed to work out which swing states Clinton now needed to win to claim the Presidency. Over the next couple of hours, Clinton's route to the White House became ever more difficult as Trump secured victories in more states including Pennsylvania, which was supposed to have been part of Clinton's 'blue wall'. A sense of dread started to spread around the party goers. Many guests left as the event didn't feel much fun anymore. By 2am, it was all over; Donald Trump had been elected.

The Washington Post event which had started in such high spirits now felt like a wake. Many of those still at the party sat quietly, holding their heads in their hands as reality hit them like a loaded truck. The electoral college system devised by the Founding Fathers to avoid the American public choosing their president directly had helped Donald Trump to victory. He had lost the popular vote by 2.1% or almost 3 million votes but won the Electoral College by 304 to 227[31]. America and the world reeled from the shock.

For the fifth time in its history, the US had elected a president for whom the majority of the American people had not voted[32]. Just 79,696 votes across three states – Michigan, Pennsylvania and Wisconsin – had secured Trump all their 46 electoral college votes and the presidency[33]. Al Gore infamously lost the presidential election to George W Bush in 2000 despite winning the popular vote by more than 500,000. In that case, the election turned on Florida where Bush won by 537 votes out of the 6 million cast and got all 29 electoral college votes[34].

US Presidents who Lost the Popular Vote

Year	President	Popular Vote
1824	John Quincy Adams	-38,000
1876	Rutherford B Hayes	-255,000
1888	Benjamin Harrison	-89,000
2000	George W Bush	-537,000
2016	Donald Trump	-2,933,224

Source: The American Presidency Project, UC Santa Barbara, www.presidency.uscb.edu

A reasonable case can be made to defend the Founding Fathers' decision to give each US state two senators regardless of their size in an effort to prevent smaller, more rural states from being consistently outvoted in Congress by larger, more urban ones. Doing so may well have helped the country hold together in times of crisis, as all could feel that their voices were heard by the federal government. But doubling down on this with the electoral college system for the selection of the most important office in the land is much harder to defend. Given how far it can skew US presidential elections, the electoral college system is arguably the most momentous US gerrymandering there is.

Al Gore's presidential election loss in 2000 was driven by the electoral college system. But it was sealed by Supreme Court decisions along partisan lines that blocked the recounting of votes in Florida despite George W Bush's margin of victory being minuscule and evidence of significant problems with the state's voting machines (the infamous hanging chads)[35]. In other words, politically influenced decisions by senior judges further undermined US democracy. Two decades later, the politicisation of senior judicial appointments is on the rise with worrying consequences for America's future democratic credentials.

After the death of Justice Antonin Scalia in February 2016, the selection of a new Supreme Court Justice came to dominate the last few months of the Obama administration with the Republican-controlled Senate refusing to consider the President's nominee to replace him. What followed was a highly partisan charade. The Democrats threw up their arms at Republicans stopping the President's nominee from getting a confirmation hearing and having the chance of being appointed; Republicans argued that so close to an election, the selection of a new Supreme Court Justice should wait until the American people had exercised their vote on the next President. In other words, the Republican Party hoped that a Republican president would be elected later in the year who would choose a conservative judge to replace Scalia, instead of confirming

Obama's more progressive nominee who would shift the ideological balance on the Supreme Court.

The whole thing was pretty unedifying to watch. But it wasn't the spectacle of yet more political dysfunction bleeding over into the selection of one of the most important judicial positions in America that struck me most. Instead I was baffled by the evident politicisation of the judiciary and why no one seemed to be raising alarm bells about the very principal. How despite the clear separation of powers established by the US Constitution between the executive, legislature and judiciary, could the Constitution also empower the President – representing a political party – to nominate who fills vacancies on the court, and the Senate – which is most often controlled by one party – to appoint? This seemed to go against the very essence of an independent judiciary and the separation of powers. And when the appointments are for life, not a fixed term, the problem is compounded further. When I spoke to one Supreme Court Justice about the whole thing he simply rolled his eyes and smiled in a 'that's just America' sort of way.

The corrosive politicisation of Supreme Court appointments was laid bare in October 2018 when the Senate controversially confirmed Donald Trump's second Supreme Court Justice nominee, Brett Kavanaugh[36]. During the confirmation process, three women made serious allegations of sexual assault against Trump's nominee. One of the women made an emotional testimony before the Senate, recalling in some detail the alleged assault when she and Kavanaugh were students. Kavanaugh, nailing his colours firmly to the Republican mast, claimed the allegations were a political witch hunt by left wing groups. President Trump, under increasing pressure not to ignore the allegations, hastily ordered an FBI investigation[37]. The FBI presented a copy of their report to the Senate within a matter of days. Republicans claimed it was thorough; Democrats that it was a whitewash. Kavanaugh was duly confirmed and, soon after, sworn into the Supreme Court. The process arguably tarnished the President, the Senate and the Court. For many women it was confirmation that their voices were still not being heard despite the #MeToo movement;

for the left, it said that President Trump would railroad through whatever he wanted even if it undermined the very core institutions of the US. Republicans, on the other hand, concluded that Democrats would stop at nothing – even allegations of sexual assault – to block their agenda. The whole thing was a car crash played out very publicly around the world and did little to bolster America's democratic credentials. And it was an unholy spectacle that would be repeated again when the iconic Supreme Court Justice, Ruth Bader Ginsberg, died just a few weeks before the 2020 presidential elections.

Nor is the Supreme Court the only judicial institution where appointments are politicised. The President, and therefore in effect the ruling party of the day, gets to nominate large numbers of senior judicial positions across America. Over the last half century, each President has nominated between two and four hundred federal judges including for the Supreme Court, Courts of Appeal and District Courts[38]. All are lifetime appointments and so the impact enduring. Most presidents probably set out to make their selections based on an individual's legal credentials, professional track record and commitment to service. But whether potential nominees are aligned with the President's political philosophy and ideology, whether they are conservative or liberal, is central to the selection process too. Indeed, presidents often take recommendations from their own parties on who to nominate rather than lead an independent selection process. This politicisation doesn't feel like a recipe for balanced judicial decision making – and there's arguably nowhere more important than in the legal system for decisions to be based on impartiality and fairness rather than politics. In the case of the Supreme Court, where justices are responsible for making some of the most important and sensitive judgements for US society, it doesn't sit well with a genuinely democratic society that they should – in effect – be chosen by the political party in power rather than impartially for their legal experience and expertise.

It's now pretty hard to conclude that America comes anywhere near to being a standard bearer for Western democracy as proclaimed in its national myths. The excessive amounts of money in US politics, widespread political gerrymandering and voter suppression, flaws in the electoral system and the growing politicisation of the judiciary are hardly the ingredients of a healthy democracy. Nor are they likely to inspire public faith in elected officials and government institutions, particularly with growing partisanship causing ever more political gridlock. In early 2020, the Economist Intelligence Unit – the research arm of the Economist newspaper – ranked the US as a 'flawed democracy' for the fourth year running[39]. The EUI measures countries against 60 democratic values in five categories: electoral process and pluralism; civil liberties; the functioning of government; political participation; and political culture. The US again fell below 'full democracy' because of increasing political polarisation, growing partisanship undermining the functioning of state institutions and falling public trust in government.

In a letter in 1814, Founding Father and former US President John Adams said: "Remember, democracy never lasts long. It soon wastes, exhausts and murders itself. There never was a democracy yet that did not commit suicide."[40] For Adams, democracy if unchecked would be just as susceptible as other forms of government to man's frailties – to vanity, pride, selfishness and greed. Two hundred years later, his views appear prophetic. US democracy is at serious risk with grave consequences for the country's future. If change isn't made quickly, and Americans' confidence in their democratic system rebuilt, the risk of further erosion seems high with disturbing consequences for the US and wider world.

Putting American democracy back on track won't be easy. It will require political leaders to stand above the partisan fray and build alliances to push through significant reforms, including constitutional change. If there was ever a time for "ask not what your country can do for you, ask what you can do for your country"[41], this is it. The alternative is even more unpalatable – an increasingly weak, divided and dysfunctional America when the Western world most needs a strong and influential example of successful liberal democracy in an increasingly dangerous world.

Chapter Two

You Can Make it. Just Work Hard

Myth number 2 – Every American can achieve success through hard work, determination and initiative in a society free from the shackles of aristocracy and class.

W hen I first travelled to the US in the late 1980s as a fairly unworldly teenager on a school exchange programme, pretty much everything I experienced seemed to confirm the American Dream. Like most young Britons at the time, I had grown up enthusiastically consuming US culture including TV shows like Miami Vice and Dallas which oozed wealth and success and Hollywood movies like Top Gun and Indiana Jones depicting all American heroes defying the odds. American technology and innovation seemed to be streets ahead too. Lessons were paused at my high school in northern England in April 1981 so we could watch the maiden launch of the Space Shuttle – the world's first reusable space craft. It was awe inspiring to see Columbia blast into the heavens against the vivid blue sky of a Florida morning strapped to three enormous rockets and, two days later, to glide safely back to earth. At the height of the Cold War, when the risk of nuclear war felt very real,

America seemed like the Western world's best hope against the malign ambitions of the Soviet Union. It was "the shining city on the hill" that would keep us safe[1]. Margaret Thatcher was standing strongly with Ronald Reagan to defend democracy from the ever-present threat of communist expansion. President Reagan was even talking about a 'Star Wars' plan – the Strategic Defense Initiative – that would make the US invincible to Soviet nuclear missiles. They were heady days of US technological dominance and moral supremacy, combined with the great promise of opportunity for all in a healthy and growing economy.

Looking back, it's no surprise that my first experience of the US confirmed the American Dream to be alive and well. To begin with, I really wanted America to be that land of prosperity and opportunity for all as seen in the movies and on TV. And then, through a good dose of luck, my exchange programme took me to a private high school amongst the elite golf courses of Pebble Beach on the Northern California coast. I could not have been sent to an area of the country that more epitomised American wealth and success if I had tried. On the affluent Monterey Peninsula, everyone appeared to live idyllic lives in expensive homes along a beautiful, rugged coastline dotted with Monterey pines and wind-sculptured cypress trees which swept into the wide sandy bay of Carmel by the Sea and onto the jaw dropping beauty of Big Sur.

To a British teenager who had grown up in a small village in the north of England built around a single factory where my dad had worked for more than 30 years, the contrast could not have been more striking. Everything in America seemed bigger and better to me – the cars, the houses, the domestic appliances. There seemed to be a gadget to automate pretty much everything, even if it didn't really need automating – from chopping to grating, can opening to juicing, ice making to popcorn popping. The fact that American fridges produced chilled water and ice at the push of a lever, and appeared bigger than many small British kitchens, was incredible to me, and still is more than 30 years later.

Everyone seemed to have more disposable income than people back at home in Britain too. Most of the Americans I met had plenty of cash to spend on regular trips to the cinema and eating out, on all the gear for surfing in the chilly waters of the Pacific, for buying the latest technology like Apple's early Macintosh home computers and for putting their children into expensive residential camps for weeks of the summer. Consumerism was just what Americans did, or at least that was my experience of life in Northern California. The majority of the older students at the school I attended had their own cars too. Some were driving models few young, working Brits could aspire to, let alone teenage school children, including convertible Volkswagens and fancy American brand trucks and SUVs. One classmate even drove a vintage Porsche. It felt like another world.

I was often asked about what I saw as the differences between Britain and America. My 'go to' example was describing the contrast between the American and British approaches to aspiration and achievement. If an American saw someone driving a Rolls Royce or Bentley, I explained, they would say, "one day I'll have one of those". Brits on the other hand would grumble under their breath, "how did they get that?" and assume it was based on privilege or class. It was a massive oversimplification of course. But it felt to me to be a pretty good explanation of the differences between the UK and US at the time. The destiny of British people in the 1980s seemed to be determined largely by their social class in a way that just didn't appear to apply to the more egalitarian US I was experiencing in California.

The private school I attended in Pebble Beach while out of reach for many Americans seemed to confirm that anyone could make it in the US whatever their background, or wherever they had started in life. Parents of the friends I made had established successful businesses from scratch, were rock stars who had made it to stardom from the tough rural hinterlands of Los Angeles or were computer geeks who had invented some innovative technology that had been bought by one of the big IT companies for millions of dollars. Social mobility – the mainstay of the American Dream – felt real. There were children of movie stars at the school too, of course. It was California after all. Clint Eastwood was even mayor of the neighbouring town of Carmel. But that just added to the allure of the place.

Thinking back to my exchange programme thirty years later and it's fair to say that the California I experienced in the late 1980s wouldn't have been described as an accurate representation of the US even at the time. Carmel, Pebble Beach and Monterey were far removed from some of the challenges faced in American cities and rural communities even in parts of California just a few miles from the school. But for the most part, this didn't really break into my consciousness. I was eighteen, away from home for the first time and lapping up new experiences in a privileged environment. I was too busy enjoying myself to want to question the reality of what I was experiencing.

I did see glimpses of a quite different America at the end of my exchange programme when I travelled across the country for six weeks by Trailways bus before catching my flight home from New York. The long distance bus network that criss-crosses the US is a lifeline for poorer Americans, students and anyone else on a budget. The busses are slow and can be uncomfortable, particularly when trying to sleep at night. But they are cheap and link up remote rural outposts and small towns across the country with all the major cities. They are a great way to get into the heart of the country; to see beyond picture-postcard America of the major tourist destinations.

During a transfer in East Miami in the early hours of a steamy July morning, I was marshalled with the rest of the passengers off our over-airconditioned bus by a couple of grizzled security guards who were waiting as we arrived. Not yet fully awake, I followed the line of people making their way into the terminal building. Once we were all in the waiting area, the guards quickly locked the doors behind us. We weren't even given a chance to warm up in the humid, night-time Florida air before we were back into ferocious air-conditioning of the bus depot. We were told that the neighbourhood simply wasn't safe for us to stay outside to wait for our connection. This was gangland Miami and we would be secured in the terminal until our bus to the Florida Keys arrived.

A while later, a young woman approached the terminal in some distress. She sobbed and screamed just the other side of the glass doors of the waiting room, wailing between her tears that she had been assaulted and needed help. The guards coldly refused to let her in unless she showed a valid bus ticket. The women appeared genuine to me. Tears were streaming down her face and there was a look of desperation in her eyes. But the guards did not budge even when she banged repeatedly on the glass doors claiming that she was in danger and pleading to be allowed in. I tried to avoid the woman's gaze as she looked around the waiting room imploring anyone for help. Making eye contact made the whole thing worse.

After what felt like an age, heavily armed Miami Police officers arrived in their squad car with its sirens wailing to handle the situation. They were still talking to the woman when my connection arrived to take me south to the Keys and I was marshalled back out of the terminal building onto the bus. I never did find out what had happened to the woman or why she had come to the bus station in such distress. But one thing was clear. In a city in the midst of a violent drug war between competing cartels, the bus station staff were not willing to take any risks by opening the door to let her in. It was my first taste of a very different America. The whole thing had been deeply unsettling.

When I arrived in Washington DC a couple of weeks later I got a further glimpse of an America far removed from the idyll of Pebble Beach. With a heavy rucksack on my back packed with all my belongings, I turned the wrong way out of the Trailways bus depot behind Union Station and soon found myself in what felt like a very shady area of the north east of the city instead of heading towards the White House and other tourists sites on the National Mall. Washington was then the murder capital of the US and in the midst of a violent crack cocaine war. Visitors were strongly advised not to go to certain parts of the city even during the day.

I began to realise my mistake when I came across a couple of young men apparently high on drugs slumped on the pavement, staring impassively into space. Until that point, I hadn't really noticed that many of the Federal-style, brick town houses that lined the streets were seriously run down. All had thick, metal bars across their windows and doors to keep out unwanted intruders. Now with heightened senses, I became vividly aware of my surroundings. I noticed groups of threatening-looking men loitering on almost every street corner. Each convenience store had an armed guard. A few of the houses were boarded up completely; some were even burnt out. There was graffiti everywhere. It really did not feel like a place a young, foreign backpacker should be. My heart was now pounding. I just wanted to get out of the area in one piece and as quickly as I could. I turned around, trying to look calm and natural so as not to draw too much attention to myself, and hastily retraced my steps back to the relative safety of the bus station. When I arrived, I was dripping in sweat from the oppressive Washington heat combined with a good dose of anxiety. The whole thing had been pretty nerve wracking, but I could finally breathe again.

Both these incidents had given me a glimpse of a different side to America. But they still felt like small vignettes when played alongside everything else I had experienced in the US for the previous six months in California. I saw them as the exceptions that proved the rule – every country had its problems, even the US. But I wasn't going to let them change my overall perceptions of the country. As a young Brit enamoured by the US in the heady days of the 1980s, I was convinced the American Dream was alive and well. I too had bought into the mythology of American exceptionalism.

Roll forward 30 years, and after another five years living in the US, the picture looks quite different. One of the first formal events I attended after arriving at the embassy in Washington DC in 2013 was a dinner reception at the British Ambassador's grand, red brick residence on Massachusetts Avenue for a retiring senior member of White House staff. Hosting the event was an impressive piece of diplomacy by the ambassador at the time as it brought together the great and the good of the Democratic Party establishment under a British roof. It gave the embassy as host an unrivalled opportunity to cement connections with senior figures in the Obama administration early on in the President's second term. And it was a chance to start talking to influential Democrats about plans for the 2016 presidential election which were already being hatched but not yet public.

But it wasn't the contact building or information gathering opportunities of the event that struck me most. Being new to Washington, it was what the reception appeared to represent that made most impact. It was, put simply, American high society in action – an event for those of position, wealth and power. I'd never been to a high society party in London before. But this was just how I imagined it would be. In this case, it wasn't the British aristocracy, but the US Democratic Party glitterati. Designer gowns and sparkling jewellery were the order of the day; and for the men, well-cut European suits and polished brogues. These were wealthy, influential and well-travelled Americans – a ruling elite by any description. Everyone seemed to know each other too, and interacted in a way tribes and elites do all over the world. It wasn't what I expected to find in the US given the myths of American egalitarianism and opportunity for all.

What I experienced that evening wasn't unique to the Democratic Party either. Other events the embassy would host during my time in Washington would be for the Republican Party establishment, but little different. Republicans of position and power formed yet another elite with all the same trappings of privilege and influence. Some were arguably more attached to landed wealth than their Democratic Party counterparts and, given Republicans' fondness for tradition, more attached to everything British too. But they were also an elite, an American-style aristocracy, by any other name.

In many ways, there's nothing surprising about any of this. Human beings have formed systems, hierarchies and elites for centuries, through the ancient Greeks and Romans to more modern societies. Even communism established elites, they just had to pretend they didn't exist as they were the antithesis of what communism was supposed be. But the existence of these elites in US society does not sit easily with American mythology which would have us believe that there is no class system or aristocracy in the 'land of the free' where everyone can make it if they just put their mind to it and work hard. The events hosted by the ambassador for the Democratic and Republican Parties were, at the very least, evidence that the myth is an oversimplification of what America in the early 21st century is really like.

You don't have to travel far from Washington DC to see that great wealth in America has bought all the trappings of a traditional European aristocracy. In Virginia, you can drive through mile after mile of rolling countryside, dotted with huge old mansions and estates behind exquisitely maintained dry stone walls and white picket fences. Stables and vineyards abound – this is horse and wine country. It has the feel of the elite rural belt of the Home Counties around London, just on a vastly bigger scale. Overlay that with the huge amounts of money that rich individuals can invest in politics in the US, and wealth can arguably buy favour in America in a way that is just not possible in other western democracies. Yet most Americans will still argue that the US is a meritocracy. Just Work Hard.

There are genuine American dynasties too. Before the 2016 presidential election primaries really got underway, the US faced the prospect of another Clinton/Bush election. If Jeb Bush hadn't performed so badly in the early primary debates particularly when taunted by Donald Trump, a race between Hillary Clinton for the Democrats and Jeb Bush for the Republicans was a distinct possibility given the money he was able to raise on the back of his family name and his record as Governor of Florida. It's only fair to say that some Americans were uncomfortable with this. But it didn't appear to be that big of a deal for most people in the country. I found this totally counter-intuitive given how much more egalitarian America is supposed to be. US mythology would have us believe that America does not have aristocracy-like dynastic traditions that have untoward influence over society. But the prospect of another Bush/Clinton race was clear evidence of the opposite.

I've lost track of the number of times Americans have referred rather scornfully to the UK class system, how it is unfair, stifles innovation and creativity, and puts the brakes on social mobility. The comments are often made without much experience of modern Britain, although the premise isn't entirely wrong. The implied message is clear: we don't have this in America; it's one of the reasons we sought independence from the British crown, and we are much better for it. There's little acceptance, or even acknowledgement, that the US has created much the same type of society. American elites might not be able to trace their wealth and influence back centuries or to aristocratic roots, although some of the oldest American families do have links to UK nobility. But they have a similar impact on US society as elites anywhere else. They guard their position and wealth, protect their interests by political and financial means and look after their own. Indeed, many of America's Founding Fathers were wealthy, slave owning landlords – another elite by any other name right at beginning of modern US history.

The fact is, inherited wealth is now increasingly a factor in future success in America[2]. The US is not the level playing field for all comers its national myths would have us believe. As early as the 19th century, historian Alexis de Tocqueville noted something of this fact: "The surface of American society is covered with a layer of democratic paint, but from time to time one can see the old aristocratic colours breaking through."[3] Nearly two centuries later, America's democratic paint seems to be flaking off in ever larger chunks. But many Americans choose not to see it, instead clinging to the belief that somehow the US is much more egalitarian than Britain and Europe and hard work will inevitably lead to moving up the ladder of society.

Drive just 40 miles north of Washington DC and you can witness somewhere far removed from the largely white political elites of the capital and old money of rural Virginia. Baltimore came to be one of my favourite places to visit near Washington. A gritty but vibrant American metropolis on the huge Chesapeake Bay that feels like a combination of the UK port city of Liverpool and the former textile town of Manchester that boomed in the industrial revolution. Baltimore's buzzing waterfront is a mix of new glass-fronted hotels, restaurants and offices alongside converted former waterfront

warehouses and the quaint 18th century red brick terraced houses of
Fells Point. Quirky neighbourhoods like Hampden in the north east
with its rows of verandaed former factory workers' cottages, have lots
of funky shops and old mills being redeveloped into restaurants, brew
pubs and yoga studios. Baltimore is a fun city in which to spend time.
It also feels more diverse, both ethnically and demographically than
the relative sterility of much of Washington.

But scratch the surface and parts of Baltimore suffer severe social
deprivation and disturbingly high levels of crime. When I first drove
to the city with a couple of British colleagues from the embassy just
a few weeks after arriving in Washington, the American friend we
were visiting asked on our arrival which route we had taken. I thought
it was a bit of an odd first question. But I soon understood why it had
been asked. Our Baltimore friend's face drained of colour as we
described our journey. Google Maps, she said, had directed us through
one of Baltimore's worst neighbourhoods in the west of the city, and
that was not at all wise given the levels of drugs dependence and gun
violence in the area. We had, on one part of the journey, noticed
crumbling social housing and multiple vacant properties which
looked pretty bleak. And when stopping at traffic lights, we had
encountered numerous people weaving precariously between the cars
begging for money holding up signs variously describing themselves
as homeless, sick or hungry. Some of the people had appeared to be
in a particularly desperate state. But we hadn't, perhaps naively, felt
threatened or at risk.

The experience got me digging into facts about Baltimore.
American friends would often mention the TV drama series The Wire
about Baltimore's drugs scene whenever I was going to the city as
some sort of warning about the risks as they saw them. As I'd never
seen the programme, the comments didn't register too much and I
wasn't going to let a TV dramatisation colour my views whatever its
reputation for accurately depicting a dark underside of the city. But
some of the statistics I found about Baltimore were shocking. In 2019,
there were 348 murders[4] – almost one every day – and more than 700
shootings[5], the majority concentrated in a number of poor

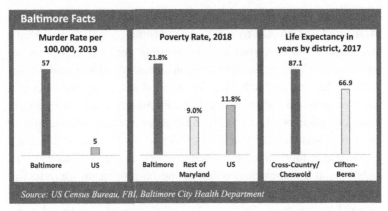

Baltimore Facts

Murder Rate per 100,000, 2019
Baltimore: 57
US: 5

Poverty Rate, 2018
Baltimore: 21.8%
Rest of Maryland: 9.0%
US: 11.8%

Life Expectancy in years by district, 2017
Cross-Country/ Cheswold: 87.1
Clifton-Berea: 66.9

Source: US Census Bureau, FBI, Baltimore City Health Department

neighbourhoods. The murder rate is more than 10 times the US national average[6]. Nearly one quarter of the population of the city lives below the poverty line, despite Baltimore being located in the richest state in the country[7]. And there's a 20 year difference in average life expectancy between two Baltimore districts only six miles apart. One is predominantly African American, the other predominantly white[8].

The depressing statistics go on. The overall unemployment rate in Baltimore is around 5% (2019)[9], but it is three times higher amongst the majority black population and reaches more than 30% for young African-American men[10]. For those with a job, White Baltimore residents earn on average almost twice as much as their African American neighbours[11]. The local Department of Health estimates that 60,000 residents of Baltimore are addicted to drugs and alcohol out of a total population of just over 600,000, with more than 25,000 suffering from opioid addiction[12]. The situation in parts of Baltimore is bleak. Whole neighbourhoods remain untouched by the American Dream. In others, it's little different from other prosperous parts of America. The contrasts couldn't be more stark, or more depressing in the most prosperous country on the planet.

Baltimore isn't an outlier either. Many other American cities face similar problems, from Chicago to Memphis, Cleveland to Milwaukee. Nor are small towns and rural areas immune. On a road trip in early 2018, I toured the southern states of Alabama, Tennessee,

Mississippi and Louisiana. When driving across the state line into Alabama I was greeted by a big sign welcoming me to "Sweet Home Alabama" from Governor Kay Ivey. Right next to the sign, alone amongst tangled overhanging trees on a dank gravel and mud lot was a large, decrepit trailer home. The wood cladding of the trailer was covered in mould and twisted and rotting. A number of windows were boarded up and others draped with roughly cut sheets as curtains. But the trailer was clearly lived in. A child's red and white tricycle and a new-looking football were outside the door. Smoke billowed from a small metal chimney poking out of the flat roof from some sort of heater. The governor's 'sweet home' welcome sign could not have seemed further from the truth. A similar scene was repeated many times as I drove across rolling countryside towards the state capital, Montgomery.

On the trip I travelled to Selma, Alabama which had played an important part in the civil rights struggle in the US. I wanted to visit the Edmund Pettus Bridge, site of the 'Bloody Sunday' confrontation where African American activists were brutally attacked with clubs and tear gas by state and local police in March 1965 to prevent them from marching to the State Capitol in Montgomery to demand voting rights[13]. When I arrived at my motel on the outskirts of the town early on a February evening, I asked the receptionist to recommend a bar or restaurant for dinner. I wasn't really expecting what she had to say in reply.

"We don't have much other than the fast food chains along the highway", she said before going on to list the options. "There's Wendy's, Taco Bell, KFC, Burger King, a Chinese take away and another fried chicken joint all clustered along the road not far from the motel".

"How about in the centre of town?", I asked. "Are there any good cafes or bars?"

The receptionist shrugged and turned to pick up the telephone which had started ringing while I was checking in.

I really didn't want to believe what the receptionist had said. It seemed so unlikely that a sizeable town in the US in 2018 would not have a few options other than fast food even in somewhere less affluent than the coastal cities of the north and west. And so I set off into downtown Selma to see what I could find.

It turned out that the receptionist wasn't entirely wrong. After driving up and down numerous streets of the downtown area which were surprisingly empty even on a cold and wet February evening, I found just one restaurant, Charlie's Place. It was a simple burger and grill joint on the ground floor of a three storey turn of the 20th century building which had once been a thriving Jewish social club complete with a fully sprung dance hall on the third floor. The owners of the restaurant, Selma locals Charlie and Sherri Morgan, were serving tasty food in a simple, but welcoming environment that was clearly popular with locals and the few visitors who had made it to Selma in the winter. The bare brick walls of the warehouse-like space were covered with old commercial signs advertising the Selma of a bygone era and black and white photographs showing scenes of the town's past. It was a warm and atmospheric sort of place.

After eating an excellent burger and fries and drinking a tasty local beer, I got chatting to Charlie and Sherri as the restaurant was winding down for the night. They told me how they were trying to do what they could to help regenerate their town. They were clearly passionate about the place where they had grown up. But, they said, it was a daily struggle to make ends meet. Charlie told me that Selma had been decimated when a US Air Force pilot-training base just outside the town had closed in 1977, an economic dividend of the end of the Vietnam war. The closure had taken millions of dollars out of the Selma economy each year.

I asked Charlie how long it had taken for the town to recover.

"It never had, and never will", Charlie said with a fatalistic shrug as he went back to cleaning up the restaurant before closing for the night.

It was a sobering conversation. I paid the bill and headed back to the hotel where I started looking a bit more into Selma's history. I learned that the population of Selma had dropped by more than a third from over 27,000 in the 1970s to less than 18,000 in 2018. The poverty rate was more than 40% and household income less than half the US national average[14]. Not surprisingly, and despite their best efforts for their town, Charlie and Sherri sadly had to close their restaurant just a few months after my visit, unable to make ends meet in a town suffering persistent economic stress[15].

Baltimore, Selma, and many other towns and cities across America are more than enough evidence that opportunity in the US is now, most often, linked to where you start in life. The mythical promise of the American Dream, that everyone can make it if they just work hard, quickly starts to break down when you see the severe and enduring social deprivation in both rural and urban communities across the country. And yet a widespread belief in the American Dream continues to survive. For many, it still defines what sets the US apart from other countries, even if it is no longer true. When asked, Americans routinely overestimate social mobility in the US. They are much more optimistic than Europeans about the chances of someone who is born into a poor family making it up the wealth ladder despite the growing evidence against it [16].

At a fundraising event in Washington in October 2017, I was invited to speak before a key note address by former Vice President, Joe Biden. The International Student House is a charity providing residential accommodation to American and international graduate students, interns and visiting scholars to "promote intercultural dialogue and global citizenship". Joe Biden was to be the recipient of the ISH's Global Leadership Award at their annual gala dinner.

The International Student House is based in what can only be described as a British manor house near Dupont Circle in the north west of the city. The former family home of the Demarest Lloyd family was built in 1912 with a Tudor design to resemble Haddon Hall in Derbyshire, England, complete with an oak panelled Great Hall that wouldn't be out of place in Harry Potter[17].

Before the formalities of the award dinner, Joe Biden spent time meeting some of the international students and ISH's patrons and donors in a small, wood-panelled anti-room complete with an imposing, carved stone fire place and glistening chandeliers. He worked the room effortlessly, radiating charisma and charm, and showing genuine interest in each student's story. In his speech accepting the award in the marquee-covered garden of the house, the former Vice President referred to the talented students he had just met. He used their example to highlight how people from all over the world were still being drawn to America because it was free from the ethnic conflict that blighted so many continents like Europe, the Middle East and Africa, and because everyone could make it in the US no matter where they came from.

I was quite taken aback that a veteran politician like Joe Biden and particularly one on the political left would make such a sweeping statement about the US and with such apparent conviction when it was at best a huge over simplification of the truth. Not wanting to appear impolite to the other guests at my table, I disguised my surprise as best I could. But my mind was trying to digest what the Vice President had said. I was sure that many minority communities in Baltimore and other US cities wouldn't agree that there was no ethnic conflict in the country. As African Americans see their neighbours routinely arrested and sometimes killed by white policeman, what Joe Biden had claimed couldn't, I imagined, have seemed further from the truth. Working class Americans across the country juggling three jobs and still finding it hard to pay their bills were also unlikely to subscribe to Biden's view. And struggling communities where few people ever seem to escape the grinding poverty that is part of their everyday lives, would almost certainly not agree either.

I shouldn't really have been surprised. Most American politicians, even the most honest and open minded about some of the challenges facing the US, often peddle the same lines about US exceptionalism and opportunity for all in one form or another. It's all part of maintaining the mythology of what America is supposed to be. There's an important place for aspiration and hope in politics, of course. Giving people something to believe in and to fight for is a good thing. It can bind communities together and encourage people to work just that bit harder to reach their goals. But it is also very easy to become blinded by rhetoric if it is repeated often enough even if it isn't true. A growing body of research shows that social mobility in the US has fallen over several decades and is now lower than in a number of other developed countries including Canada, Australia, Sweden, Denmark and Japan. US social mobility is also particularly low for those Americans born to the poorest families[18]. By some analysis, social mobility is higher in the UK too[19]. But Americans continue to believe strongly that hard work is the simple key to getting ahead.

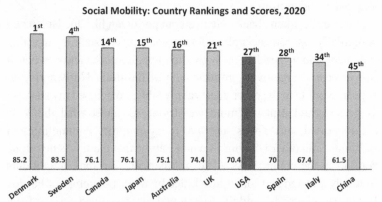

Social Mobility: Country Rankings and Scores, 2020

Denmark	1st	85.2
Sweden	4th	83.5
Canada	14th	76.1
Japan	15th	76.1
Australia	16th	75.1
UK	21st	74.4
USA	27th	70.4
Spain	28th	70
Italy	34th	67.4
China	45th	61.5

Source: World Economic Forum, Global Social Mobility Report 2020

When staying on a small camping resort in northern California close to Big Sur in summer 2018, I got chatting to the general handyman. He spent every day cleaning the pool, tending the lawns, clearing the rubbish and generally keeping the place spick and span for the guests. He was always good natured despite being at the resort from early in the morning until late in the day and never seeming to stop working even for a break. The groundsman was no more than 20 years old, an archetypal Californian with floppy sun-beached hair, baggy shorts and a laid back style. On one Monday morning I asked him if he had had a good weekend.

"I've been working", he said with a shrug as he carried on emptying the waste bins around the pool.

He went on to explain that he had two other jobs – working in a bar in the evenings after his shift at the resort and then laying concrete at the weekends just to try to bring in enough money to help his single-parent mother pay the rent, keep food on the table and allow his younger brother to finish school.

"Life is really expensive here", he said. "It is hard to earn enough just to make ends meet".

I now understood why the groundsman was rake-like thin and often looked physically and mentally exhausted. But even so, he was positive and optimistic about his future. He still believed he would get a break before too long and secure a job earning enough to have a decent life, even if the social mobility statistics were increasingly against him.

Some argue that lower social mobility in the US can be explained away by a bigger financial step up from the bottom to the top of the wealth tables given America's greater overall affluence compared to other developed countries and the more significant disparities between rich and poor. But the fact remains whether its relative or absolute movement up the economic ladder. US social mobility is falling behind its competitors despite the promise of the American Dream that has attracted people to the country from all over the world for generations. In the US in the early 21st century, every American's likely future success is increasingly tied to the circumstances of their birth. Hard work alone is unlikely to deliver economic advancement.

America's falling social mobility is driven, at least in part, by the fact that the US has much less of a social safety net than other developed countries to help people bounce back when they fall on hard times[20]. An almost visceral aversion to government means fewer Americans support a role for the state or federal authorities in helping those in need through welfare benefits, healthcare and retraining. The stubborn attachment to the belief that hard work alone is the ticket to making it in the US also creates a strong sense that Americans only have themselves to blame if they aren't successful. So why should the state intervene to help? In essence, the US practices a form of extreme Darwinism for humans; only the strong deserve to survive. It creates a tough and unforgiving environment where it is much harder to be poor than in other developed countries and one where it is increasingly difficult to get out of the poverty trap too.

For all Americans, access to a decent education is essential to be able to climb up the socio-economic ladder. Wealthy families can afford the best private schools and colleges for their children many of which charge huge fees. But these are out of reach for most American parents leaving their children in the public school system which is much more of a lottery. With almost half of US public school funding coming from local property taxes, the available resources can vary widely between rich and poor communities. More wealthy areas tend to have more expensive homes and therefore correspondingly higher taxes which get ploughed into the school system[21]. The state and federal governments do try to adjust for these differences – to level up the education offer at least to a degree. But significant disparities in spending per student persist across the country. Some states spend three times more per pupil than others with obvious implications for the quality of the education that can be provided[22]. In some of the poorest communities, public schools have been seriously neglected leaving Americans most in need without access to a quality education.

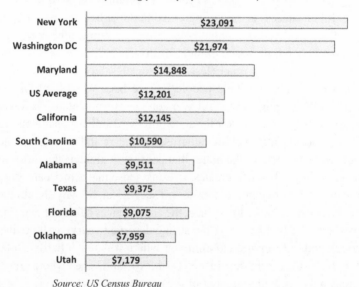

School Spending per Pupil per Year 2017, US dollars

New York	$23,091
Washington DC	$21,974
Maryland	$14,848
US Average	$12,201
California	$12,145
South Carolina	$10,590
Alabama	$9,511
Texas	$9,375
Florida	$9,075
Oklahoma	$7,959
Utah	$7,179

Source: US Census Bureau

Even in affluent Washington DC, where the average education spend per pupil is one of the highest in the country, there can be a marked variation in quality between the public schools in different parts of the city and the surrounding suburbs. Some have very high performance ratings; others surprisingly poor[23]. This caused a great deal of anxiety for many Washington families I knew who understandably wanted the best education for their children but couldn't always afford to live in the areas where the better schools were located. Many middle class families therefore choose to move out of the city to Virginia and Maryland where the schools are decent and housing more affordable. But this sets them up for a long and painful commute in Washington's infamous traffic, and seeing their children much less as a result. Many poorer families, of course, simply can't afford to move and so they have to rely on their neighbourhood school however good or bad. In such circumstances, it is easy to see how disadvantage can quickly be baked into the American way of life. The US education system – an essential element of individual advancement – just doesn't deliver for all Americans.

If you spend enough time in the US and scratch the surface, it's hard to avoid the conclusion that the enduring belief that America is a meritocracy – that everyone can make it if they just work hard – actually works to perpetuate divisions in US society and makes it even harder for many Americans to improve their lives. Overlay this with the American aversion to government stepping in to help when people fall on hard times, and this creates something not seen in many other Western countries, something exceptional but not in a positive sense. The US has perfected an 'exceptionalism of neglect' where the less fortunate are left largely to fend for themselves or to rely on charity while facing a decreasing chance of being able to improve their lives.

Ironically perhaps, the American Dream is being smothered by an unquestioning conviction that it still exists. The conviction allows the US to underplay serious and growing problems that prevent people moving up the socio-economic ladder even when they do work hard – problems that include access to good education and training, a lack of affordable healthcare and social support and the scarcity of working class jobs that pay a living wage. In the meantime, the US elites have stacked the system in their own favour and become increasingly wealthy, widening the gap ever further between rich and poor.

In a speech in 1965, President Dwight D Eisenhower felt able to proclaim: "We are, proudly, a people with no sense of class or caste. We judge no man by his name or inheritance, but by what he does and for what he stands."[24] And yet, less than 70 years later, the American Dream has been snuffed out for all but a tiny number of Americans who are lucky enough to have been born to wealthier families and those 'one in a million' cases where someone does make it out of the poverty trap against all the odds. For everyone else, the chance of bettering their lives in 21st century America is very small and fading.

Unless something changes, the American Dream will soon be little more than distant history. The myth that everyone can make it in the US if they put their mind to it and work hard will only again ring true if the country can move back to its more egalitarian roots and provide genuine opportunity to all Americans whatever their background. The risks of not changing course are obvious – further social upheaval as a growing American underclass faces diminishing opportunities to improve their lives. And, ultimately, it would hasten America's decline as the country would fail to unleash the potential of all its people. No one in the US should want that to be their future.

Chapter Three

The Most Successful Capitalist Economy

Myth number 3 – The US is the most dynamic and innovative economy in the world where competition is king and the market delivers.

There's no doubt that the US is a highly successful economy; it's an economic superpower. It is still the world's largest economy by a number of measures and produces around one quarter of total global output[1] - an astonishing figure when Americans makes up only 4.3% of the planet's total population. US GDP per capita is firmly in the top 20 in the world, and higher than in all other large developed nations[2]. Parts of the US are also known the world over for their innovation, entrepreneurship and economic dynamism. San Francisco and Silicon Valley lead the pack having produced so many globally dominant technology companies including Apple, Intel, Cisco, Facebook and Google. But other areas have an impressive record of innovation and economic growth too including the booming city of Austin, Texas; Boston, Massachusetts around the leading universities of Harvard and MIT; and Raleigh, North Carolina with its research and development driven economy.

Like many embassies, we worked hard to learn from the US where it has particular economic strengths. We set up programmes to study the economic eco-systems around America's world-leading centres of innovation – looking at everything from the regulatory environment, financial infrastructure and business/academic links to try to understand the 'secret sauce' that makes them crucibles of so many incredibly successful companies. I visited funky incubators and cool accelerators in San Francisco, Boston and Los Angeles that provided everything you could think of for start-ups including shared work spaces, high speed internet, workshops on how to get finance and build your business and, of course, trendy relaxation areas in bright colours complete with fully stocked kitchens with artisanal coffee and craft beer on tap – all the Millennial 'must haves'. In Boston, the accelerator I visited even provided lab benches and gene mapping equipment to support those hoping to commercialise their medical discoveries.

We didn't find a silver bullet in our investigations. Each location was slightly different. But we did learn a great deal about how different parts of the US support innovation. We passed our conclusions to government departments in London so they could apply lessons to the UK's efforts to drive up innovation in places like Tech City (aka 'Silicon Roundabout') in south east London and other economic development zones all over the country. We shared best practice with the US administration too in areas where the UK is leading the world, including in the digitisation of government services and international development innovation.

But the indisputable facts about the US' economic strengths just make some of the truths about the US economy all the more surprising. It soon becomes clear to anyone spending a reasonable amount of time in the US that it isn't always the highly competitive, super-innovative, consumer-driven economy you might expect, and in some particularly unexpected ways. Parts of the US economy are surprisingly old fashioned and bureaucratic and some economic behaviours verge on the criminal. The reality can be strongly at odds with the myth of America's world-leading, free market capitalism.

Take internet services for example. A small number of companies have the broadband market sewn up. From all the glitzy billboards and expensive TV commercials advertising the big companies – Comcast, Verizon and AT&T – the market looks dynamic and highly competitive. But this belies a very different reality. The internet and cable service providers often fail to compete. Even in large cities, most apartment blocks and even some whole districts only have one choice of provider, or at most two. Rural areas have even fewer options. The result is obvious – inflated prices and poor services for US consumers. I've heard stories from American friends living not far outside of small towns facing a bill of thousands of dollars to lay cable or fibre to their home so they can get a reasonable internet speed for their work. Others are left to rely on expensive satellite links, even cutting down trees to create a clear line of sight to their home and, even then, having to compromise seriously on service levels.

When I arrived in Washington in 2013, I had to set up broadband in my embassy-allocated house. I was living in a leafy residential district in north west of the city, a stone's throw from the embassy and just a couple of miles from the White House. It was hardly remote by any description. But getting reasonably functioning internet took four months of endless emails and telephone calls to Comcast – the sole provider in the area – and several visits by company engineers. After one particularly exasperating exchange with the company more than three months into my internet saga, Comcast agreed to send one of their "best engineers" to the house with a more powerful small business router which, they said, would resolve the ongoing connection and speed problems around the house. When I got home that evening, Comcast had in fact installed a tiny router for a small apartment in a large detached home and so the WiFi reached even less of the house than before and at snail-like speeds. The whole thing was exasperating. At this point, and after a couple of glasses of wine to reduce the stress levels, I decided to take matters into my own hands and call in an independent expert to sort out the problem.

Despite this terrible service, Comcast was charging more than $250 (£192) per month for an internet connection and basic cable TV package – a shocking amount of money, but apparently a reasonable deal in the US; many people were paying more. I had no choice but to pay this if I wanted broadband and TV of course. No other company provided a service in the area. It was free market forces, American style.

I wasn't alone in my battles to get decent broadband either. Many colleagues had similar war stories about their long and frustrating struggles to get set up and the eye-watering costs for a poor service which was common to all the US internet companies. Foreign journalists in Washington would regularly express their exasperation at the laughable service levels, low speeds and high cost of a utility so fundamental to their work. They expected challenges in developing countries and conflict zones, but not in America[3].

Despite prices dropping and speeds increasing in the last few years, the cost of broadband internet in the US is still almost double that in France and Germany and more than 40 percent higher than in the UK[4]. The greater cost can't be explained away by wealth differences either; US GDP per capita is only between 12 and 36 percent higher than in countries in Western Europe[5]. Fixed-line broadband penetration is also lower in the US, falling behind twelve

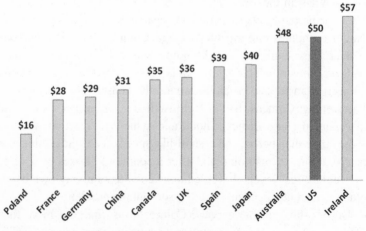

Average Fixed-line Broadband Price per Month in US Dollars, 2020

Source: Cable.co.uk, Worldwide Broadband Price Comparison

European countries including the UK, France and Germany[6]. It is a pretty sorry state of affairs in the most advanced economy on the planet.

There is little doubt that the problem is the result of an excessive concentration of market power among the three big internet and cable companies[7] who routinely fail to compete to keep prices high and maximise their profits[8]. In an industry with such high costs to entry given the infrastructure required to set up a nationwide broadband service, the chances of new competitors emerging through natural market forces is low to non-existent. And that means the big US providers come under little pressure to up their game and reduce their prices. American consumers have little power to bring about change. Only regulatory intervention could make a difference by forcing the existing broadband companies to offer access to their infrastructure to other companies at reasonable cost. But that seems unlikely with the providers working hard to prevent this from happening – the telecommunications companies are some of US industry's biggest spenders on political lobbying in Washington to protect their privileged position[9]. Such a state of affairs would be bad enough in any industry. But with access to high speed internet at reasonable cost so critical to economic development in the digital age of the 21st century, the failings in the US must have serious implications for future American competitiveness and prosperity. It's just not what

Top 5 Sectors by Lobbying Spend 2019, US$ millions

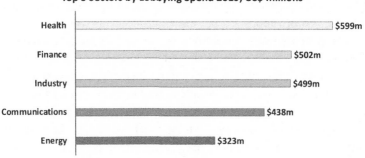

Source: Center for Responsive Politics - OpenSecrets.org

you would expect in the US where the American consumer is supposed to be king and the market deliver.

If that wasn't enough, the big internet companies work hard to stifle international competition too. British Telecom lobbied persistently with embassy support over a number of years for the 'special access' market to be regulated more effectively by the Federal Communications Commission (FCC) to ensure the legacy infrastructure owners – Verizon and AT&T – couldn't charge prohibitively high rates for other companies to access the 'last mile' of fixed line connections necessary to be able to offer broadband services in the US at competitive prices. BT was almost successful in getting the necessary regulatory changes towards the end of the Obama administration[10]. But 2016 election jitters prevented the FCC from following through. Verizon and AT&T argued vociferously that the change would reduce investment spending in the US on new broadband services[11]. This may or may not have been true. But the outcome was clear – fewer providers could offer services in the US market. Less competition inevitably meant higher prices for American consumers and greater profits for the existing internet and cable companies. To add insult to injury, the big US internet providers, with a nod from the regulators, are now busy consolidating even further by buying up big content providers like TV and movie studios which doesn't bode well for future choice and competition.

The other essential service of the digital age – the mobile phone plan – is also considerably more expensive in the US than in Britain and the rest of Europe[12]. Like most Europeans arriving in the US, I was taken aback by the huge difference in cost which was greater even than that for broadband. I just couldn't understand how a similar mobile data plan could be four or more times more expensive in the uber-capitalist US market. Much to the amusement of friends and colleagues who had been in the US for longer, I spent many hours in my first evenings and weekends in Washington DC searching the internet to try to find a more reasonable offer which I thought must exist if I looked hard enough. The cost difference was so big, it just didn't compute. Wasn't the US supposed to be the place where

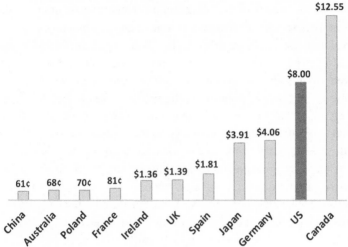

Source: Cable.co.uk, Worldwide Mobile Data Pricing

consumers ruled and drove excessive pricing and dubious practices out of the market place by the power of their choice?

So why is America so much more expensive than other countries for mobile services? The answer again is the small number of companies that dominate the market combined with limited regulation of the sector and weak implementation by the federal government of antitrust and competition laws that do exist. So, in many ways, the problem is more a reflection of US politics than pure economics. But the result is the same – high prices and limited choice for American consumers. Not surprisingly, my hours of scouring the market failed to find a plan comparable to those in the UK at reasonable cost. I just had to bite the bullet, pay the money and accept the fact that I would be paying considerably more to get less. As a small consolation, I did at least have another conversation piece on how the US just isn't what you would expect from the world's most successful capitalist economy.

In essence, the behaviour of the US internet and mobile phone companies is protectionist and monopolistic, driven by the desire to make maximum profit for their executives and shareholders, not to provide the best products and service for American consumers or facilitate the growth of the US economy. The argument often peddled by the companies – that the US is a huge country and so the costs of developing networks are much higher than elsewhere – doesn't really stack up. The US market is significantly bigger too and so the profit potential greater than most other developed countries. California alone is 5th biggest economy in the world; Texas is the 10th[13]. And when you do travel to more remote rural areas around the US, there's often very little cell phone coverage as the companies simply haven't built the necessary infrastructure, instead focusing on more heavily populated areas where there are bigger profits to be made. The American laissez-faire capitalist model – where competition is supposed to be king and those who don't provide high quality services or who make excessive profits are quickly replaced by alternatives on the back of consumer choice – clearly isn't working. In these cases at least, the market does not deliver and the US economy and consumers suffer as a result[14]. I still haven't worked out why Americans don't demand better.

It doesn't stop at internet and mobile service providers either. There are surprises in the banking sector too. While there has been a great deal of innovation in some areas, it has not always been in places you would necessarily expect, or that were widely beneficial. The big financial players in New York and London were arguably at their most creative in the 2000s when they came up with complex repackaged mortgage instruments that eventually triggered the global financial crisis of 2007-8. More than ten years later, working and middle class Brits and Americans are still paying for the massive losses incurred during the crash through stagnant wages or under-employment. The US and UK economies might have been nominally bigger a decade later than they were on the eve of the crash, but little of the rebound has trickled down to the average worker. The economic shock of the coronavirus pandemic is also likely to be much worse because of the numbers of people forced into the gig economy by the financial crisis who no longer have the protections of a salaried job and benefits like healthcare.

But that's not the whole story of what US banking shows about the American economy. The unexpected extends even to the basic operations of the sector. Much consumer and business banking in the country is antiquated and inefficient when compared to other developed countries. Almost everyone's first experience of this when arriving in the US is the lack of apparent security in the US credit card system. While chip and pin is finally being rolled out for debit cards across the US, it is almost non-existent for credit cards where arguably much more can be spent in a single transaction. To make matters worse, signatures are rarely checked when credit cards are used, negating even that limited security feature. Consequently, I used to give an increasingly random squiggle when signing for purchases with my credit card. There seemed to be no point in taking the time to sign properly as my signature wouldn't ever be verified. And yet, despite this, I never had my card rejected for payment.

The US banks just seem to accept all this despite the obvious risks. They sometimes even compound the problem by their own actions. When my Citi Bank card was renewed on one occasion, the signature strip on the new card was a slightly lighter shade of blue than the rest of the card, not the traditional white. I was duly instructed, in the accompanying letter from the bank, to sign the back of the card immediately to guard against fraud. But with a mid-blue strip, the signature couldn't be seen even when signed firmly in black pen. So if anyone had ever decided to check my signature for a purchase, they would not have been able to as the one on the credit card was impossible to read. It felt like such a basic, and avoidable, security flaw. Not surprisingly the US easily tops the chart for payment card fraud globally reaching almost 11% of card spend compared to less than 6% in the rest of the world[15]. When I was in Washington, it was rare for a week to go by without hearing a story from a colleague or friend about fraudulent spending on their card and often to the tune of several thousand dollars. Why banks and credit cards companies would operate in this way in one of the most advanced economies is difficult to fathom, particularly when there is a tried and tested technology widely used elsewhere which significantly reduces fraud.

Cheques are surprisingly widespread in the US too despite being around since the 18th century and largely superseded by new, safer digital payment methods in most other developed economies. When buying a car soon after my arrival in Washington DC, I telephoned the dealership before I was due to pick up my new VW Golf to get details of their bank account so I could arrange an electronic transfer to settle what I owed. At that point, I had only paid a deposit of a few hundred dollars. I assumed the dealer would want to see the full remaining payment in their account before handing over the keys to the car. But to my surprise, that wasn't necessary.

When the salesman picked up the phone he appeared slightly surprised by my question.

"Just bring your cheque book", he said.

His answer didn't really compute. When cheques had been in widespread use in the UK, a bank guarantee card had been needed to make a payment of just £50, let alone thousands of dollars for a new car.

"Are you sure you don't want a bank transfer or a guaranteed bank draft?", I replied with a slight sense of incredulity.

"No. A cheque is fine", the dealer confirmed. "We trust you".

So, the next day, I did what I had been asked. I wrote out a large cheque to the dealer and was soon driving my new car off their lot without leaving a secured payment for more than $20,000 (£15,500). I almost felt like I was doing something wrong when driving away. I wondered what would have happened if my cheque had bounced. I knew I was honest, but the dealer didn't really know that. How long would it have taken for them to get their money if I had been acting with criminal intent? The whole thing felt rather anachronistic in such an advanced economy. It was endearing in a way, given the implied trust in the transaction. But it did make me feel rather uneasy about the risk of fraud in the US banking system.

Cheques are still widely used in the US for paying for everything from rent to credit cards bills despite being slow and expensive to handle. More than 14 billion were written in 2018 with a value of $26 trillion, compared to just $7 trillion spent on credit and debit cards[16].

Cheque usage is slowly declining in the US. But most other developed countries have already replaced cheques with quicker, safer and cheaper online payment systems or are well on the way to phasing them out. It is much harder in the US to set up automated monthly debit transfers to pay utility, credit card or other bills too. I often wondered whether this was a ploy by the banks and credit card issuers to increase the chance that their customers would forget to pay on time and therefore rack up interest charges and late payment penalties to add to company profits. But that would all seem rather Machiavellian. A better explanation is simply that the US banking system is failing to keep up with the times.

In an innovation of sorts, many of the banks came up with a nifty feature in their mobile banking apps to photograph and then deposit a cheque without needing to go to the bank itself. I used this from time to time and it worked well. But it still felt like it was missing the point. It just partly automated a process that many countries have deemed obsolete and inefficient. I remember someone in the financial technology sector who had developed the feature rather excitedly asking the embassy whether the innovation could be exported to the UK. He looked rather crest fallen when told there would be no market for it. Britain had already moved well beyond cheques.

So why is the US so apparently sluggish in modernising the banking sector? There are many reasons for this. With more than 5000 banks across the 50 states[17], there is much less sector consolidation than in other countries which makes agreeing and implementing innovations much more difficult. Interstate banking was even prohibited until the mid 1990s[18]. The regulatory environment is different too. But the result is the US not keeping up in a sector so crucial to its economic development. By contrast, the fintech industry is booming in the UK and Europe with innovative companies disrupting the market and keeping the bigger, traditional players on their toes. The fact this is happening much less in the US is good for UK and European exports, just not so good for the US maintaining its position as the world's leading economy.

Strong economic protectionism is another surprisingly significant part of the US system and one that existed well before the most recent wave of populism that spread across the country following Donald Trump's election in 2016. Legal requirements to 'Buy American' have existed at federal and state level since 1933 in various forms covering federal government contracts, transportation infrastructure, Department of Defense purchases and more[19]. In just one recent example of new legislation, New York State enacted further Buy American provisions which came into force in 2018 and covered iron and steel used in construction projects[20].

The ostensible motivation behind these laws is to support American manufacturers and protect US jobs. Politicians and policy makers around the world understandably want to boost their local industry and help workers, particularly in times of economic stress. That's not unique to the US. But there's always a balance to be struck between supporting local businesses and jobs and allowing competition so the best products and services can be procured at the best price. It's one thing to *encourage* or *incentivise* people and businesses to buy American wherever possible, but legislating reduces competition and increases costs to the US taxpayer[21]. With fewer competitors bidding for contracts, US companies also have less incentive to innovate which is not good for their future competitiveness or profitability. Americans arguably get poorer goods and services and pay more for them as a result – hardly the free market forces that the US myth would have us belief are central to the American economy and its success.

Buy American provisions also create some strange quirks for international companies. World-leading British ejection seat manufacturer Martin-Baker has to use American sourced and processed leather on any seats it sells to the Department of Defense for F35s fighter jets for the US Air Force because of an obscure American-only textile provision in Department of Defense procurement legislation. UK based Martin-Baker does not, of course, have to use American leather on ejector seats for any other nation buying the same or other aircraft. The legal requirement just adds complexity and cost to the production of the product for the US and increases the price.

In the infrastructure sector, Buy American provisions have arguably contributed to failing US transportation networks by reducing competition and innovation in the market place. Contracts instead go to 'locals' at higher prices, reducing the number of projects that state and federal governments can afford. The parlous state of US infrastructure is quickly evident to anyone driving in the country. Using a car in Washington DC requires quick reactions and adept slalom skills to avoid the huge potholes that appear in the roads on a regular basis particularly after heavy rain and then stay unrepaired for months or years. I lost my sense of humour when I destroyed a second tyre on my car from hitting a large, new pothole only a few weeks after having to replace another one from a similar incident. The pothole was deeper than a coke can, but had been impossible to see in the dark and wet of a Washington winter night. It caused an immediate flat tyre and meant shelling out $200 for another replacement.

So much of US infrastructure is crumbling, not just the roads. In 2017, the American Society of Civil Engineers graded US infrastructure 'D+' (meaning "poor and at risk") and estimated that $4.5 trillion needed to be spent over 10 years to bring it up to a reasonable standard[22]. US airports fare particularly badly having suffered from years of underinvestment. Anyone who has travelled through JFK in New York, Chicago's O'Hare, Boston Logan and many other American airports has seen the aging facilities that simply can't cope with passenger numbers, leading to long queues and delays. Many airports in Asia, the Middle East and Europe are now streets ahead of the those in the US. Protectionist 'Buy American' legislation is not the cause of all of the problems with US infrastructure. There are many other reasons why US infrastructure is failing. However, Buy American provisions have played a significant role in increasing project costs and causing delays[23]. Consequently, the US is quickly falling behind many other countries on the critical physical infrastructure that is so important to the continued success of the American economy.

Quality of Infrastructure: Rankings by Country, 2019

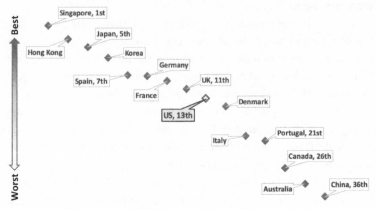

Source: *World Economic Forum, World Competitiveness Report 2019*

Some large British companies do try to operate in the infrastructure sector by incorporating in the US to the level needed to be badged American and therefore able to bid for contracts under the "Buy American" terms. But they still have to work hard to hide the nationality of their parent companies, even to the point of excluding any executives with British accents from key meetings with potential American buyers so as not to risk being ruled out as bidders from an over-zealous interpretation of the rules. The companies are also wary of overt support from the UK government's trade and investment services for fear of revealing that they are not entirely American, even if they are registered in the US, employ Americans and pay US tax. It's a weird dance to get around legislation which is damaging to the US economy. By contrast, nationality provisions largely don't exist in UK and EU public procurement which frees up the market to international competition.

American protectionism also saw the popular Virgin America brand disappear from the US – an airline that was shaking up the market and challenging other US domestic carriers to up their game. US law limits foreign ownership of domestic airlines to a maximum of 25% – much less than the 49% permitted in the EU. As a result, Richard Branson could not hold even close to a controlling share of the company and was powerless to stop its sale and subsequent absorption by Alaska Airlines in 2017 when other shareholders wanted to cash in on its success[24]. The consolidation saw the end of an innovative company, meaning less choice for US consumers.

In another aviation-related example, Norwegian Air – a UK and Republic of Ireland-based European airline – submitted applications to the US Department of Transportation in 2013 for permits to operate more transatlantic flights into regional US airports. The application met fully the requirements of the EU-US Open Skies Agreement and relevant American regulations and laws. But US airlines and transportation unions immediately launched a shrill lobbying campaign to block the applications claiming Norwegian Air's business model would contravene US labour laws, threaten US airline jobs and reduce aviation security. Large amounts of money were spent to win over members of Congress and petition the federal government. A number of senators issued a bipartisan amendment to try to block the applications; the House Transportation Committee wrote to the Transportation Secretary urging him to deny the airline's request[25].

After more than two years of analysis and consultation, the applications were ready to be signed off by the Transportation Secretary. The Department of Transportation had considered the opposition to the permits, but confirmed the applications met all US requirements[26]. But this turned out not to be enough. With the 2016 presidential election approaching, politics would now get in the way. The Transportation Secretary didn't want to risk upsetting the airline unions so close to polling day even if there were no grounds on which to block the applications – the Democratic Party needed union support. So, although the Transportation Secretary had no formal power to prevent the approval of the applications, he delayed the process, effectively kicking it to the next administration. In the end, it was almost four years before the applications were finally approved despite the fact that the company met all US legal requirements, would create many jobs in the US, bring thousands more tourists to the country spending dollars in the US economy and offer American consumers a greater choice of transatlantic flights. An \$18 billion order of Boeing jets needed to fly the routes had also been significantly delayed on the back of fearmongering by the US airlines and unions because they didn't want international competition[27].

The list of examples where protectionism in the US hobbles the free market goes on. The US understandably banned the import of British beef and lamb following the outbreak of BSE in the UK in 1989. But more than 30 years later, British farmers still can't sell their lamb in the US; the ban on British beef was only lifted in 2020. The delays can only be attributed to protectionism and broader trade politics to stop high-end products competing in the US market. There have been no health grounds to block the sale of UK beef and lamb in the US for many years. Most of the rest of the world has permitted British exports for a long time, satisfied with the actions the UK took after the BSE crisis to eradicate the disease.

But perhaps the biggest surprise about how the US economy really works came from my experience of running the UK government's offices across America. With more than 700 staff in 14 locations in the US, the British network – the embassy in Washington, plus consulates and UK government offices in other major cities – operates daily in the US economy, employing several hundred Americans, procuring goods and services and managing a range of owned and rented real estate.

The first shock was quite how litigious the US can be, and despite America's international reputation on this front. Not long after my arrival in Washington, we had to make a small number of staff redundancies because of enduring pressure on UK government budgets following the 2008 economic crisis. Letting people go is never desirable or easy. But it was considerably more fraught in the US. Around half of those we made redundant claimed discrimination for their departure on the grounds of race, age or something else, even when this was patently untrue – we simply had to make redundancies to cut costs. Perhaps even more surprising were the staff who chose themselves to resign from their jobs to take up opportunities elsewhere – usually for more money than a government employer could offer. Some then tried to claim they were owed extra pay or some other form of additional compensation on a range of spurious grounds and threatened legal action if their demands were not met. No win, no fee lawyers were always on hand to offer their services and stir up trouble. I got the sense that the lawyers saw embassies as soft targets on the grounds that foreign governments wouldn't want to risk potential damage to their reputations from labour disputes that went public.

The embassy therefore faced fairly regular investigations by the Equal Employment Opportunities Commission (EEOC) or written demands from private lawyers with the clear objective of us agreeing some form of paid settlement to our former staff. The implicit threat was obvious. If we didn't comply we would risk going to court which would have been eye-wateringly expensive and time consuming, and could have damaged the UK's reputation. I soon learned that this whole pseudo-legal industry was fuelled by the behaviour of other US employers who would just offer some cash to make the whole thing go away when former staff made claims, however unfounded. That was just the way business worked in the US.

I spent a lot of time explaining to our embassy lawyers and EEOC mediators that as a UK government operation we could not make payments to former staff on a whim when there was no case to answer even if that meant risking litigation. The UK Treasury, rightly, does not permit transactions which could be classed as "novel or contentious" and this includes special severance payments – payoffs by any other name[28]. This led to quite a lot of head scratching on our lawyer's part. It wasn't the American way. Very often, they advised that we should simply press the Treasury harder to agree to pay up, to make the cases go away and avoid the risk of ending up in court. We didn't. And in every case, we managed to avoid formal litigation and making any form of payoff. But this was far from cost free. It came from many hours of hard work constructing our defence and significant bills for legal support for no reason other than to see off an opportunistic merry-go-round of claims, fuelled by unscrupulous lawyers in the US legal business.

When running the UK government network, I also came face to face with surprising amounts of arcane employment legislation that significantly increased the burden on US employers and was widely disliked by our American staff. The Fair Labor Standards Act of 1938 created important protections for US workers against unfair pay practices and work regulations at the time[29]. But the law hasn't kept up with the times and is hard to apply to many aspects of a 21st century intellectual-capital based business like an embassy or consulate without creating significant bureaucracy, adding cost and causing divisions between staff. The Act requires all employees to be put into two categories: "non-exempt" for lower-level, hourly paid workers who are entitled to overtime as defined by the act; and "exempt" employees who have more responsibility, are considered salaried and not entitled to overtime. These categorisations might work in a factory scenario where there's a clear distinction between the shop floor and management. But classifying staff in this way in the embassy was often controversial and unpopular particularly at mid-levels where the lines around the law's definitions are blurred. It also meant we had to have expensive electronic clocking in systems in all our offices to manage hours like some sort of Victorian factory. We followed the rules because that's what Brits do and, of course, to avoid the inevitable litigation that would be stirred up by opportunistic lawyers if we didn't. But it did feel rather disruptive, arcane and unnecessary.

Even worse were some shark-like business practices the embassy experienced that smacked more of the New York of Salvatore Maranzano or Chicago of Al Capone than a highly advanced economy in the developed world in the 21st century. In one location where we had offices in New York, there was a single cleaning contractor for the building. The company was significantly over-priced and gave a pretty poor service, no doubt comfortable that they had the building stitched up. When we investigated replacing them with our own cleaners, we were warned off by the office management company because of the risk of ugly picketing outside the building by the cleaners' union complete with a large inflatable rat or worse[30]. We were strongly advised to stick with what we had; other tenants in the building wouldn't appreciate the disruption of angry labour protests.

In the end, we did find a way to adjust the contract for the cleaning company, reducing their responsibilities in our offices for a reduced fee and taking on the rest of the work with directly hired staff. It saved money and delivered cleaner offices. But we hadn't been able to get rid of the cleaning contractors completely. We had more important things to do than face some long and disruptive local employment dispute that upset our office neighbours and risked becoming very public. It was ultimately a case of 'choose your battles' and we decided not to fight this one. Of course, that was exactly what the cleaning company and building management had banked on. It was a New York version of the free market in action.

In one condominium building in New York where we owned a large apartment, we faced what can only be described as behaviour verging on extortion. The apartment had been bought several years earlier with the express purpose of having an entertainment space to host events to showcase the UK. The building owner had been delighted at the time to have a prestigious customer like the British government in his condominium which he almost certainly used to market other units in the newly renovated building. A few years later, however, the owner took against how we used the apartment. He and other members of his family still lived in units in the building. He claimed that our events were disturbing the residents and placing extra wear and tear on the lifts. The developer had no evidence to support his claim. We had not received a single complaint from anyone else living in the building and we knew many of them through the block's management board. Most of the events we hosted were over by 10pm at the latest; few were held at weekends. None were wild or noisy parties. We called in experts anyway to assess our lift usage with a view to paying a fair share if we were causing extra wear and tear. The experts told us that the lifts were designed for much heavier use than would ever be the case in a small condominium building even if we did regularly invite guests to events. We were making no difference whatsoever to their expected life.

This didn't satisfy the building owner. As he still held more than half the units in the block, he had a majority of the votes on the condominium management board to push through whatever he wanted. He set about changing the building's rules and regulations to impose additional management fees on a sliding scale for each event we hosted from a small dinner party to a larger reception. He took the revised regulations to the board and nodded them through himself. The impact was immediate. If we continued to host events as we had done for years, we would rack up thousands of dollars in extra charges each month.

We took legal advice on our options given the serious impact on how we could use the apartment. Many events would become unaffordable. It just wasn't reasonable for the UK taxpayer to have to spend hundreds of extra dollars for a British minister to host a reception or dinner in an apartment we owned. It felt like we had a strong case to overturn the new condominium rules. But the legal advice was surprising and frustrating. We were told that we could take legal action as the building owner's behaviour was unreasonable. But we would have no more than a fifty percent chance of winning the case as New York courts tended not to intervene in condominium building disputes unless the actions were expressly fraudulent or criminal. To make matters worse, the costs of taking action would likely amount to half a million dollars, the whole thing would take at least a year and we probably wouldn't be awarded costs if we won.

We learned later that the building owner had skimped on regular maintenance over a number of years, despite taking hefty annual management fees from all the residents which was supposed to cover the work. He was therefore facing a significant bill to rectify a number of problems and was probably trying to find a way to cover his costs. But the law was going to be no help even though we had watertight case. Either we had to accept the restrictions on how we could use the apartment or pay the charges imposed unreasonably by the building owner. Neither were sustainable. The only alternative was to move.

There are plenty more sharp practices in New York and other US cities that seem equally difficult to stop. The embassy and our consulates would often partner with British theatre groups and musicians to showcase the UK creative industries in the lucrative US market. When playing at New York venues, the groups were often obliged to pay extortionate rates for support from the venue's technical staff in addition to the venue hire costs. But those stage hands, carpenters and electricians – some of whom were earning the sorts of six figure salaries that brain surgeons would recognise – were then rarely available to help, leaving the groups to do all the set up work themselves. It soon became clear that this was well-known feature of the New York entertainment industry. Highly unionised venue employees have negotiated outrageously lucrative contracts by, in effect, holding the venues to ransom by threatening to remove their labour[31]. The contracts are so valuable that the technical staff do everything they can to pass the jobs onto their children when they retire in a mafia-like system of patronage. No other similar jobs in New York would pay anywhere near the same amount of money, so it's important to keep them in the family. The practice has effectively smothered out competition. The venue owners have little choice but to pay the exorbitant salaries – and to recoup them from visiting companies – to keep their operations open. In this case, the US free market feels more like the wild west, or mafia exploitation, than a thriving capitalist economy.

In many ways, little of this is unique to the US. All economies have their quirks. As far as protectionism is concerned, for every story of one country's restrictive behaviour, there's often an equivalent on the other side. Many countries' leaders champion free market forces while at the same time passing legislation to protect their domestic industries from competition or at least to give them a competitive advantage. But what is surprising in the US case is just how far the reality diverges from the myth of America being the world's foremost capitalist economy, where competition is king and the market delivers. When the very essence of a country is wrapped up in a particular narrative, it's all the more surprising to discover the narrative doesn't really reflect reality at all.

The unexpected truths about the US economy are also problematic for two reasons. First, in some areas absolutely critical to America's continued economic success – the internet and mobile phone services, banking, infrastructure and the legal and regulatory environment – the US is falling behind its peers and, in some cases, rapidly developing countries too that are looking to attract international investment away from the US and other Western countries. Political grid lock combined with powerful commercial interests backed by lobbying dollars are stopping these problems from being tackled, or slowing down agreement on solutions. Second, as far as protectionism is concerned, the US appears to impose more restrictions than many other developed economies despite the myth of the US being the country most committed to the free market. The result is stifling competition and innovation and pushing up costs. Neither is good for America's future prosperity.

Even more importantly, the US economy appears to be increasingly weighted towards benefiting the rich. Anti-competitive behaviours are commonplace to protect big corporate profits. Parts of the economy are run by effective monopolies and activities verging on the criminal or fraudulent are not unknown. But there appears to be little government push back to try to address this.

In his inaugural address in 1937, Franklin D Roosevelt said: "The test of our progress is not whether we add more to the abundance of those who have much; it is whether we provide enough for those who have too little."[32] And yet the US economy is now enriching an increasingly small elite of the super-wealthy while impoverishing a growing underclass. Despite pockets of incredible innovation and economic dynamism, significant parts of the economy are falling behind America's competitors. Without change, the US will struggle to retain its position as an economic superpower. And if the US economy were to falter, the knock on effect for the economic health of the rest of the developed world would be significant. The Great American Delusion has many real-life consequences.

Chapter Four

Separation of Church and State

Myth number 4 – the US is a secular republic as established by the Founding Fathers with a clear dividing line between church and state.

B ack in the late 18th century, as they grappled with establishing a guiding framework for their newly independent nation, America's Founding Fathers envisaged the clear separation of church and state. They wanted a new system of government for a new country based on secular principles, free from a state religion that had come with being ruled by the British monarchy[1]. Many of the Founding Fathers were men of faith. But like most of the population of the American colonies at the time, they were from different Protestant denominations, not the same church. The Founding Fathers understood from experience and history the oppression that could be associated with a state religion and the risks of religious conflict. It was therefore no accident that they crafted a constitution which makes clear that no religious test will be required to hold public office[2], or that the First Amendment to the Constitution protects the freedom of all religions[3]. Quite purposefully, the Founding Fathers made no reference to a link between church and state.

Roll forward 230 years, and you wouldn't easily guess the Founding Fathers intentions from the political landscape in the US. Formally and legally speaking, America is still a secular nation where the worship of any religion, or indeed being atheist or agnostic, is accepted and is separate from government. Overall religious adherence is also falling in the US just as it is in other parts of the West[4]. But the role of religion in US politics, driven largely by the evangelical Christian right, is considerable and growing as America becomes ever more polarised. And all this is happening despite the US becoming significantly less Christian as increasing numbers of Americans identify with no religion at all[5].

One of the first things Western Europeans notice when they arrive in the US is how much more religion, and particularly Christianity in its various forms, is an integral part of American life. The US is a significant outlier among wealthier, developed nations as far religion is concerned. It is much more religious than most other Western countries. More than five times as many Americans than Britons, Germans and French say religion is an important part of their lives[6]. Around a quarter of all Americans consider themselves to be evangelical, or 'born again', Christians at the conservative right of the

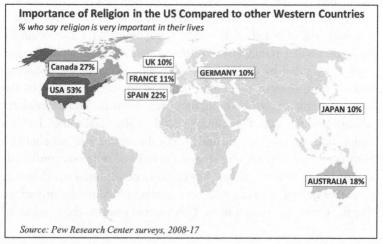

Importance of Religion in the US Compared to other Western Countries
% who say religion is very important in their lives

Canada 27%

UK 10%

FRANCE 11%

GERMANY 10%

USA 53%

SPAIN 22%

JAPAN 10%

AUSTRALIA 18%

Source: Pew Research Center surveys, 2008-17

religious spectrum[7]. Church going, although declining, reaches numbers not seen for decades in most of Western Europe[8]. While in Washington, I soon learned that the best time to visit supermarkets and shopping malls, or anywhere else that is usually crowded on a weekend, was on a Sunday morning when many Americans would be in church. You just had to be careful to avoid driving near popular places of worship around the times of their services. I got this wrong more than once and was quickly stuck in traffic as faithful Americans all tried to park as closely as possible to their church, causing local gridlock.

This enduring strength of faith is pretty surprising for many Europeans. But it is the influence of religion on politics, particularly that of the Christian right, that I found to be most alien and more than a little disturbing. The extent to which election candidates have to go to 'out faith' each other to win support from powerful evangelical groups and Americans of faith more generally can be quite disconcerting. It is hard to fathom why politicians in the 'land of the free' would kowtow to movements that want to constrain the rights of the American people if they somehow clash with a particular set of religious beliefs. It's equally difficult to grasp how evangelicals themselves reconcile their own strong attachment to personal freedom with their efforts to ensure US society is firmly moulded around their own religious views. Most evangelicals sit squarely on the right of the political spectrum and individual liberty is a cornerstone of American Republicanism. But for evangelical Christians in the US, personal freedom has to fit firmly within a staunchly traditional and conservative view of America's future otherwise it should not be permitted. In other words, it's not personal freedom at all, and evangelicals are investing heavily in politics to try to achieve their aims.

The 2016 presidential election followed the pattern of every other recent US national election in terms of the role of religion, at least early on in the campaign to choose the Republican and Democrat presidential candidates. I watched, both fascinated and uneasy, as those standing for their party's nomination would parade their religious credentials during public appearances, often before even setting out what they stood for on critical issues like health, education and national security. In the evangelical heartlands of the south and south west, the lengths to which the candidates felt they had to go was even more discomforting. They went out of their way to be seen in churches, with Christian communities, or alongside well-known evangelical religious leaders. They spoke profoundly about their belief in God and usually alongside their perfectly turned out wives and children to drive home their commitment to the traditional, Christian family unit.

For some of the candidates, their efforts were more than a little dishonest given faith was clearly not an important part of their lives and their behaviour could hardly be described as compatible with religious sensibilities. But the votes of the quarter of Americans who claim to be evangelical and others who profess the Christian faith were too important to pass up. And so all the candidates flaunted their religious credentials, whether real or not, as genuinely as they could muster. Some did hold profound religious beliefs. But that wasn't necessarily any less disturbing. Most Western democracies don't tend to mix religion and politics beyond expecting their elected representative to have certain core human values that may or may not come from religious beliefs. Despite the recent rise of populism in many parts of the Western world, most democracies tend to try to embrace the growing diversity in their societies, not constrain their citizens around some traditional values of a bygone era. But that is exactly what evangelical Americans were looking for in 2016 and what some candidates promised in an effort to win their votes.

When evangelicals swung behind the candidate for president who least embodied their strongly-held religious views, many rationalised their choice by claiming it wasn't about the vehicle but rather about securing a Republican Party election victory at any cost. Only a Republican win would ensure the next Supreme Court Justices would be chosen by a nominally conservative president. And stemming the tide towards liberalism as they saw it was paramount[9]. The Supreme Court's decision just a year before to legalise gay marriage was still raw for many on the Christian right. But how evangelical voters were able to block out so much about the vehicle they chose to hitch a presidential ride with remains a mystery to me, unless they were somehow able to convince themselves that the alternative was the devil incarnate itself – the 'Devil Wears Clinton'. Could that really be possible in 2016 America? Many evangelicals certainly came close to this in their visceral hatred for Hillary Clinton despite the fact she was more a person of faith than her opponent[10].

I got a revealing insight into conservative Christian thinking when I visited the headquarters of the evangelical movement, Focus on the Family, outside Colorado Springs soon after the 2016 election. The visit was also a clear reminder of the power and wealth of the evangelical movement in America. The vast red brick campus includes a palatial welcome centre offering guided tours detailing the movement's mission and showcasing its radio station, websites, publishing arm, conference centre, family helpline and internet monitoring station. The centre also includes children's play areas, a discovery centre, a gallery and shops, and even features on TripAdviser with 4½ stars as the 10th best thing to do in Colorado Springs. Evangelicals are clearly obliging when it comes to writing online reviews to promote their cause.

After a personal tour of the centre I sat down for lunch in a bright, modern meeting room with two representatives of the movement to talk about their mission and the role of evangelicals in the presidential election. I was told about Focus on the Family's aim to help families stay together, its pro-life commitment, its belief in the 'sanctity of the man and woman' (code for homosexuality being sinful), its efforts to spread evangelism around the world and its work against cyber bullying. The representatives wisely chose not to mention the organisation's support for sexuality conversion therapy. When I asked about the strong evangelical vote for Donald Trump a few weeks earlier, the answer was simple. Evangelicals wanted to ensure a conservative president would nominate the next Supreme Court Justices – to stop the erosion as they saw it of traditional Christian values in the US. Nothing else mattered. Evangelicals hoped a more conservative Supreme Court might even re-open Roe vs. Wade and outlaw abortion again across the US.

The two Focus on the Family staff described the importance for the evangelical community of Americans being free to make decisions based on their religious beliefs – including for businesses to refuse to serve same sex couples or to limit healthcare to their employees so as not to include contraception or the morning after pill. They railed against a case a few months earlier where a cake maker from Masterpiece Cakeshop in Lakewood, Colorado was judged by the Colorado Court of Appeals to have discriminated against a same sex couple for refusing to make a cake for their wedding[11]. Evangelicals, they said, believed they were in a battle to preserve the sacred over the secular, and secularism went against the very foundations of the US as they saw it. Holding their noses to support a flawed candidate to ensure the Republicans took the White House was simply what they needed to do to try to advance the values of their faith. Indeed, they argued, every human being was flawed but anyone could still be a vehicle for God's work, wittingly or not.

I asked about the obvious tension between the rights of those with strongly held evangelical faith and the rights of others with different views or beliefs, religious or not. By way of example I probed what Muslims living in America should be able to do in pursuit of their faith from a Focus on the Family perspective. Should mosques be able to broadcast calls to prayer in American communities just as churches rang their bells to mark their services or celebrate events? The Focus on the Family representatives did not have a good answer to this. For them it was all about the rights of people with evangelical faith who should be free to act in accordance with their religious views, period. That was the American way and, from their perspective, what the Founding Fathers had intended for the country. Somehow, the Focus on the Family representatives appeared to have managed to convince themselves that their approach would have little impact on others, that their freedom to choose would not have broader consequences. In effect, other religions or non-religious beliefs could be seen, but not heard.

I left the centre in no doubt that Focus on the Family did some good work, including supporting couples getting into marital difficulties, encouraging the adoption of children in need and working against internet bullying. I heard stories of Focus on the Family staff intervening directly in chat rooms when distressed individuals were being encouraged to commit suicide by unknown cyber bullies. We talked about the parallels between their work on cyber bullying and governments' efforts to ensure terrorists did not have a safe space on the internet to incite violence.

How much Focus on the Family proselytises to anyone who comes to them for help was unclear from my conversation. But "sharing the gospel of Jesus Christ with as many people as possible" is a core element of their mission[12]. So it's hard to see the organisation not taking the opportunity to steer people with whom they come into contact towards their particular version of Christianity. Doing so, when many people approach Focus on the Family at their most vulnerable, has to raise questions of integrity and morality. The need to spread 'the word' appears to justify almost anything for some American evangelicals.

Like many religious organisations, Focus on the Family is also politically active to advance its cause. They work through a partner organisation – the Family Policy Alliance – to get around the legal restrictions on churches being involved in politics. The Founding Fathers' formal limitations on mixing church and state remain. But loopholes – or rather creative use of the law to establish firewalls between churches and their lobbying arms – allow religious organisations to be significant political players. The Family Policy Alliance trains and supports political candidates who are aligned with Focus on the Family's evangelical mission; it lobbies against LGBT rights including the right of gay couples to adopt; it campaigns against federal contributions to the sexual health organisation Planned Parenthood because it provides contraception and abortion services; and it was active in trying to prevent gay marriage before the US Supreme Court ruling in 2015[13]. Armed with considerable resources, often from anonymous private donors, evangelical groups can be very effective lobbyists. By 2010, there were more than 200 religious lobbying and advocacy organisations in Washington DC, up from around 40 in the 1970s, and spending more than $350 million a year[14].

My visit to Focus on the Family helped to explain why 81 percent of white, evangelical Christians voted for Donald Trump in 2016[15]. But some evangelicals were almost certainly motivated by more sinister aims than trying to ensure a conservative president would nominate the next Supreme Court Justices in the hope of stopping the spread of liberal values in the US. Some were undoubtedly attracted by the populist and nationalist messages of a number of the candidates, and the promise of a return to a more traditional America – an America which was largely white, almost exclusively Christian and certainly less diverse. It's hard to avoid the conclusion that racism played a part in this[16]. The sense among evangelicals that their country was becoming unrecognisable on the back of a slew of liberal policies under the Obama administration could easily be linked to immigration. It was then just a small step psychologically to see immigration as the cause of violent crime, stagnant or falling wages and joblessness.

Early in 2018, when visiting a beautiful old Catholic church in Florida with its origins dating back to the first Spanish settlers in north America in the 16th century, I got chatting to the docent who was welcoming visitors. The docent was a petite woman probably in her late sixties, with an engaging but gentle manner. She explained with great passion the story of the saint after whom the church was named, depicted in striking, colourful stained glass windows around the building. The saint, she said, had lived a sinful life for many years but had converted to Christianity after hearing the voice of God calling him to return to the Church. The docent explained the impact of the saint's teachings on Catholic thought and was clearly touched personally by the story of God winning out over sin and bringing another soul to the goodness of Christianity.

As I was about to leave the church, our conversation turned to more mundane things. The docent asked what was I doing in the US and how I liked the country. I tried to answer the question in a way that would avoid a conversation about politics, which didn't feel right in a church. But I gave a nod to the tumultuous developments since 2016; it was impossible not to without sounding completely out of touch. This usually resulted in a knowing nod or smile from Americans on either side of the political aisle who probably wanted to avoid yet another conversation about politics too. But the docent dived straight in and our conversation immediately took a darker, but more revealing turn.

"You have been in America during an interesting four years", she said.

I nodded and smiled.

"But America is no longer what it was", she explained.

I could sense that she was genuinely anxious about her country.

"I am praying for immigrants to stop coming", she added, dropping her voice to a whisper. "The America I love is becoming unrecognisable".

The docent didn't mention the word "white"; she didn't have to. But the meaning was clear. It didn't feel malicious or even overtly racist, at least not on the part of this particular docent. Rather it seemed to reflect a genuine fear about her country and how quickly it was changing. But the contrast was stark with what churches are supposed to teach about faith, love and compassion and helping those in need. I couldn't help thinking how perverse and disturbing it was that some right-wing Christian organisations in the US would stoke these fears, and politicians prey on them in pursuit of election success.

I shouldn't have been surprised, of course. Only a few months earlier, pro-Brexit campaigners in the UK had successfully played on the same fears of change. They pedalled populist promises with their lightly veiled nationalism of "taking back control" from the EU including to stop immigration which, they claimed, was increasing crime, forcing down wages, leaving 'real' Britons without jobs and making the UK unrecognisable for 'genuine British people', whatever that meant. Just like the US, the UK has faced waves of immigration over its history. We are both countries of immigrants and highly diverse. Great Britain's colonial past and open economy have brought people from all over the world to make the UK their home for centuries. The modern US was founded on immigration. Trying to define a 'true British person' or 'true American' or indeed some perfect and idyllic time in our countries' histories around a particular belief system makes no sense. But that is what happened on both side of the Atlantic.

The 2016 presidential election in the US saw these messages of fear deployed extensively, fuelled by the huge amounts of money in US politics, and amplified through an unholy, and perhaps unintentional alliance – at least on the part of some churches – between evangelicals, White nationalists and the Republican right. In Democracy in America, Alexis de Tocqueville talked about religion as providing the moral framework for a successful democracy[17]. But that's hardly the role religion is playing in the US today, with evangelical organisations allied to fringe groups and pursuing a return to an illiberal and backward-looking America that would impose its views on an increasingly diverse and vibrant society. The Founding Fathers may not have foreseen the growing polarisation of political views in the US, or the rapid growth of a particular conservative interpretation of Christianity. But they did understand the consequences of allowing one religious viewpoint to dominate others through the mixing of church and state. And that was to be avoided at all cost.

The 2016 election revealed the true aim of religious groups in seeking political influence in the US today. It is not only about trying to uphold a particular sense of human morality that de Toqueville would recognise and that conservatives, religious or otherwise, fear is being lost in modern American society. At least part of the motivation is fear that growing ethnic and religious diversity will weaken the influence of traditional Christian religions in the US and, with that, the white, largely Protestant Americans who have governed the nation since its independence. In other words, it's about power and control, which also means money. What we are really seeing is a rear-guard action by evangelicals to try to ensure their brand of Christianity is ever more influential in the US political system so that white Christians continue to dominate American society and wealth.

The Christian right pursues these aims vigorously through religious advocacy and political lobbying. But it also has an extensive and growing media presence across radio, TV and the internet to feed its base and extend its influence across all parts of the country. Its reach goes well beyond churches and preachers, evangelical organisations like Focus on the Family and their lobbying arms. I've lost count of the number of times when driving around rural America that the only FM radio stations I could find from a full scan of the airwaves were evangelical, broadcasting in various formats including contemporary Christian music, talk shows, spiritual teachings and church services. Non-religious alternatives often just don't exist.

Christian radio stations, now numbering more than 3000 around the country, outstrip National Public Radio by a factor of three[18]. When taken together in their various formats, Christian radio even outnumbers stations playing country music – America's most popular single radio genre. A number of Christian radio networks have national reach through hundreds of local channels that rebroadcast their content[19]. And many of the broadcasters have a significant internet presence too, offering programmes to stream and podcasts to

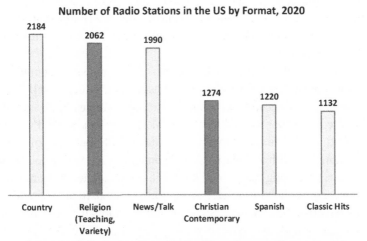

Number of Radio Stations in the US by Format, 2020

Source: Inside Radio, http://www.insideradio.com/resources/format_counts/

download and, of course, evangelical merchandise to purchase to fund their mission[20]. Scrolling through American TV channels on cable or satellite anywhere in the country will also quickly lead to one of many evangelical stations. As with radio, some of the Christian TV networks have greater reach than the big mainstream commercial channels through hundreds of re-broadcasters. Their output is often highly polished and professional. At first glance it is easy to think you are watching a conventional national TV channel, not the broadcasting arm of an evangelical religious movement.

When I first travelled to the US in the late 1980s, TV religion was mainly dominated by simple, low budget broadcasts of church services and religious teachings. A few, flamboyant televangelists had developed huge followings and become national and sometimes international celebrities, amassing great fortunes in the process and living lavish lifestyles – the reality TV celebrities of the time. Some like Jim and Tammy Faye Bakker established a popular Christian theme park, Heritage USA, on the back of their hugely successful Praise the Lord TV network until Jim was embroiled in a sex scandal and later jailed for fraud[21]. Others like Jim Swaggart hosted a show that was broadcast on more than 3000 stations in the US and in many other countries around the world at the height of his fame. But he too fell from grace after a sex scandal involving a prostitute in a Louisiana motel and was soon being investigated by the Internal Revenue Service for fraud[22]. Glitzy TV evangelism lost its sheen a little, but didn't disappear.

The US still has many televangelists today and some continue to court controversy[23]. Over the years, I have often found myself filling time in an American hotel room by scrolling mindlessly through the hundreds of channels on American cable TV. After a while, I will get sucked in, Louis Theroux-style, to the weird spectacle of a US televangelist with all their passionate oratory, laced with a good dose of fear, predicting that something terrible will happen to mankind if watchers don't turn to Jesus through their particular brand of conservative Christianity. Some of the televangelists can be both fascinating and disturbing to watch in equal measure. But it's their shopping slots that quickly have my blood boiling. Before I know it, I'm shouting at the TV in outrage and grabbing for the remote control to change channels before I become too incensed.

The shopping slots offer everything from branded bibles and prayer books to healing CDs, as well as self-penned books by the channel's star preachers on leading a more faith-filled life. More disturbingly, the televangelists offer 'wishes' and prayers for sale with techniques little different from the exploitative selling of religious indulgences in Europe in the Middle Ages. The televangelists explain how the extra donation will be spent to advance their godly mission. But it's little more than preying on the vulnerable to make money with the promise of some sort of religious redemption. It distasteful and immoral. I still don't really understand why the US would not have legal protections to prevent this type of consumer manipulation and exploitation. All the televangelists are really doing is accumulating wealth by dishonest and unsavoury means. 'Let the buyer beware' is one thing; this sort of malign manipulation in the name of God quite another.

More sinister still is the fact that evangelical media organisations no longer shy away from politics. Some of the major Christian TV networks now feature shows exclusively focused on the day's news and politics interpreted from an evangelical perspective. One is even hosted by former Arkansas Governor and 2016 candidate for president, Mike Huckabee[24]. Other programmes with talk show formats are a little more subtle, but no less slanted. The networks carefully select contributors who will put across their station's preferred political/religious messages, including praising certain conservative election candidates and their evangelical-leaning policies. The show's host can then simply ask 'neutral' questions to keep the conversation going, safe in the knowledge that the station's viewpoint will be delivered to their audience. The objective is clear – to make sure the network's chosen political message gets across to their audience while setting up a defence against claims of religious interference in politics. If challenged, the station could say that they were only providing a platform for individual Americans to exercise their right to free speech. If only it were that simple.

Some of the evangelical media organisations have moved even further beyond religious programming and now have the apparent aim, whether stated openly or not, of being the sole source of entertainment, news and political analysis for their followers. Their platforms include TV and radio stations, full news websites, print media, podcasts and more[25]. In other words, they hope their viewers or listeners will have no need to go anywhere else for their doses of religion, information and entertainment. If they are successful, they will significantly reduce the chances of US evangelicals hearing a different perspective or something which challenges their point of view. And with politicians and their proxies now increasingly comfortable appearing on Christian TV and radio to court evangelical voters, there are even fewer reasons for evangelicals to turn elsewhere for news and information. Slowly but surely, the role of a single religion in US politics is being cemented in a way the Founding Fathers clearly sought to avoid.

Some American Christian conservatives also have no qualms in using heart wrenching stories in other countries to advance their cause, and sometimes in both shocking and callous ways. More than once during my time in Washington, the Christian right used the unbearably sad cases of terminally ill children in the UK for political purposes. Pious American individuals and religious groups would weigh in on the cases claiming with some moral indignation to have the best interests of the British child at heart and to be proponents of parental choice against a 'socialist' healthcare system in the UK which, if you followed their logic, was in the business of allowing children to die unnecessarily. They argued that if the parents wanted to bring the child to the US for experimental treatment, they should be allowed to even if it was against the advice of multiple British doctors and specialists who believed it would increase the infant's suffering and would not change the prognosis. Nor did it seem to matter if the American doctors being proposed to try to save the child had not assessed the child's medical condition or even tested their experimental treatments on humans.

Many of those who intervened undoubtedly felt genuinely moved by the cases and the unbearable anguish being endured by the family. No one wants to see a child die. But some on the religious right intervened largely for political purposes. They were seeking to advance their agenda in the US, wrapped in a shroud of greater care for the sanctity of human life as if the doctors and nurses treating the children in the UK somehow didn't want to make the children better. If you followed the logic, pious Americans 3,500 miles away across the Atlantic somehow felt more for the infant and their parents than those immediately involved in the fight for the child's life.

The motivations of the evangelicals were simple: to claim some moral deterioration of a more secular society in the UK which, they believed, allowed children to die unnecessarily; and to scare Americans about universal healthcare. The messages were clear. First, if only Britain was still attached to some higher, moral and religious code the children would miraculously survive, and so Americans should stick with the church or reap the chilling consequences of greater secularisation. Second, the 'socialist medicine' of the UK's National Health Service was not able to provide cutting edge care and as a result killed children. Americans should therefore resist any calls for universal healthcare as some on the left had proposed as otherwise the US would suffer the same fate.

Those intervening also, perhaps wilfully, misinterpreted the role of the British State in these cases. For the Christian right in the US, the National Health Service is an embodiment of state overreach which, with the courts, had overruled the will of the family to force a child to die. The will of the family as they saw it should be sacrosanct, whatever the consequences. But the religious conservatives failed to understand the independence and professionalism of the doctors and nurses in the National Health Service and how, if cases do go to the courts (which are, of course, also independent), both the family and the child have formal advocates alongside medical experts to ensure reasonable, albeit sometimes agonising, decisions are taken about the best course of action. It is also very rare that cases get as far as the courts, but that's just an inconvenient detail. What the Christian right fails to mention is that children tragically die in the US every day and in higher numbers amongst the poor and ethnic minorities. But that doesn't provide a vehicle for advancing a politico-religious agenda. Instead it would muddy the waters with unhelpful facts that the richest country in the world doesn't provide healthcare for millions of its citizens and that American medicine has limits just like everywhere else.

It is, of course, almost impossible to comprehend the sense of anguish and grief of parents facing the death of a young child. But the intervention by American evangelicals, usually without full knowledge of the facts, risked extending the pain for domestic US political purposes. The noise made in one of the cases reached such levels that the White House felt the need to comment – offering help to the family concerned – to burnish its own credentials with the religious right. Members of Congress weighed in too, sometimes in lurid and opportunistic terms. So much for the Founding Fathers' aims of separating church and state. The church, or rather the evangelical Christian right, is fighting hard to dictate the future direction of the US, politically as well as religiously.

Americans should be wary of attempts to link church and state, religion and government, and instead defend what the Founding Fathers envisaged for the US – a clear separation between the two. Countries where a conservative or nationalist form of religion dominates the state and society have not proved the most successful or stable, whether they be Christian, Muslim or following any other belief. America's arch nemesis, Iran, which is so reviled by evangelicals and the conservative right – is just one example. Any form of government that reflects only a particular doctrine, religious or otherwise, is doomed to be less successful, economically, culturally and socially. Dogma stifles innovation and flexibility, and alienates a significant part of society. Americans should know this more than most with their genetically-coded attachment to liberty and personal freedom which has been so important in the success of the country over the last 250 years. The Founding Fathers certainly understood the perils of governing through one interpretation of faith. Instead they foresaw a new country where all people could thrive, whatever their religious views.

In a letter in 1822, Founding Father James Madison wrote: "religion and government will both exist in greater purity, the less they are mixed together"[26]. But the lines between the two are being blurred in the US today as political polarisation cements an alliance between evangelicals and the conservative right, and as politicians see electoral advantage in pandering to religious groups in their search for votes. Some evangelical groups would undoubtedly like to see the US redefined as a Christian state and even campaign for the loosening of the restrictions on churches explicitly supporting particular political candidates. They claim that the restrictions amount to targeting pastors and censorship, and are a restriction on the right to freedom of speech. But such a change would perhaps fatally undermine the constitutional separation of church and state in the US, and increase division across America's increasingly diverse population, not heal it.

The Founding Fathers would almost certainly be disturbed by these efforts and would instead vigorously defend the guiding principles behind their constitution and the First Amendment. If the US wants to stay on top, both politically and economically, it would do better to continue to focus on tolerance and living together in an increasingly diverse society, rather than opening the door to the imposition on the whole country of the beliefs of one particular conservative interpretation of religion. Democracies thrive on the basis of everyone having a voice, not powerful groups having undue influence. That should apply equally to churches as it should to major corporations or individual billionaires. All mainstream religions share the same core values; they are human values. So there is no real threat to a Christian way of life in America as the country becomes more religiously diverse or simply less religious overall. It is certainly no justification for one church trying to impose its particular views on others in a way that goes against everything the Founding Fathers intended.

Chapter Five

Good Government is Small Government

Myth number 5 – The US has smaller and more efficient government than other developed nations, with lower taxes fuelling individual enterprise and economic growth.

Most people complain about their government; it's a common human pastime in all countries. Either government is not delivering enough or spending too much. It is wasteful and inefficient or even criminal and corrupt. But Americans tend to grumble about their government more than most given their genetically coded sense of individualism and corresponding scepticism of the role of government in society. Those on the political right campaign vigorously for smaller government. Conservatives and libertarians both routinely hark back to Ronald Reagan's presidency in the 1980s and his drive to cut government spending under the mantra: "Man is not free unless government is limited". According to Reagan there was a "clear cause and effect … as neat and predictable as a law of physics. As government expands, liberty contracts"[1]. At the same time, many conservatives often want much higher defence spending and so their position doesn't entirely add up; defence, of course, is nother branch of government. That expenditure counts as government spending too.

Whatever their politics, most Americans will claim the US has smaller government than other Western countries and is much better for it. It's a badge of honour for many if the federal, state or local government doesn't get involved, leaving individuals to provide for themselves and industry to self-regulate. Europe is widely perceived to have large government, socialist-style, and socialism is almost never a positive word in the US. Not surprisingly, this is an oversimplification of the reality in both America and Europe. Scratch the surface in the US, and government often doesn't feel very small or particularly efficient compared to those in other advanced economies. It can be unwieldy, surprisingly bureaucratic and pretty antiquated.

My first experience of this was during a visit to a Social Security Office soon after my arrival in the US. A Social Security number is essential to function in the country. It is required for everything from opening a bank account to getting a driving licence, and I needed to collect the number in person. Having been warned about how long the process could take, I tried to make sure I arrived at the central Washington DC Social Security office as soon as it opened in the hope of beating some of the daily rush of customers. But Washington's notorious rush hour traffic quickly put paid to that.

When I finally arrived about 10 minutes after opening time, I was greeted by long lines of people already struggling to work out which queue to join, from which ticket dispenser to take a number for their interview slot – supermarket deli counter-style – and what form they needed from racks of obscurely labelled wooden pigeon holes on the walls of the waiting area. There was no one in front of the counters to direct customers or provide advice. A couple of unsmiling security guards standing by the main entrance doors onto the street were constantly being asked for help as the only staff accessible to the public. But as contractors there to ensure order, they didn't have answers and usually just shrugged or pointed vaguely towards the queue ticket dispensers. The office itself looked like it hadn't been renovated since the 1970s, with tired office furniture, dulled and chipped paintwork, worn carpet and stark fluorescent lighting. It was a spirit sapping sort of place. I felt for the staff who had to spend all their working day in such an uninspiring environment. It couldn't be good for morale.

I passed the time waiting for my slot by people watching. The clientele seemed to come from all over the world - a microcosm of melting pot America milling about. Some were trying to entertain children who were clearly bored and griping from all the waiting. Others grappled with forms and piles of paperwork balanced on their knees. A few were staring blankly into space as the time passed slowly. After what felt like an age, my number was finally called and I was invited forward to one of the counters by a polite but largely expressionless member of Social Security staff. I handed over my application forms and some ID and then waited quietly. After just a couple of minutes of cross checking and stamping, the person behind the counter handed back my ID and then passed me a social security number on a small, flimsy piece of grey card. That was that. I smiled, said thank you and headed for the door.

I kept looking at the card as I made my way out. How could such an important number be on such a thin bit of paper? Why wasn't it on a chipped, plastic card, or even digital? Why wasn't the service available online. The whole process had taken more than an hour for just two minutes of interaction. It all felt rather bureaucratic and inefficient, like some communist-era public service in Eastern Europe rather than an essential government function in one of the most advanced economies on the planet. The Social Security Office isn't unique either. Very similar experiences can be repeated at other government agencies from the Department of Motor Vehicles to the US Postal Service and more. Many of the departments are obviously suffering from years of underinvestment and more general neglect. It was not what I expected to find in the US.

There's plenty of duplication and overlap in the US government system too. Traffic would sometimes grind to a halt in Washington when I was travelling across the city for meetings with the administration or on Capitol Hill. But it wasn't always the notorious Washington traffic or an accident that caused the blockages. Instead, it was police officers who had been called to an incident on the National Mall. So many different agencies would turn up at the scene that the number of police vehicles would quickly block the road. The Metropolitan Police Department would be there as Washington DC's main city police force. The United States Park Police would attend as the National Mall is part of the National Park Service which has its own law enforcement agency. The Secret Service would usually turn up given the proximity to the White House and government departments where it has responsibility for protecting senior figures. And the Capitol Police would often appear given their role in providing security for Members of Congress in their buildings on the south east end of the Mall.

With so many police on the scene, most appeared to have little to do other than loiter around or sit in their cars stopping the traffic. A few then had to work out which service had overall jurisdiction for the incident depending on what had happened. If you were stuck in your car close enough to the location of the incident, you could watch all this playing out between the different police forces. Calls were clearly being made to seniors to reach agreement on who had primacy and once a decision was reached most of the officers could return to their bases taking their squad cars with them. You could see Washingtonians getting seriously frustrated by the whole thing as they sat gridlocked in traffic, blocked from moving by the very people who were supposed to facilitate order and to solve traffic chaos, not cause it.

The competing police forces on the National Mall in Washington are just a small illustration of a much wider issue in the US where there are almost 18,000 law enforcement agencies across federal, state and local authorities[2] compared to around 70 in the UK[3]. US law enforcement agencies range from large national bodies like the Federal Bureau of Investigation which has jurisdiction over serious federal crimes, to small and sometimes private police forces that have responsibility for a single entity like a university campus, hospital or even the Washington National Cathedral. I first became aware of these small, individual police forces when the media reported the tragic murder of a Massachusetts Institute of Technology police officer at the hands of the Boston Marathon bombers in April 2013 as they were trying to evade capture[4]. Beyond the sad loss of another law enforcement officer in the line of duty, it struck me as odd that a university would be responsible for its own policing. Why wouldn't the university just be subject to the jurisdiction of the town or city police where it was based? Wouldn't the different police forces just end up tripping over each other, particularly if a more serious crime was committed that required state or federal police involvement? And wouldn't this just lead to higher police numbers than really necessary, as well as wide varieties in policing procedures and skill levels, and ultimately greater cost to the American taxpayer. Public confusion was likely too, which wouldn't help with confidence in US policing.

The American approach to law enforcement of multiple agencies with overlapping responsibilities made international cooperation more tricky too. Establishing which agency to work with on a particular problem would test an American expert let alone foreigners given the scale and complexity of the US system. But that's what UK law enforcement agencies had to do. Given the extensive cooperation between Britain and America on national security and international crime, understanding exactly who did what within US system was critical to working together effectively. Colleagues in the embassy from the UK law enforcement agencies couldn't simply dock in with their main partner agency the FBI. Representatives from the UK intelligence community could not just focus on their CIA opposite numbers. All had to navigate multiple law enforcement organisations for different challenges, with complex variable geometry depending on exactly what the issue was from international terrorism to cross-border financial crime.

The very act of cooperation with the UK could lead to better join up across American organisations too. Given their size and scale, US agencies don't necessarily feel the need to cooperate with their domestic counterparts in the way that those from smaller countries are forced to do to maximise the impact of their more limited resources. Instead, with terrorists and other international criminals turning to new technologies to turbo charge their activities and hide their tracks, US law enforcement agencies often establish their own dedicated teams to develop new techniques and technologies to try to stay one step ahead. Very often, the teams work in silos, with multiple staff dedicated to the initiative and a healthy budget, but little or no collaboration with other domestic agencies trying to crack the same problem. At the same time, the agencies do often seek UK cooperation where there is an international dimension to the challenge or threat. The Americans know that their British counterparts will be facing the same problem and might already be working on a solution which could be shared and developed further. And if not, joining forces with a partner country will bring wider skills and perspectives to the problem, and the prospect of additional resources too.

On a number of occasions when I was at the embassy in Washington, US agencies only became aware of the work going on elsewhere in the American law enforcement community when the UK was brought on board. British liaison officers either had already been approached about cooperation on the same issue by a team in another part of the system or they were simply aware of activities going on across different US agencies from their regular conversations about the new threats and challenges everyone was facing. When they shared this information, it did often then lead to greater join up across the American law enforcement community. But even this wasn't always straightforward given ingrained rivalry and competition between some of the agencies, or more mundane challenges like mutual recognition of security clearances and incompatible IT across the US system.

On the up side, the American approach does mean that large amounts of human capital and financial resources are often dedicated to solving some tough national security and law enforcement problems. But on the down side, there is a serious risk of duplication and waste in a world of finite resources and pressure on government budgets. The UK undoubtedly benefits from its collaboration with the

US on law enforcement technologies, by sharing costs with a bigger and therefore better resourced partner, and drawing on both US and UK expertise to find the best solutions. But from an American tax payer's perspective, the siloed approach doesn't seem like the most efficient use of tax payer dollars. It makes for bigger, not smaller government.

Another government-related phenomenon that Washingtonians complained bitterly about was the disruption caused by large official motorcades frequently travelling across the city. New Yorkers get even more wound up during the great global jamboree of the UN General Assembly each autumn when senior leaders from all over the world descend on the city at the same time. In the US, if a senior government figure is moving between locations, roads are temporarily blocked to allow the unhindered passage of multiple police and other vehicles guarding the principle, causing traffic chaos. When it comes to the President and Vice President, the motorcades include dozens of police outriders on CHiPs-style superbikes to move people out of the way, several bespoke "The Beast" armoured limousines to carry the President or VP and to act as decoys, numerous accompanying police vehicles, mobile communication and hazmat centres, an ambulance or two and more police outriders[5]. It's quite a sight, but not great for traffic flow.

With the embassy located next to the Vice President's official residence, I was regularly held up on my way home in the evening waiting for the VP's motorcade to pass. I seemed to have a unique knack of timing my departure with the moment the nearby roads were closed a few minutes before the motorcade arrived bringing the Vice President home. When the motorcade finally raced past with sirens wailing and lights flashing, it could take a couple of minutes for all 40 or so vehicles to enter the Vice President's compound and the roads to be opened again. The whole thing could last 10-15 minutes, causing gridlock at rush hour and frustrating many tired commuters just wanting to get home.

The motorcades are bigger than anything else I have experienced around the world on multiple trips with British ministers to Asia,

Europe and the Middle East. The costs to the federal government budget are significant too. There are numerous sets of motorcade vehicles ready to be shipped around the US and abroad when the President or Vice President travel. The US never relies on foreign governments for the security of its travelling leaders, even when they are visiting their closest allies like the UK.

The threat to political figures in the US is particularly high, of course. More than one American president has been assassinated and so considerable protection is needed. The prevalence of firearms in the country also means that those with designs against senior figures have easy access to lethal, precision weapons. But the motorcades still feel like overkill when watching dozens of vehicles and around 100 police and security staff whizz by in a blaze of noise to move US leaders around their own city. The contrast with the handful of vehicles and outriders used to transport the Queen or British Prime Minister in the UK, both of whom are also high profile targets, couldn't be more stark. But the American way is for the government to throw money and resources at a problem on an unprecedented scale rather than to manage the risks.

When local, state and federal spending is added together, overall US government expenditure as a percentage of GDP was 37.8% in 2018. By this measure, US government spending is more than Australia, Ireland and Switzerland, similar to Japan, a bit lower than

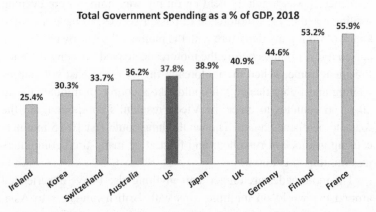

Total Government Spending as a % of GDP, 2018

Source: OECD General government spending, National Accounts at a Glance

Total Government Spending per capita (US$ thousands), 2018

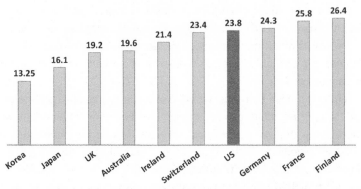

Source: *OECD General government spending, National Accounts at a Glance*

the UK (40.9%), but significantly below France and Finland where spending reaches more than 50% of GDP[6]. In other words, the US is on the lower end of the middle of the pack in terms of size of government in developed countries. It is not uniquely small. When considered in absolute US dollar terms, US government spending moves up the table and is well above the OECD average. And when most other Western governments provide some form of universal healthcare as part of their services for only a few additional percentage points of national expenditure, US government spending appears less small and efficient than many Americans would like to believe. By some analysis, when personal healthcare contributions are included to fill the gap left by government, US spending is higher as a percentage of GDP than comparable developed countries for a similar level of core services[7].

The rather obsessive American focus on the size of government also rather misses the point. It's not just about volume of spending, but efficiency, value for money and the level and quality of services delivered. There's quite a lot of evidence that the US doesn't do particularly well on this front. While the World Economic Forum again ranked the US second in its Global Competitiveness Index in 2019 because of market efficiency and American strengths in innovation, the US doesn't fare well on some basic requirements for competitiveness including the reliability of water supply, transport infrastructure, the quality of electricity supplies, tackling crime, judicial independence, workers' rights and overall health outcomes. And yet most would describe these as fundamental services which every government in an advanced democracy should provide to their citizens at reasonable cost either directly or through a well-regulated private sector.[8]

Despite the US being the world leader in many areas of technology and the internet, it has also done much less than many other developed countries to digitise government services to improve public access, increase efficiency and reduce cost. I shouldn't really have been surprised by this, even if it doesn't fit with the US national myth. When I travelled to New York with Foreign Secretary Jack Straw in November 2001 shortly after the 9/11 terrorist attacks on the World Trade Center, we went to see Mayor Rudi Giuliani in City Hall to thank him for the support New York had provided to British nationals affected by the attacks. The French Renaissance-style building is one of the oldest city halls in the US and sits elegantly at the end of a small park in Lower Manhattan, dwarfed by the surrounding glass skyscrapers that glisten in the sun. As we entered the building through the grand rotunda and were led down a traditionally tiled corridor toward the mayor's office, I was distracted by a long wall of wooden pigeon holes full of manila, internal mail envelopes typical of 1950s offices around the world. Smartly uniformed mailmen and women were distributing trolley loads of more mail with the addressee marked in a numbered box on the outside of the brown envelopes.

How could there be so much physical mail in a US office in 2001, I wondered as I followed the minister down the corridor? Why wouldn't they be using email? When we arrived at Mayor Giuliani's suite of offices, I started to understand the answer. I could only see one computer between several secretaries and personal assistants. Instead, multiple in and out trays were piled high with envelopes and documents. Paper was everywhere. It's fair to say that few governments are renowned for being at the cutting edge of IT. Britain is certainly not one of them. But by 2001, even the UK government was using a form of electronic mail system, even if clunky and bespoke. New York City Hall, while dealing with the aftermath of the biggest terrorist attack in history on US soil, seemed surprisingly behind the times.

Much has changed since 2001. President Obama set up the US Digital Service in 2014 to drive the federal government to catch up on digital access to public services after the embarrassing failure of the IT system to launch a critical element his signature healthcare reforms, Obamacare[9]. The service survived into the Trump administration and has achieved some good results on veterans' services, immigration and college selection[10]. It has worked closely with its UK counterpart which is considered to be a world leader having helped move significant proportions of UK government services online via a single, dedicated website. It's no accident that the US government portal "US.gov" looks quite like its British equivalent, "gov.uk". But there's still a long way to go in the US to achieve the levels of digitalisation reached by many competitor countries[11]. As a result, interacting with the US government online can be surprisingly painful and time consuming.

Part of the slowness of the US government to modernise can be explained by the multiple players in the US system – at local, county, state and federal levels which often jealously defend their independence from each other. This just makes it harder to join up and agree new standards, make decisions on new technologies and then implement change at a national level in an effective way. But it's also about comparatively less investment in government in a country that is instinctively sceptical about public institutions, leaving US government agencies struggling to keep up with technological advances and, consequently, falling behind their foreign counterparts.

Congress itself often doesn't help in the drive to modernise government services. Agreement on Appropriation Bills – the main vehicle for authorising federal government expenditure – is routinely won by buying off individual members with various, additional and unrelated funding commitments which are attached to the bill before it is passed. These commitments can be anything from continuing to fund defence production in a particular factory to not closing a civilian government office in the district of a member of Congress whose support is needed to get the bill through, and even if the military equipment being produced is obsolete or the facility no longer required. It can also be 'earmarks' to bills assigning government spending to the pet projects of particular members of Congress to benefit their districts, even if they are not a priority for the federal government or the US public as a whole. Both can help secure sufficient votes for an important bill to pass, particularly when Congress is so polarised and agreement otherwise difficult. Either way, the result is the same. The costs of government projects increase leaving fewer resources to provide essential services, which then compounds Americans' scepticism of government and what it delivers. With growing partisanship making it ever harder for Congress to agree the federal government budget, these practices are unlikely to stop any time soon.

If Congress can't agree new Appropriation Bills before the end of a budget cycle, or pass a temporary Continuing Resolution to maintain government spending at current levels, the federal government is shut down until an agreement on funding is reached. Shutdowns are typically the result of political disputes between the President and Congress over specific policies. But the fact that America's elected representatives would even countenance closing down the whole federal administration over a policy disagreement reveals a great deal about US perceptions of government.

A shutdown sees hundreds of thousands of government employees sent home without pay and others who are classed as "essential", such as air traffic controllers and border security agents, continuing to work but without a salary. It sees many government services stop, and contractors temporarily laid off. Despite all this upheaval, and significant financial hardship for many, Congress apparently sees little harm in closing the US government for a while for political aims. Some on the political right even try to argue that shutdowns prove that some government activities are unnecessary as US society didn't fall over without them for a few weeks when the administration was forcibly closed. Others, with no sense of irony, suggest that critical national services like air traffic control should be privatised so they can't be affected by future government closures[12].

My first experience of a government shutdown in October 2013 centred around a dispute between the Republican-controlled House of Representatives and the Democrat-led Senate over continued funding for President Obama's flagship health bill, the Affordable Care Act. The government was closed for 16 days[13]. The whole thing was pretty strange to witness. Washington was like a ghost town, with eerily quiet streets and none of the typical rush hour traffic which brings the city to a standstill every working day. More than 800,000 federal government employees were sent home. Another 1.3 million in roles deemed essential continued to work. Neither were paid.

The shutdown also put much business of the embassy on hold for more than two weeks as many of our US government interlocutors were absent, and those in work were not permitted by the terms of the shutdown to do anything that wasn't deemed critical or essential. Some were even nervous about taking our phone calls in case they opened themselves up to criticism for doing 'non-essential' activities. Numerous visits by ministers and officials from London had to be postponed or cancelled as there would be few people to meet. It wasn't even possible for Washington residents or visiting tourists to go to the monuments on the National Mall. As these are managed by the National Park Service – a federal government agency which was also forced to close – the monuments were rather bizarrely cordoned off for the duration of the shutdown even though the whole National Mall is normally an open area without restrictions at all other times of the year.

The 2013 shutdown cost the US economy $24 billion (£18.5 billion) or 0.6% of quarterly GDP in just over two weeks[14]. Since then, there have been a further three shutdowns with the most recent, which ended in January 2019, closing the federal government for a record 34 days[15]. It's a pretty sorry state of affairs in a leading Western democracy when the very functioning of the government is used as political leverage by the most powerful in the land, the President and Congress. It shows an element of contempt for the

US Federal Government Shutdowns since 1990, Length in Days

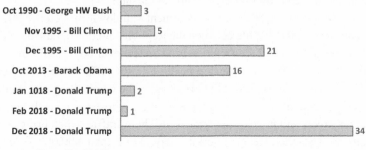

Source: New York Times

institution and a lack of empathy for government workers and many other businesses who suffer financially from the shutdowns, and particularly when significant political gain is far from guaranteed. In the 2019 case, the shutdown ended when the President backed down and accepted pretty much what had been on offer 35 days earlier[16].

When the US government is working, departments can feel large and unwieldy compared to their UK and European equivalents. Part of this is simply scale; the US is a bigger country and its departments therefore correspondingly larger. But that's only part of the story. US departments tend to be much more hierarchical and delegate much less responsibility down the chain than their UK counterparts. While at the embassy, I was challenged more than once by senior US State Department colleagues to explain why British diplomats were not keen to apply for their department's flagship international exchange programme. The programme enables young foreign service officers from America's allies to spend a year working in the State Department to get to know the US government and make useful connections for their future careers. On paper, it is a fantastic opportunity for ambitious British diplomats.

Despite this, few Foreign Office staff were interested in applying. Word had travelled quickly from previous British participants that the bureaucracy and security clearance processes in the State Department would mean successful applicants spending the first few weeks of the programme without direct access to their assigned department or even a computer. But it wasn't just the start up challenges that put British diplomats off. Once eventually set up, the size and hierarchy of the State Department meant the secondees were given little challenging work or responsibility. At their level, they were just one of thousands of US staff and far below the decision makers around much more senior political appointees. British officials who had come on the exchange programme in the past had found the whole thing pretty frustrating and advised their colleagues not to apply. By comparison, young American diplomats seconded into the Foreign Office on the UK's equivalent programme are – like their UK counterparts in a smaller and flatter organisation – given responsibility for a policy area and allowed, under direction and supervision, to make recommendations directly to senior officials and ministers. Not surprisingly, the programme is popular among State Department officials as it stretches them much more than jobs at the same level in their own organisation.

State and local governments in the US suffer from considerable bureaucracy and inefficiency too. After a review of the embassy's physical defences by visiting UK security experts in 2015, we were advised to make some upgrades to our vehicle entrance gates to improve protection from potential lone shooters or vehicle borne attacks. We already had partial protection through a combination of gates and anti-ram blockers. But they were aging and did not amount to a total airlock which would stop people or vehicles getting into the embassy compound without proper checks or searches. So we set about working with a contractor to install the new defences. The whole project amounted only to putting in new automatic gates and a bit more fencing to create a sealed vehicle entrance system in exactly the same locations as our existing gates and blockers. But after much consultation with experts we discovered that we would need fourteen separate permits from the Washington authorities ranging from the fire department, water service, historical society and building department to be able to do the job. The system was so complicated we had to hire a consultant to navigate the system on our behalf. And even then, I had to write personally to the city council to complain about how long the process was taking as it was significantly delaying important security enhancements to keep our staff safe. It was not an example of streamlined government or efficiency by any stretch of the imagination.

The system of political appointees which sees thousands of senior jobs change when a new president is elected creates further bureaucracy in the US government. On the plus side, the process brings in new blood and energy to drive policy, drawing on expertise from both within and outside government. Fresh perspectives can accelerate innovation and change. But on the negative side, every four or eight years, the process of nominating political appointees and getting them confirmed by Congress takes a great deal of time. In normal circumstances, most new presidents don't have their full team in place until 6-12 months after they have taken office. During the interim, government departments have largely to free wheel waiting for their new politically appointed seniors to set the direction of policy and launch new initiatives. In other words, it can be largely dead time when governments have many pressing issues to deal with. Simply moving thousands of people out of government positions and new ones in also has direct costs of tens of millions of dollars, and untold indirect costs in delays to government activities as the new staff get settled in and learn the ropes.

Most governments in developed countries have some political appointees alongside professional civil servants. But the American approach is of a totally different order of magnitude. In the UK, each Cabinet Minister can appoint two or three political staff – their Special Advisers. The total number of UK political appointees is therefore tiny compared to the thousands in the US. UK Government departments are run by civil service professionals under the political direction of the elected government. Officials are expected loyally to serve the government of the day, whatever their own politics. On the face of it, it's a much more efficient approach and better value for money. British ministers from all parties do sometimes complain that they feel thwarted from pursuing certain policy objectives by civil servants who – as experts in their fields – can outmanoeuvre their political leaders if they disagree with the government's approach. But it's a charge that most civil servants would vigorously deny. The politicians remain fully in charge.

The inherent scepticism of government in the US also drives American administrations to spend more on outsourcing to private companies rather than delivering goods and services themselves. It's much easier politically to get budgets agreed for spending on private sector contractors than securing government funding itself, even if this could ultimately mean US taxpayers paying more. At around two million, the number of federal government employees has changed little over the last four decades despite widespread US public perceptions of an ever-growing government. At the same time, the number of private contractors has increased. Contractors now make up more than 40 percent of all staff on the federal government's books and outnumber tenured federal government employees two to one[17]. The Department of Defense is the biggest direct employer of private contractors at more than 500,000. But this does not include the very large number of staff employed by defence companies working on contracts awarded by the Pentagon to the tune of $360 billion in 2018[18].

America's increasing reliance on contractors raises questions about accountability, oversight and value for money. There's no doubt that private companies can bring in specific expertise that doesn't exist within government or can stand up an important project more quickly. But as commercial enterprises, companies providing contract staff to the US government often pay higher salaries to their employees. They also have to factor in a decent profit margin and the hefty cost of bidding for the contracts in the first place. In other words, the government can end up paying significantly more for the private contracts than if it had used its own employees. That's hardly value for money for American taxpayers[19].

Just as importantly, few governments have a good track record of overseeing external contractors or ensuring delivery of outsourced contracts on time for the original price. Government staff often simply don't have the skills, time or resources to do this effectively. In the

US case, when the number of contractors is so high, proper oversight arguably becomes almost impossible. Add in the reality of the revolving door – with good federal employees regularly being offered jobs by the contractors for much higher salaries than the government can afford – and genuine oversight becomes even more difficult. American tax payers are not always getting the value for money or accountability they should.

In some cases, US federal, state and local governments don't deliver sufficient critical services to the American people, either directly or through contractors, because they don't have the funding or the political desire to do so. In these cases, philanthropy often steps in to fill the gap. This can include anything from providing mobile doctors and dentists in rural areas for those who can't afford health and dental care, to food banks and clothes supplies for the homeless or those living in poverty. The levels of giving of both money and personal time in the US are really impressive. Many Americans I met were regularly volunteering through their local community or church or donating items to charity. It's just what Americans do.

Healthy tax breaks for donations to charity certainly help to drive this philanthropy, although it's by no means the full story. When I had a clear out at home after Christmas one year in preparation for leaving the US, I was surprised to find a very long queue of cars waiting to donate at my local Goodwill store during the holiday period. My first thought was that my Washington neighbours were being very efficient and donating unwanted gifts or having a post-Christmas clear out too. Both could have been true. But the actual driver for the frenzy of donating was the approaching end of the US financial year on 31 December. This was the trigger for dozens of Americans to queue up in their cars overloaded with household items to donate to Goodwill in return for an Internal Revenue Service form which would reduce their overall tax bill if submitted with their end-of-year tax returns. Goodwill was obviously aware this was going to happen and was ready and waiting with dozens of extra staff and a car park full of shipping containers to store the donations until they could be sorted. The process of tax efficient giving was very slick.

Much larger scale philanthropy is also more common in the US than in the UK and many other countries. It is the norm to see museum wings, university libraries or hospital annexes named after a family who has donated the lion's share of the millions needed to build them. Multi-billionaires like Bill and Melinda Gates, Mark Zuckerberg and others have committed to giving away considerable amounts of their fortunes to good causes. All this is hugely worthy and clearly makes a difference to the lives of many Americans and others overseas too. But it isn't an efficient or necessarily well-targeted way of providing products or services to those in greater need. Instead of a collective decision being taken by government and society about what the most critical needs are in America, wealthy individuals alone get to choose.

Most of the spending undoubtedly goes on good causes. Personal freedom and choice is also important. But those who have made large amounts of money usually on the back of American and international consumers may not know what the most critical needs of society are or may not want to spend their cash on priority areas for personal or political reasons. So while Americans are rightly proud of their tradition of philanthropy and generosity, it doesn't always lead to money getting to where it is most needed. Instead, it can end up with vast sums of money being spent on vanity projects or obscure causes, while leaving Americans short of critical services from good education to healthcare, suitable housing or even adequate food because they are not provided by government. In other words, the heavier reliance on personal generosity over government for important services leads to uncoordinated and inefficient spending and continuing gaps in essential services. It doesn't really feel right in a wealthy, modern democracy.

In essence, government in the US is somewhat smaller than most other Western countries. But it's not significantly smaller, and increasing numbers of projects and services are being delivered through profit-driven private contracts which are largely unaccountable to the American public and don't always have a good track record of delivering value for money. At the same time critical services like healthcare aren't provided. So the myth of effective, small government is seriously eroded. The better question – do the American people get reasonable services for the money their government spends – remains unanswered. But the evidence would suggest that this is not always the case.

The innate US skepticism towards government seems to create an environment where the American people don't hold their government to account in quite the same way as taxpayers in other countries. Somehow, Americans just don't want to think about government and so would rather be distracted by a philosophical debate about levels of taxation instead of thinking about how their money is spent by government departments. Overlay that with politically motivated budget decisions in Congress and large parts of the US government remain unreformed and others poorly resourced to deliver really critical services to the American people. That in turn fuels further American skepticism about government which simply perpetuates the negative cycle.

The US can do much better than this. Americans should demand more from their government instead of continuing to bury their heads in the sand and allow politicians and the media to focus the debate simply on who will raise or lower taxes. There is considerable scope for streamlining US government agencies, modernising services including through digitisation and reducing duplication at the local, state and federal level. By doing this, the American public would see services delivered more effectively and at better value for money. And it might even allow the US government to provide additional services for a similar cost. Only then would the US myth of smaller, more efficient government start to ring true.

In a speech in 1910, Theodore Roosevelt acknowledged Americans' dislike of big government: "I am a strong individualist by personal habit, inheritance and conviction", he said. "But it is a mere matter of common sense to recognise that the state, the community, the citizens acting together can do a number of things better than if they were left to individual action"[20]. America would do well to find a president who has the courage to try again to realign this debate.

Chapter Six

Free Speech Fortifies American Democracy

Myth number 6 – A vibrant media underpinned by the constitutional right to the freedom of speech provides quality, breadth and choice of information to the American people and reinforces American democracy.

After watching President Obama's penultimate State of the Union Address to a joint session of Congress in January 2015, I decided to do an experiment in comparing how the speech was being reported by the big American cable news channels. I didn't expect to be surprised. The ever-growing political partisanship in the US was already well embedded in the news media. But I spent a couple of hours switching between the main news stations to do a side-by-side comparison in real time. Despite expecting to see some partisan commentary, I was still shocked by just how different and slanted the coverage was.

On the right, Fox News was slamming Obama's claimed achievements on the economy and healthcare and doing what it could to undermine his new proposals on paid family leave, increasing the minimum wage and tackling climate change. In what can only have been pre-prepared material to attack whatever the President said, a series of different conservative experts with graphs and charts set about disabusing Obama's claimed economic achievements in a way that was clearly meant to appear rigorously scientific and hard to dispute. The host presenter was mocking and sarcastic, almost baiting viewers watching from the comfort of their sitting rooms around the country to scoff with disbelief at what their President had said.

By contrast, on the left, MSNBC was praising the tone of the speech and its message of hope and progress. The presenter enthused about the President's economic record and lauded his new proposals although quickly highlighted how difficult they would be to implement because of unreasonable resistance from the political right who would do anything to scupper the President's agenda. If you hadn't actually watched the President's address to Congress you could easily have concluded that Fox and MSNBC were commenting on two quite different speeches, or even two different presidents. The Fox and MSNBC approaches came from parallel universes.

Fifteen years or so earlier I had travelled to New York to visit a Portuguese diplomat friend who was serving at his country's mission to the UN. I remember him complaining bitterly about the lack of decent TV news. The only credible source covering both domestic and international stories, he said, was the BBC World Service's US-focused TV news programme. But that was broadcast just twice a day on BBC America and not at particularly convenient times. So, if you missed these two programmes because of work or other commitments, that was quality broadcast news forgone for the day. I found this really quite hard to believe at first. But after just a few days in New York, I began to understand what he meant.

Arriving in Washington in 2013, I naively assumed things would be better. After all, I was going to be based in the US capital which would surely have numerous credible sources of TV news to feed the market of policy makers and politicians. But I quickly ran into the same problem. While the number and variety of TV channels available to the American public is mind-blowing, try as I might, I could not find a US TV news bulletin that provided coverage of the main American and international news stories in a comprehensive and balanced, yet digestible way. All I was looking for was a 30 to 60 minute slot that allowed busy viewers to get a good fix of news in one sitting at a convenient time of day. I made repeated attempts to find something that fitted the bill. It simply didn't compute that a good, mainstream, primetime TV news service wouldn't really exist. I fruitlessly scoured the channels of my cable provider. I asked American colleagues for advice on where they got their TV news – the answer was usually vague but increasingly pointed to news websites, not TV. It was pretty desperate. I even repeated my search every few months, convinced that I must have missed something in the overwhelmingly long cable TV channel guide. I hadn't.

The mainstream national TV networks – ABC, CBS and NBC – do have nightly news bulletins and most do a reasonable job at being factual. But around half of their 30 minute bulletins are commercials, and the remaining programme time includes the weather, quite a lot of commentators or other journalists giving their personal take on the news rather than news stories themselves and a daily heart-warming or "also in the news" story. So the actual, serious news content is limited to just a few minutes per bulletin and most of that is reporting about the US. Only the biggest international stories get any coverage at all and, even then, these are usually limited to the same handful of countries or issues. Travel outside the big US cities and local affiliates of the major national channels provide even less breadth of information, focusing instead on small local stories, despite being the main source of news for their local community.

The 24/7 cable news providers are arguably worse despite having plenty of scope to put together a comprehensive news roundup with so much time to fill. But instead of producing focused, inclusive news programmes that efficiently inform their viewers of the main US and international news stories of the day, the cable channels fill multiple hours with "experts" often on grainy home webcams commenting on the day's chosen stories. Or they feature seemingly endless in-studio talking heads or other journalists debating the news with each other. Like some strange TV zoo, all the commentators are shown on the screen at the same time in individual boxes alongside the programme presenter while just one is talking. Rather than listening to the person speaking, I find myself being distracted by the facial expressions or fidgeting of the silent panellists or wondering why the presenter has to be front and centre throughout the whole programme even when they are not contributing to the debate. It's really odd to watch, and certainly not genuine news reporting or a decent source of factual information for American viewers.

Overlay all this with the intense partisanship of much of the output of the popular cable news channels like Fox News and MSNBC and it makes it almost impossible for viewers in the US to get balanced, impartial TV news anywhere. To make matters more sinister, some of the cable news channels and their presenters claim repeatedly that they are the 'go to' source in America for fact and honest news when they are quite evidently providing nothing of the sort. Instead, the presenters repeatedly spout highly politicised personal opinion dressed up as news reporting. The language is increasingly shrill – with claims that those reporting from the other side of the political spectrum are shameless, full of lies, or disgraceful in their promotion of "fake news". The atmosphere could not be more febrile, or the results more frightening in terms of American access to unbiased, factual information.

If the poor state of TV news in the US isn't worrying enough, Foreign state actors are also manipulating the American media to their own advantage. In a meeting with the Alliance for Securing Democracy in Washington DC in late 2017, I learned about the techniques Russia was using in the US and Europe to anger, provoke and distract the public with the ultimate aim of destabilising Western society. The Alliance for Securing Democracy is a small, bipartisan non-profit organisation that was established after the revelations of Russian interference in the 2016 US elections "to defend against, deter and raise the costs on Russia and other state actors' efforts to undermine democracy" in the US, Europe and globally[1]. With just a small budget and a few people, the Alliance is trying hard to document and expose the activities of Russia and others, and to provide policy makers with recommendations on how best to safeguard our democracies.

The Alliance representatives described how Russia cleverly played to the growing divisions in American society and had found an unwitting ally in the US media. Stories created or amplified by the intelligence services of the Russian state were routinely released on social media to feed the divisions and increase distrust in American institutions. These were picked up first by fringe US blogs, but quickly found their way onto populist websites like Breitbart or InfoWars from where they moved onto cable TV like Fox News and became 'mainstream'. After that, the stories were reported widely even if untrue or a particularly selective interpretation of the truth. In other words, Russian state actors were skilfully feeding the ever-growing partisan appetite of the US media in order to undermine American democracy and sow dissent. The cable channels were simply lapping up the content while applying little journalistic rigour to check the facts.

It turns out that it wasn't always like this. Until the 1980s, there was a requirement for American TV and radio broadcasters to cover stories of public importance in an honest, equitable and balanced way. The Federal Communication Commission introduced a Fairness Doctrine in 1949 with the objective of ensuring that TV and radio stations exposed viewers to a variety of viewpoints when covering controversial matters of public interest. In other words, political programming had to include opposing views to an equal degree[2].

But it wasn't long before the doctrine came under challenge from American conservatives claiming that it violated the constitutional right to the freedom of speech. In 1987, with opposition building and growing fears that the now conservative-led FCC was planning to revoke the Fairness Doctrine, the Democratic Party took the opportunity of controlling both houses of Congress to pass legislation enshrining the doctrine's requirements into federal law. It didn't work. Their efforts were thwarted when President Reagan vetoed the bill[3]. And just as Congress had feared, the FCC, led by a chairman appointed by Ronald Reagan, then quickly abolished the doctrine[4]. A further attempt to re-establish the provisions of the doctrine failed in 1991 when George Bush senior threatened to veto similar proposed legislation[5].

It's hard to conclude anything other than the revocation of the Fairness Doctrine contributed significantly to the growth of increasingly partisan broadcasting in the US and arguably to political polarisation too. The rise of radio 'shock jocks' in the late 1980s including Rush Limbaugh, Michael Savage and Opie and Anthony started to feed their listeners with a never-ending meal of politically slanted outrage, bombast and exaggeration. The presenters cleverly used humour to endear themselves to their audience and normalise what they said, however offensive. The desensitising of extreme political discourse had begun[6]. Michael Savage reached such levels of outrage that he was banned from the UK by the Home Secretary in 2009 for provoking others to commit serious criminal acts and fostering hatred because of his pronouncements on Islam and immigration[7]. But he continued to broadcast unconstrained in the US. Many radio shock jocks like Glenn Beck and Sean Hannity also moved onto cable TV, expanding their reach to millions more Americans[8]. Sean Hannity's prime-time TV show on Fox News was drawing in an average of more than 4 million viewers in early 2020, with Hannity prominently positioned as President Trump's media supporter-in-chief[9].

US Public television (PBS) and National Public Radio are legally required to be objective and balanced in their programming[10]. They do an impressive job producing quality, in depth news reporting and making efforts to hold politicians of all persuasions to account. But their finance mechanisms – with the majority of funding coming from private membership contributions and donations – leaves them unable to match the reach of the big commercial channels. Partnerships with other public media organisations like the BBC help. But just 1.1 million Americans watch PBS' flagship daily TV news programme, Newshour. That's just a fraction of the viewership of the mainstream commercial network news programmes and the cable news channels, and a minuscule proportion of the US population[11].

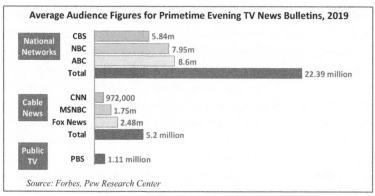

Average Audience Figures for Primetime Evening TV News Bulletins, 2019

National Networks
- CBS — 5.84m
- NBC — 7.95m
- ABC — 8.6m
- Total — 22.39 million

Cable News
- CNN — 972,000
- MSNBC — 1.75m
- Fox News — 2.48m
- Total — 5.2 million

Public TV
- PBS — 1.11 million

Source: Forbes, Pew Research Center

American Public media's regular on air telethons and pledging drives needed to keep themselves afloat undoubtedly put viewers and listeners off too. I for one would regularly turn to other channels or even go without broadcast news for a while rather than be subjected to week-long fundraising campaigns several times a year full of endless pleas for donations in return for a branded tote bag, reusable water bottle or some other random gift. I am sure public broadcasting's presenters would rather not have to beg for cash to keep their services going either. It's a bizarre state of affairs in the world's wealthiest democracy.

To make matters worse, growing political partisanship has also led to increasing numbers of conservatives concluding that public broadcasting is 'liberal' or 'socialist' because it tries to give a balanced perspective by questioning both sides of the political debate, including those on the right. Right wing politicians, and sometimes Presidents, now routinely attack US public service broadcasting for liberal bias and threaten to cut its already limited federal funding[12]. So far, they haven't succeeded. But their actions almost certainly encourage more conservative-voting Americans to turn off public media and rely more heavily on the echo chambers of right-wing news shows that simply reaffirm their views.

As for print news journalism, the US still has some of the world's best including the New York Times, the Wall Street Journal, the Washington Post, the Los Angeles Times, the Chicago Tribune and the Boston Globe. Despite falling circulation, advertising revenues and staff numbers, many American newspapers refuse to dumb down and still invest as much as they can in traditional investigative journalism which helps keep the US government and American corporations honest. On numerous occasions while at the embassy I would sit with US print journalists for an off-the-record conversation about the UK angle on a particular international policy issue – from the Iran nuclear deal to Russian interference in Western elections. The journalists would build stories over weeks or months to ensure their readership was well-informed and to try to hold the government or businesses to account. But, once again, these publications can't compete with the reach of American cable TV news channels or social media. They too are increasingly attacked by the political right for liberal bias and "fake news". They are a small, but incredibly important, voice in an overall media environment that leaves most Americans without fair, balanced and comprehensive news.

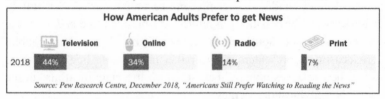

How American Adults Prefer to get News

Television	Online	Radio	Print
2018 44%	34%	14%	7%

Source: Pew Research Centre, December 2018, "Americans Still Prefer Watching to Reading the News"

The rapid growth of social media and online news sources is seriously compounding this problem. While more Americans on average still prefer to get their news from the TV than any other single source, news websites and social media are quickly growing in popularity and are now the preferred source of news for the under 50s[13]. And yet, despite their vast reach, social media and internet news sites are even less regulated than broadcast and print media and often make little effort to provide balanced and impartial information. Instead they can act like repeated doses of crystal meth to their users, amplifying and intensifying partisan information through automated algorithms that instantly circulate news stories to the like-minded, reaffirming their beliefs and prejudices and stimulating a meth-like high of a sense a belonging and wellbeing. Social media also energises those with extreme views by giving them easy access to a wide audience in a way that simply wasn't possible before the

News Source Preference by Age

% of each age group who often gets news from each platform

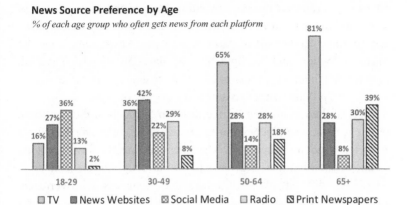

Source: Pew Research Center, survey of US adults, Jul-Aug 2018

internet, turbo-boosting their ability to organise and influence. The long term effects of social media and internet news are arguably as damaging as crystal meth too. They cause user addiction from the buzz of being repeatedly fed things we want to see and hear and ultimately to irreparable damage to the critical organs of society: factual information, sensible debate and a willingness to compromise.

In June 2013, not long after I arrived in Washington, National Security Agency contractor Edward Snowden leaked millions of stolen top secret documents to the Guardian and other newspapers about NSA and GCHQ mass internet and telephone data collection[14]. Snowden's actions triggered a frenzy of government activity on both sides of the Atlantic to work out the full extent of the leak and assess the impact it could have on critical NSA and GCHQ operations. I attended numerous meetings in the embassy to discuss the British response which was trying to limit the very real damage the leaks were likely to cause to US and UK national security[15]. Even now, seven years later, there's an ongoing debate between privacy advocates and the security establishment about whether Snowden was a hero or a traitor for leaking the information he stole from the NSA. But what was even more revealing about the leaks as far as I was concerned was how differently Americans viewed government and private sector collection and use of data. Although the NSA and

GCHQ programmes revealed by Snowden had the ultimate aim of keeping America and its allies safe, details about them were greeted with outrage on the part of many Americans. At the same time, the mass collection and manipulation of data by hugely powerful, commercial internet companies usually triggered no more than a shrug. The private sector was somehow largely benign.

Part of the explanation for the reaction of much of the American public was the fact that NSA programmes were collecting data about Americans, not just foreigners. The latter was fine; the former crossed a fundamental red line. The leaks played directly into the instinctive American distrust of government and concerns of overreach. Interestingly, the reaction in the UK was almost the opposite. When I travelled home just a few weeks after the Snowden leaks hit the press, most people I spoke to expressed little concern about the NSA and GCHQ programmes. There was an acceptance, indeed assumption, that government would (and should) collect data to help keep the public safe from terrorists and other malign actors. A long history of largely benign government in the UK certainly played its part in this viewpoint; the reaction in Germany with a history of the Stasi in the former East Germany spying on innocent members of the public was, understandably, quite different. At the same time, there was unease in the UK about how large US internet companies could use the massive amounts of data they collect to manipulate consumer behaviour, albeit with no sense at that point that anyone was about to switch off their smart phones and stop using Facebook or Google.

The way social media and internet news services work is simply adding fuel to the fire of the growing political partisanship in America and elsewhere, and making it even harder for policy makers and politicians to reach the compromises needed to tackle problems affecting the US and wider world. The companies are amplifying divisions in society through the unrestricted spread of fake news which is purposefully directed to the most susceptible targets by the huge amounts of personal data they hold about us. The first victims are sensible dialogue and social cohesion. We will never know exactly how far Russian social media activity to influence the outcome of the

2016 US presidential election in Donald Trump's favour skewed the election result. But we can be sure that Russia and others will continue to try to interfere unless there is a concerted effort by governments and the technology companies to stop it from happening. Indeed, there's plenty of evidence already that this is the case.

In the run up to the 2020 US elections, the big internet companies did make some efforts to remove fake accounts as they came under growing pressure to stop foreign exploitation of their platforms. In autumn 2019, Facebook announced that it had removed four networks of accounts – three from Iran and one from Russia – for "coordinated inauthentic behaviour", with the activities of the Russian accounts reminiscent of 2016[16]. But the scale of the challenge is enormous given the numbers of social media users and the changing tactics of foreign actors to stay ahead of the game. Facebook's Sheryl Sandberg has admitted the company "can't stop the interference by ourselves"[17]. And yet, few Western countries have amended their election laws to help them fight back effectively. In the US, the Trump administration tried to avoid focusing on the issue for fear of undermining the legitimacy of the president's 2016 election victory. The president himself weaponised his Twitter account to whip up his base and attack his opponents with little concern for fact.

With no single federal data protection law in the US[18], the technology giants are also largely free to do what they want with the vast quantities of personal data they collect. In effect, they get to determine their own rules despite the self-evident conflict of interest given data manipulation is the main source of their vast profits. Individuals are left to 'self-regulate' – to either accept the companies' data policies or not to use their platforms – and to try to work out which social media and internet news sources are trustworthy. In an incredibly complex and fast moving space, this is almost an impossible ask. And yet with so much power in the hands of a tiny number of very large technology companies that have vast reach, none of the major players have really chosen to take responsibility for the content they deliver despite how much it can damage society. A few have acted to remove material in areas like child pornography where there is a strong consensus around its abhorrence and its devastating impact on individuals and society. Google, Facebook and Twitter have also made efforts to remove misleading information about the Covid-19 virus[19]. But social media and the internet news services still remain a largely unregulated space.

Several years on from the Snowden leaks and the debate about the responsibilities of the big technology companies has heated up. Public concern is growing about their power and influence, their ability to manipulate user data for commercial gain, and how they can be used by malign actors like Russia, Iran and North Korea to destabilise Western society. In part, the debate has moved on because legislative changes in America and Britain have placed the government surveillance programmes revealed by Edward Snowden under a tighter legal framework. But the revelations about Russian efforts to influence the 2016 US presidential election were a loud wake-up call for many as they highlighted the very real dangers from an unregulated digital space. More recent reports of serious leaks and abuse of data by the technology companies are further fuelling the debate. Pressure is now finally growing for them to take more responsibility for the content on their platforms and how their algorithms influence society.

At the same time, the big players like Facebook and Google are investing heavily in lobbying to see off any significant new regulation of their activities[20]. They continue to argue vehemently that they are not publishers of news or information, just conduits which should have limited, or preferably no, legal responsibility for the content placed on their sites, despite their vast reach and power. With billions in the bank, the social media companies have almost limitless budgets to protect their interests through a growing army of lobbyists. And while money talks in US politics, the odds have to be in their favour of either seeing off any meaningful regulation completely or eviscerating any new legislation that might cut across their interests with disturbing consequences for American society and democracy.

It's never been entirely clear to me why Americans would fear the owners of the massive internet companies much less than their democratically elected governments. The internet companies have the tools to influence the behaviour of tens or even hundreds of millions of people with little oversight. Democratic governments work within a much stronger legal framework and can be voted out of office if the public is dissatisfied with their actions. Ideally, we should have a healthy scepticism of both, and hold them equally to account. But that is not yet happening in the US, or at least not on a scale to make a significant difference to the reckless behaviour of the internet giants.

So how can we explain this rather complacent American approach to a media environment which has changed beyond recognition in 20 years and could now be a threat to democracy itself? Part of the answer is America's purist approach to the freedom of speech as enshrined in the First Amendment to the US Constitution. In essence, Americans are able to say whatever they like, however distasteful to many people, unless it falls within a few, limited categories where the constitutional right to the freedom of speech is not protected. These include obscenity, blackmail, incitement to *imminent* lawless action and child pornography[21].

Freedom of speech is a cornerstone of all Western democracies, not least the UK. But that didn't stop a surprising number of American colleagues suggesting to me when I was in Washington that the UK, unlike the US, did not have genuine freedom of expression because we had legislation restricting the incitement of terrorism and hate speech on the grounds of race, religion, disability and sexual orientation. When I pushed back, highlighting the dangers of the American approach, one colleague even argued that the UK's limited constraints on the freedom of speech undermined British credentials as a democracy. The UK legislation is, of course, not without controversy in Britain. But the laws are largely accepted as a benefit to UK society as long as they are applied sensibly and equitably which, by and large, they are.

The purist American approach, with its dogmatic attachment to the freedom of speech, has its own serious limitations in a rapidly changing media environment. Social media and the internet more broadly have given potentially dangerous fringe elements of US society much more power and leverage. In the past, to protect First Amendment rights, it might have been reasonable to turn a blind eye to some hate speech or the incitement of violence when the individual had limited means to propagate their views or incite others to action. But that has all changed in the digital age. Anyone, anywhere can now connect with thousands of other people at the click of a mouse from wherever they are. The far right demonstrations in Charlottesville in summer 2017 which ended in violence and murder were organised on the internet and social media and saw extremists from all over America travelling to the protests to cause trouble. Even in the more traditional media space, with cable news channels ever more partisan, it feels increasingly irresponsible to argue that national broadcast organisations with very large audiences should be able to skew their programmes however they want in line with the extreme political views of their wealthy owners because Americans can change channels if they want a different perspective.

Parts of the traditional US media and certainly the social media giants seem to have no sense that with reach and power comes responsibility. Their approach to news and information is little different to falsely shouting *"fire!"* in a crowded theatre and inciting panic which would not be protected by the First Amendment right to the freedom of speech because of its potential to cause harm[22]. Repeatedly allowing their platforms to be used to stir up anger and contempt towards those with different political views or of a different religion or sexual orientation doesn't meet the definition of responsible by any reasonable definition. Falling back on the argument that someone else will cover alternative viewpoints or that there are other channels to watch with different perspectives does not recognise how people consume news media. It's little more than a cop out to avoid a difficult debate about how, sensibly and reasonably, to constrain some speech which is now clearly harmful to Western society but without unduly cutting across the fundamental right to freedom of expression. Most consumers of news media don't go hunting for alternative perspectives. They simply watch or listen to the news shows that match their own perspectives and prejudices, or consume stories fed to them by social media algorithms that play on their emotions as well as their interests. At best the approach of the American media is naïve; at worst it's reckless and a risk to US cohesion and stability. Purist free speech advocates are simply playing into their hands.

At a dinner on digital media policy for a visiting senior British colleague in summer 2017, I got into a heated debate with US government officials, privacy campaigners and technology company representatives about the benefits and risks of the digital revolution. The technology companies unsurprisingly argued strongly against regulation of their businesses. One non-profit advocate of a literal interpretation of the First Amendment suggested that the American public simply needed to be better educated about what sources were genuine news, fake news or opinion so they could make choices accordingly. Americans, he argued, could not then be manipulated by the proponents of any particular viewpoint or a foreign power seeking to influence events in the US or undermine its democracy.

We were soon debating whether this was realistic or fantasy. I argued that the approach might have worked in a pre-digital era where there were limited numbers of broadcasters and publications. But in the digital age, awash with unlimited information sources, it was wishful thinking to expect the public to be able quickly to work out what information was accurate and what was fake, dishonest or distorted, not least when new, professional and credible looking Twitter feeds or Facebook pages could be created very quickly. The First Amendment advocate was not convinced. He argued that we shouldn't second guess the intellect of the American people. Putting any constraints on free speech would, from his perspective, have worse consequences than the existing free for all, however limited any regulation or legislation might be. He didn't go on to explain how this would be the case despite the very real risks to society and democracy of the current approach.

Regulation is a poisonous word to many Americans, even though the US like all other Western countries has plenty of legislation at federal and state level to ensure everything from American food and product safety, a clean environment and to protect US domestic industries from damaging or unfair international competition. So it shouldn't be a big stretch to conclude that better regulation of the US media is necessary to keep Americans safe too. More effective regulation of the traditional broadcast media, and new rules and requirements for the large social media and internet companies, are now arguably essential to protect democracy in America and around the world. Government policy needs to respond to a transformed media environment, not continue to rely on systems designed for a totally different era largely dominated by print journalism with mainly regional reach and a limited number of national TV and radio channels.

Solutions can be found which would not cut across any sensible interpretation of the constitutional right to the freedom of speech or constrain any legitimate and peaceful political activities. It just needs political will and an open, inclusive debate. Taking action would strengthen, not weaken American democracy. In essence, the major national news broadcasters should again have an impartiality requirement enshrined in US law – a duty to cover all mainstream points of view equally. And the technology giants, just like other publishers, must take responsibility for all their content rather than hiding behind the argument that they simply provide platforms for other people's material. If the internet companies won't take ownership of the content voluntarily, they should be firmly regulated to ensure their products cannot be used to manipulate the public or spread lies which cause untold harm to American society and Western democracy.

Fake news and press manipulation are not new phenomena. In 1807, Thomas Jefferson wrote: "Nothing can be believed which is seen in a newspaper. Truth itself becomes suspicious by being put into that polluted vehicle"[23]. But a transformed media environment over the last 20 years has increased these threats to unprecedented levels. Unless the American people can agree a way forward that balances the freedom of speech with sensible oversight of the media and internet, it's hard to see an outcome other than further division in US society and continued political gridlock which could weaken the very foundations of American democracy. The only beneficiaries of this would be political extremists who would attract more support on the back of America's continued disfunction and foreign powers who seek to gain from a weaker, self-absorbed US. History has shown repeatedly how easy it can be to whip up whole societies through twisted and slanted information, leading to growing anger and hatred and ultimately fracture and violence. America, as an advanced democracy, is no more immune to this than any other country. Indeed the very freedoms enjoyed in the US give malign actors even greater space to act. America ignores these risks at its peril.

Chapter Seven

Our Guns Keep us Safe

Myth number 7 – Gun ownership is an essential part of being an American and keeps the country safe.

So much has been written about guns in the US. Every mass shooting triggers another wave of newspaper articles and heated television debates pitching advocates for greater gun control against the proponents of largely unfettered rights to own and bear arms. Those who have been touched by the gun violence try desperately to change the debate despite their trauma, courageously calling for action as they battle all-consuming grief in the hope that what they have suffered does not have to happen to others. But nothing ever really changes, even with repeated opinion polls showing a majority of Americans wanting greater gun control[1] and politicians promising that, this time, something will be done. When President Obama met yet more families of the victims of mass shootings later in his presidency, his personal anguish and frustration at being unable to bring about change was sobering to watch. The message was clear. One of the most powerful leaders on the planet was apparently powerless to stop the unending cycle of senseless deaths wreaked by

America's guns. And if the President couldn't do it, there didn't appear to be much hope for change.

My first experience of America's attachment to gun ownership was while on an English Speaking Union student exchange programme to Robert Louis Stevenson School in Pebble Beach, California in 1987, more than 30 years before President Obama took office. A school friend invited me to spend spring break on his family's ranch in the far north of California, close to the Oregon border. The ranch was 50 miles from the nearest town. Even the family's mailbox was 15 miles from the farm in a tiny settlement which was little more than a gas station, a few small houses for ranch hands and a couple of churches dotted across a flat dusty plain. There was nothing else as far as the eye could see other than scrub and dust.

Arriving at the ranch early on a March evening, I was given a tour before dinner. The ranch house was set on a small hill overlooking thousands of acres of farmland spreading out in all directions. Large centre-pivot irrigation systems had created vast circles of green across the barren landscape, skirted by low rocky hills that were turning ever more golden in the evening sun. The single-storey homestead was a fairly plain-looking wooden structure. But inside, it was a large, comfortable and welcoming family home. I was fascinated by the kitchen which seemed to have more and bigger appliances than I'd ever seen. In the room next door, there was a grand piano where my friend's sister would practise for hours every day. And then there was the large pet pig, Floyd, who would try every which way to get into the house and cause havoc if given a chance.

But it was the wood-panelled basement which held the biggest surprise. As you entered from the stairs, it had a warm, country club-type feel, with a bar and small lounge area and glass display cabinets full of model Ferraris and other Italian super cars. Just off the bar, a separate room contained what looked like a significant armoury of rifles and shot guns stored in lockable racks. I really didn't know how to react when shown the gun store. The sight was so alien to me that my stomach was quickly doing somersaults. I had never seen so many guns, except perhaps historic pieces in a museum display. I tried being as cool and nonchalant as possible, so as not to give away my shock to my American hosts. But I was more than a little uneasy at the prospect of spending a few days in a house surrounded by so much fire power.

I wasn't able to conceal my discomfort for long. After dinner that first night, my school friend asked if I wanted to go porcupine hunting. He explained that porcupines were a pest, damaging trees and plants on the farm and so they needed to be controlled. Before long, I had to admit that I had never even held a gun let alone shot one. And I didn't really want to try. My school friend was pretty understanding if a little bemused. I'm sure he was as surprised at my lack of gun experience as I was of his comfort with weapons at the age of 17. Instead he roped me into joining him on the hunt with a high-beam torch to help spot the porcupines for him to shoot. So that was it. We set out in a battered old pickup truck to track down some porcupines, using a rack of multiple spotlights on the roof of the truck to light the fields and bush in front of us. My portable torch was to be deployed if we spotted something moving out of the blinding beam of the truck's lights. I was more than a little relieved when, by the end of the evening, we hadn't found a single porcupine and so returned to the ranch without a kill.

A few days later I was to get an even more revealing taste of America's relationship with guns. On Easter Sunday, friends and family arrived at the ranch for a festive BBQ lunch on the lawn of the house overlooking endless fields of freshly sprouting alfalfa. The afternoon's fun was going to be some competitive shooting. Ground squirrel were to be the target of the day, but not in any sense as effective pest control. Firing at ground squirrel from a fixed spot on a ranch of thousands of acres was hardly going to make any difference at least as I saw it. The Easter Sunday shooting was all about entertainment, and quite a lot of macho bravado thrown in. When the basement armoury was emptied of .22 rifles – the weapon of choice for ground squirrels I was told – shotguns and a higher calibre 'deer-killing' rifle were handed out.

What followed is still etched in my mind more than 30 years later. A group of middle aged men and teenage boys were lined up on the ranch lawn firing down onto the fields below in an artillery-like assault on an attacking ground squirrel army. Some of the men didn't even bother to get up from their seats at the picnic tables where they had been eating copious quantities of barbecued meat before firing their weapons. Cheers and laughter filled the garden as squirrels somersaulted and flew in all directions when the bullets made impact. But the loudest cheer rang out when the bigger shell from the deer rifle caused a ground squirrel to explode instantly into a number of bloody pieces. There was much high fiving and back slapping, and more beer drinking as the shooting went on. Others wanted to try the deer shooter to see if they too could inflict a catastrophic explosion on a small rodent. It was the perfect day out.

While the experience was a real culture shock for a small-town Brit in his late teens, I could still make sense of the presence of guns on American ranches where genuine pests have to be dealt with. What I found much more difficult to understand was the thrill of inflicting destruction on a small animal simply for entertainment. I knew this wasn't just an American phenomenon. People hunt all over the world. But there was something about all the bravado of the 'Easter Sunday Squirrel Massacre' that made it feel different, and not just a little disturbing.

There are more gun shops in America than supermarkets and McDonalds combined[2]. Visit any one of them or some of the many firing ranges all over the country and the connection between weapons, machoism and being a 'real' American is clear. The outsides of the shops are often emblazoned with the Stars and Stripes and, in the south, the provocative Confederate flag too. Others are decorated with the emblematic American bald eagle, powerful bears or even the Statue of Liberty. Posters advertising guns themselves are held by rugged men, in powerful poses like mythical gods. The aim is clear – to stylize US history and American ideals and link gun ownership to patriotism and strength.

Vicksburg, Mississippi, February 2018

Entertainment is a major sales pitch too. I've seen gun stores advertising themselves with colourful inflatable gorillas, and Hollywood-style superheroes. Firing ranges offer targets of cartoon zombies and comic-book villains to increase the enjoyment of the shoot, but also with the obvious intention of down-playing and dehumanising what discharging a powerful handgun or semi-automatic weapon at another person really means. One store I saw on a trip around Louisiana claims, "We don't just sell guns, we sell fun". Others specifically entice women to gun ownership by offering brightly coloured handguns specially designed for a handbag, and hosting "Babes and Bullets" nights for women to practice their shooting skills. The US gun industry clearly has no issue with tired, old stereotypes.

From trips across many parts of rural America, through the forests, swamps and old plantations of the south and particularly the deserts and mountains of the west, it is easy to get a sense of the pioneering spirit and sheer grit of those early settlers who tamed the US, battling natural barriers of the Rockies and Sierra Nevada, fighting Native American tribes and coping with extreme weather. Even now, many places are a very long way from anywhere else – from the nearest law enforcement, fire department, or any local, state or federal government service. The land can be hostile too, with blazing sun, or icy cold, little or too much water, tornados, hurricanes or the ever-present risk of fire. So it is easy to understand why there is such a strong independent spirit and sense of self-reliance in US culture. Americans feel they have to look after themselves in ways that most Europeans don't. And this, in turn, can breed an instinctive distrust of government and authority in case they dare to curtail individual freedoms.

This deeply ingrained aspect of American culture helps to explain the continuing attraction to guns. But it's only part of the picture in a country very different from the pioneering days of the 18th and 19th centuries. I've often wondered who would really make the effort to travel large distances to isolated homesteads in rural America today to commit a crime which might justify the caches of powerful weapons that many have in their homes. Would anyone really go to such lengths to steal a laptop, iPhone or some cash, or for some depraved sexual or violent purpose in today's rural America? The threat from an indigenous population faced by those early American pioneers is long gone as Native Americans were all killed or rounded up and placed in reservations miles from anywhere as the pioneers pressed west. Animal rustling and the theft of expensive farm machinery can be a problem for ranchers. But the overall threat from crime is low even with law enforcement a long way away.

Violent and property crime has dropped significantly across America since the 1990s[3]. It's true that if anyone did travel to rural areas to commit an offence, they would likely bring a gun – what criminal wouldn't take a weapon with them given whoever they meet is likely to have a stockpile of handguns or semi-automatic AR-15s? But therein lies the rub. Gun ownership breeds gun violence. If hand guns and semi-automatic weapons were outlawed in the US like other western countries, anyone who did set out with criminal intent would have much less ability to do serious harm as it would so be much harder to get hold of a powerful weapon. People would be safer. It's as simple as that. But the National Rifle Association, America's biggest pro-gun lobby organisation, and other gun advocates will have Americans believe the opposite. Guns don't kill people. Deranged people kill people. According to the head of the NRA, "the only thing that stops a bad guy with a gun is a good guy with a gun".[4] In other words, gun ownership keeps Americans safe.

And what about the vast majority of Americans who live in towns and cities or the sprawling suburbs of most urban areas? Crime is significantly down in urban and suburban parts of the country too[5]. But I stopped being surprised when Americans living ordinary lives in the types of suburban neighbourhoods that surround every US town offered to show me their gun collections. Some had a cache of weapons the likes of which a criminal warlord would have been proud including hand guns, sporting rifles and even semi-automatic weapons. In these cases, the self-reliance argument just doesn't stack up. The crime threat is low and heavily armed law enforcement officers are only minutes away. Simply by owning guns, these Americans are massively increasing the likelihood that they will be shot if they happen to be unfortunate enough to be caught up in a crime. They are also more likely to face a gun if they suffer domestic violence. And the risk of a serious gun accident at home is real too[6]. The enduring US fascination with guns simply doesn't make sense, at least not to an outsider.

All that said, I learnt quickly that trying to discuss the issue with American friends is usually best avoided. It's hard enough between Americans given the deeply held views and emotions involved. After one mass shooting, I overheard a conversation between two retired couples sitting at the bar in a laid back beach cafe in St Augustine, Florida. In typical British fashion, I was trying to order a beer at the bar rather than waiting for table service and therefore was having to reach over the couples to get the attention of the barman. One of the couples, almost certainly liberal "snow birds" from the north east wintering in Florida, was advocating that something had to be done after yet another mass shooting; the killings couldn't go on. Within seconds, the elderly man in the other couple had stood up abruptly, and was declaring red faced that no one would ever take his guns away. It was about "individual liberty and personal responsibility", he blustered. The man's wife encouraged him to sit down with a gentle pat on the knee. He did so, shaking his head. But the conversation was over. Both couples turned to staring quietly into their drinks. The gun debate, even amongst Americans, can be explosive.

After a particularly heart-wrenching school shooting in 2018, I did manage to have a lengthy conversation about gun control with a travelling businessman from Virginia who I met in an old fashioned bar and grill in Charleston, South Carolina. We got chatting over the best beers on the menu as I struggled to choose one from a seemingly endless list of creatively named options, from Elysian Space Dust IPA to Pumpkin Down Scottish Ale. With multiple TV screens behind the bar showing the harrowing aftermath of the shooting on seemingly permanent loop, it was impossible not to mention the incident. Like everyone else in the bar, we were both drawn to the images of distraught school children, their parents and teachers trying to come to terms with what had happened.

"The whole thing is really awful and sad", I said turning away from the screens to avoid yet more distressing pictures.

The Virginian nodded in agreement. "Teachers should be armed", he said casually before taking another sip of his beer. "We need to make our schools safe again".

That night, for some reason, I couldn't help myself but jump right in. The liberal European in me needed to come out. Being British, you can get away with quite a lot in the US; a British accent often has Americans in raptures and anything out of the ordinary which may be said is likely to be put down to British eccentricity. Americans are fabulously polite too. But talking guns is different. A short conversation can quickly descend into a tense and emotional exchange. Many Americans, understandably, don't take kindly to someone from outside challenging their views. But on this occasion,

I asked if the businessman minded me explaining why I thought arming teachers was a bad idea. To try to avoid the whole encounter becoming confrontational, I apologised for myself upfront, explaining that I was British, with a very different background, and so I couldn't possibly fully understand the American perspective nor claim to have answers for the US. But I just had to point out all the problems as I saw them.

The Virginian nodded again and so I set out my arguments. Most school shooters, I said, were current pupils or former students, so wouldn't they know who the armed teachers were and simply avoid the areas where those teachers had their classes when going on the rampage? It only took seconds to kill or injure many people with a semi-automatic weapon and so the armed teachers wouldn't make a significant difference. It would be impossible to keep secret who the armed teachers were. They would have to go away for regular training, have lockable but accessible stores for their weapons in or near their classrooms or even carry their guns around the school at all times. And what about the teachers arming themselves when hearing there was a shooter in the school and leaving their class alone as they set off to find the gunman? As the armed teachers searched the school, law enforcement would arrive. How would the police know the armed teachers weren't the gunman and shoot them before asking questions given the pressure to stop the killing? And what about the more fundamental issue of teachers not wanting to be law enforcement officers, but educators, and children not wanting to be in schools surrounded by weapons. The whole idea, from my perspective, was crazy. There was a much simpler answer.

The Virginia businessman looked bemused from my impassioned stream of consciousness. He also seemed far from convinced. His first reaction was to tell me he was a concealed carry permit holder which gave me immediate pause for thought. At this point, if we had been in the movies, he would have pulled out a .44 Magnum and placed it on the bar to make his point. But he didn't. Instead, to my relief, he quickly reassured me that he wasn't currently armed as guns weren't permitted in bars in North Carolina. He told me that he owned a number of different guns and had recently bought his wife a small, designer handgun "for her purse". It was all about staying safe, and protecting his family, he said. From his perspective, armed teachers would deter shooters from coming to schools in the first place. And that would mean fewer school shootings.

I couldn't help but jump right back in to disagree. Almost all school shooters ended up being killed by the police, I said. So why would the risk of being shot by a teacher rather than law enforcement deter them from going on a killing spree? That didn't make logical sense either.

At this point, the businessman tried to change the direction of the discussion. He mentioned recent terrorist attacks in the UK and Europe and argued that greater gun ownership could have stopped these from happening or, if not, limited the number of deaths. I acknowledged that it had been a bad year for terrorist attacks in the UK after a long period when our police and intelligence services had successfully thwarted a number of plots. It was never going to be possible for all attacks to be stopped. But I also pointed out that many fewer people had died in three terrorist incidents combined in the UK than in one recent mass shooting in the US. And because guns were not widely available, anyone with designs to be a terrorist had to deploy other less effective means to try to kill their victims. I was comfortable with that; indeed, I was reassured by it.

The businessman tried again, turning to reports of growing knife crime in Britain. I acknowledged this too. The attacks were disturbing, I said. But if we accepted that some people would always commit violent crimes, wasn't it better for them to have to use knives rather than guns and assault weapons as the scope for killing was so much less? Limiting the havoc that criminals could cause by sensible gun control was a no-brainer, at least as I saw it.

I sensed the businessman was now getting quite tired of the discussion. Americans would never give up their guns, he declared, trying to close down the conversation. There would be a rebellion if anyone tried to take them away. Nothing was ever going to change that, even if there were many more school shootings.

I jumped in again. It didn't have to be about taking away all guns, I said. The UK, Australia and many other western countries permitted the ownership of sporting and hunting rifles under licence but outlawed more powerful handguns and automatic weapons. America could do something similar without infringing the constitutional right to bear arms.

The businessman was still not convinced. Gun control would simply never happen, he said. Gun ownership was just part of being American. I couldn't help myself at this point and pushed back yet again. Over time, I suggested, Americans would come to accept much greater gun control. Public opinion was already shifting. I just hoped the US would make sensible changes to its gun laws without needing the catalyst of some particularly catastrophic attack by a deranged American or foreign terrorist. Something more terrible would inevitably happen if guns weren't controlled.

At this point the Virginian businessman evidently wanted to end the conversation. He was clearly getting tired of my barrage of arguments. We would have to agree to disagree, he said politely but firmly. And so that was that. We turned back to our beers and the TV screens still showing interviews with traumatised survivors of the school shooting. Not long afterwards, the American nodded goodbye and left the bar. Although we had come nowhere near to agreeing, it felt good to have been able to have a conversation about US gun control without it degenerating into a tense standoff. The issues had been aired calmly and constructively. I hoped, probably naively, that this might just be a sign of a small shift in the debate.

Switching on the TV later that evening in my hotel room, I was quickly drawn in by a CNN town hall discussion between survivors of the school shooting, local and national politicians, law enforcement officers and a representative of the National Rifle Association[7]. Senator Marco Rubio, when pressed repeatedly by a teenage survivor, did remarkable contortions trying to avoid answering whether he would stop accepting campaign donations from the NRA. When he wasn't let off the hook, the senator said he would continue to accept funds from anyone who "supported his overall agenda". It wasn't about individual issues or lobby groups buying influence, he claimed (the crowd scoffed in disbelief at this point). And in any case, he argued, the problem wouldn't be solved by gun laws alone.

The NRA spokesperson was disturbingly effective at putting across gun lobby messages. The shooting wasn't about guns, she said, but a combination of failures by law enforcement and mentally ill Americans getting hold of weapons when they shouldn't be able to. It felt like a particularly cold and callous presentation so soon after a mass shooting of children and young people. You could feel the anger in the room rising as the spokesperson referenced the safety of her own children, and all American children, as being the driver behind the NRA's stance on almost unfettered access to guns and the arming of teachers. The senior law enforcement officer on the podium – the county sheriff – heroically challenged this approach, calling for greater gun control and describing how his officers had to put their lives on the line every day to face down armed Americans because of the prevalence of weapons in US society.

The sheriff's intervention reminded me of the shocking scenes on TV a few years earlier when the killing of an unarmed black teenager by police in Fergusson, Missouri triggered days of demonstrations, looting and violence. The police response to the rioting looked like some sort of dystopian hell from a Mad Max movie, with law enforcement officers equipped as if they were heading into battle in Iraq or Afghanistan rather than policing disturbances in a small town in middle America. In some ways, the militarisation of US law enforcement is hardly surprising when police officers are faced every day with Americans who can buy powerful handguns and semi-automatic weapons more easily than a car or mobile phone. But the fact is no less shocking. In their military fatigues, helmets and body armour, armed with high-powered weapons with night-sights and using armoured personnel carriers to move around, the police in Fergusson, Missouri were an intimidating presence[8].

Under a programme established by Congress in 1990, $7.4 billion of surplus military equipment has been transferred to more than 8000 federal, state and local US law enforcement agencies in 49 states over

Surplus Military Equipment Transferred to the US Police, 2006-14

432	435	44,900	533	93,763	180,718
MRAPs	**Other armored vehicles**	**Night vision pieces**	**Aircraft**	**Machine guns**	**Magazines**
Mine-Resistant Ambush Protected armored vehicles	Including cars and trucks	Including sights, binoculars, goggles, lights and accessories	Planes and helicopters	5.56 mm and 7.62 mm rifles	No ammunition

Source: New York Times, War Gear Flows to Police Departments, Matt Apuzzo, 8 June 2014

the last 30 years[9]. According to a New York Times report in 2014, US police departments had acquired almost 94,000 machine guns, more than 800 armoured vehicles and 530 military aircraft from military surplus over a six year period from 2006[10] – a frightening arsenal of equipment. In 2015, on the back of the disturbing images from Fergusson, Barack Obama restricted the transfer of some of the more controversial types of equipment available under the programme including tracked armoured vehicles, grenade launchers, bayonets and camouflage uniforms. But President Trump reversed the decision just two years later[11].

On the face of it, the transfer programme has laudable aims. It's about re-using and recycling equipment and saving money. But more violence was its inevitable consequence. The militarisation of police forces simply drives them to become ever more remote from the people they serve. At the same time, it puts more lethal options at the fingertips of law enforcement officers for those split second decisions when confronting potential criminals who could be armed[12]. It was never going to turn out well.

Mass gun ownership in the US also has an insidious impact on everyday American life which is often overlooked in the gun debate and despite the depressing flow of news reports of deadly shootings. Many Americans appear to have become largely desensitised to what it does to US society although it is profound and disturbing to an outside observer. Schools and businesses in many countries have drills to practice what to do in case of a fire, or maybe even a bomb threat in more high profile institutions. But few have to drill for a crazed gunman getting into their place of education or work with a semi-automatic weapon, even with a heightened terrorist threat in many western cities. And yet, that what's you have to do in the US, and it isn't cost free. I have heard parents recount stories more than once of their children coming home from school in some distress after an 'active shooter' drill, worried that an armed gunman might actually come to their school and start shooting them and their friends. And for some children that anxiety sticks around despite reassurance from their parents and teachers that a gun attack is unlikely to happen; the daily news tells a different story.

I've also witnessed parents frantic with worry when they receive a text alert about an incident at their child's school, terrified that it might be an active shooter only to be able to relax again once a false alarm or minor incident is finally confirmed. It just doesn't feel right that this should be the norm in a peaceful Western democracy. The US is neither a failed state nor a conflict zone. But children at school and employees at work have to learn drills to keep themselves alive lest an armed gunman decides to go on a killing spree. And then there's the even greater impact in communities where gun violence is prevalent, with parents fearful of letting their children play outside, no one able to go out at night without taking a risk of being caught up in a deadly incident, and everyone having to protect their homes with bars on the windows and doors to keep armed criminals out.

All Americans are advised by the federal government to consider what they would do if someone started shooting in their workplace, at a shopping mall, in a bar or restaurant, at their church or even in a hospital. The US Department of Homeland Security produces guidance for all Americans on how to prepare for an armed attack[13]. Providing the advice makes sense in the circumstances of a country awash with guns. But it does feel wrong that Americans should have to think about where they could hide at school or work, how they could escape an incident while shopping or eating out with friends, or even whether they should get tourniquet training so they could help anyone who got shot. Wouldn't it make more sense to tackle the cause of the problem instead?

When I arrived at the embassy in Washington in 2013, we didn't have a plan for how to respond to an armed intruder. As a British-led organisation, it hadn't really crossed anyone's mind that this should be necessary. But after a civilian contractor at the Washington Navy Yard killed 12 people[14] and a lone shooter murdered two at a nearby Maryland shopping mall in the space of just a few weeks[15], I set about putting together a response plan. We worked closely with the Secret Service and Washington DC Police to make sure we got our preparations right. We strengthened our internal defences by putting access control on all corridors and bolts on multiple doors to help slow the progress of any gunman who might get into the building. We identified hiding places that could be secured most effectively. And we organised presentations for staff on how to react in an active shooter situation guided by the Department of Homeland Security's recommended response of "Run, Hide, Fight".

We debated whether to follow the British police's slightly different advice of "Run, Hide, *Tell*" on how to respond if caught up in a terrorist incident. But we concluded that "fight" as a last resort was better advice in the US given the greater fire power available in the country. If someone were to be cornered by an active shooter with a semi-automatic weapon, there was a simple choice: fight with anything you could find or be killed. That didn't apply in the same way in the UK where guns are more effectively controlled.

Not surprisingly our active shooter preparations caused some anxiety amongst staff who worried that we were putting plans in place because we saw the embassy as a particular target. We did lots of reassurance on that front, making the argument that it just made sense to be prepared given the prevalence of guns in the US and the unpredictable nature of gun violence. The chance of the embassy itself or any of our staff or their families being caught up in gun violence was pretty small even in America. But it wasn't insignificant and so we had to be ready. The very fact that we had to have such plans felt like a sad reflection of American gun culture which no one seems able to address.

Despite the seriousness of the whole thing, we had some more light-hearted moments too when drilling our new intruder response plan. We learnt that our intercom system didn't reach all corners of the embassy building and particularly some of our newly designated hiding places. So some staff didn't hear the announcement that the drill was over and spent an extended period of time in their chosen hiding place wondering whether it was 'safe' to come out. When they finally emerged, they were greeted with cheers from colleagues who had been back at their desks for some time. We also made sure we remembered to advise staff not to be tempted to refer to the drill on social media. We didn't want local law enforcement thinking we were under genuine attack and sending in a SWAT team which would have caused quite a stir. But we also had to have some tough conversations with staff about possible scenarios in a real incident. We discussed what should be done if a colleague were to get left outside a locked zone and therefore at the mercy of an active shooter. Even worse, we talked through the scenario of an armed attacker taking a hostage and trying to force their way into the building by threatening to kill if doors weren't opened. It was a sobering exercise.

The prevalence of guns and gun violence in the US also had an impact on the normal business of the embassy. Every time there was a shooting in a place possibly frequented by British tourists – a Las Vegas concert, an Orlando nightclub, a Florida airport – we had to mobilise either in Washington or in one of our consulates around the country to try to establish whether British nationals might have been caught up in the incident and need our assistance, or worse, have been killed. Not only was this a distraction from our core business, it was pretty distressing for the staff concerned as they dealt with worried family members and tried to track down the facts in often chaotic circumstances.

Just the financial costs to American society of all this planning and preparedness is significant: from the extra security staff required in schools, hospitals and office buildings to the additional physical defences that must be installed to slow the progress of a potential gunman; from the productivity lost when doing drills on how to respond to a possible gun attack to the police time spent advising businesses on preparedness rather than tackling crime. But these are just the tip of the iceberg. The immediate medical costs alone of dealing with firearm injuries in the US average $2.8 billion a year[16]; the wider costs to US economy are estimated to exceed $230 billion[17]. And that's without mentioning the almost immeasurable cost of the thousands of lives lost every year to gun violence and the trauma for the families of those killed or injured.

Some Americans routinely cite concerns about being caught up in act of terrorism as a reason for thinking twice about travelling to Europe. But even with some of the recent attacks in Britain, France and Belgium, the chances of being affected by terrorism in Europe are so much less than those of being caught up in gun violence in the US. I still haven't worked out why, for Americans, mass killings by their compatriots with guns are considered to be different from acts of terrorism. The motivations might not be quite the same, but the outcome is – a significant and needless loss of human life. And in America the numbers killed are almost always higher because of the availability of powerful hand guns and semi-automatic weapons. It is also impossible to fathom how so many Americans can still believe that guns make them safe when all the evidence confirms otherwise. More guns mean more gun violence. It is as simple as that.

There were almost 40,000 gun deaths in the US in 2018, with just over 60 percent from suicide, one third being homicides, and a small proportion from accidental discharge and police shootings[18]. In total, that's 12.2 gun deaths, or 4.3 gun homicides, per 100,000 Americans. In the UK there were 35 gun murders in 2019[19] or 0.053 per 100,000 people[20]. The US is five times bigger than the UK in

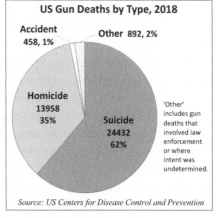

US Gun Deaths by Type, 2018

Accident 458, 1%
Other 892, 2%
Homicide 13958 35%
Suicide 24432 62%

'Other' includes gun deaths that involved law enforcement or where intent was undetermined.

Source: US Centers for Disease Control and Prevention

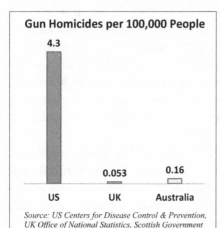

Gun Homicides per 100,000 People

4.3

0.053   0.16

US   UK   Australia

Source: US Centers for Disease Control & Prevention,
UK Office of National Statistics, Scottish Government
Publications, Australian Bureau of Statistics

terms of population, but has more than 80 times the gun homicide rate. In raw numbers, there are 400 times more gun homicide deaths in America than in Britain. For Australia, another country that enforced strong gun controls after a mass shooting, the figures were 0.16 gun murders per 100,000 people in 2019, or a homicide rate more than 26 times lower than the US[21].

None of this should be surprising. The US makes up just 4.3 percent of the world's population but has almost half of all civilian owned guns. There are almost 400 million of them in circulation in the country, more than one for every American[22]. The US arms industry manufactured more than 9 million new guns in 2018 alone, and exported just 6 percent of them[23].

When talking to the Virginian businessman in the bar in Charleston in February 2018, I took the arguably risky step of suggesting that Americans needed to take a deep look at themselves to answer the question why they were so attracted to guns. Why did so many find it thrilling and fun to own and shoot powerful weapons that can kill and maim in seconds? Why did Americans apparently feel so at risk – other than from the availability of weapons in civilian hands in the country which was evidently fixable – that they wanted to arm themselves and their families with powerful handguns and semi-automatics? And why were they so distrusting of authority to feel unable to rely on law enforcement to keep them safe? I guess this is what really prompted the businessman to close down our conversation. Asking such pointed questions about the US psyche was a step too far, even coming from a Brit. But whatever the reasons for the businessman ending our conversation that night, the questions remain largely unanswered in the highly charged US gun debate. They are questions that gun advocates and the gun lobby are keen to avoid.

Another deadly school shooting in 2018 led to an unprecedented mobilisation of people calling for greater gun control. In a campaign led courageously by inspiring teenage students who survived the attack, politicians were put under serious pressure to do something about the problem. Tens of thousands of people in many cities across the country marched in support of change. Many politicians promised action. No one was even suggesting anything radical like bans on certain types of guns, which might really have started to tackle the problem. Just a few more limited controls on buying semi-automatic weapons were proposed, and greater efforts to stop those with mental illness from buying guns. But again, despite all this, nothing changed. The arms lobby led by the National Rifle Association immediately mobilised to thwart any significant policy change and politicians quickly backed off fearing they might lose support from gun owning voters or see their NRA campaign money dry up. The prospect of real gun control died almost as quickly as the victims of the mass shooting.

The National Rifle Association spent an astounding $419 million in 2016 including operating costs. $140 million of this was spent on "legislative programmes and public affairs" – a euphemistic term for lobbying and direct support for political campaigns and candidates. $30 million alone was invested in Donald Trump's presidential campaign with at least a further $20 million helping Republican Senate candidates[24]. More was spent attacking Hillary Clinton too for fear she might, like President Obama, advocate greater gun control. The gun lobby denies that it wields much weight or that its spending influences politicians and policy. But no one would invest this amount of money, not least in the uber-capitalist economy of the US, unless it delivered results. And for the NRA this is blocking any attempt to increase gun control even though this would make America safer and prevent thousands of needless deaths each year.

If you wanted to make a case that the American political system is broken, and that rich lobby organisations have too much power, then the inability to do anything about the scourge of gun violence would be the perfect vehicle. If Americans can't even agree action to protect their own children, their own husbands and wives, from the deadly impact of their gun culture, there seems to be little prospect of them tackling other knotty issues that face the US and wider world.

The Second Amendment to the US Constitution established the gun rights of American citizens: "A well-regulated Militia, being necessary to the security of a free State, the right of the people to keep and bear Arms, shall not be infringed."[25] But what began as a cost effective means for a new nation to defend itself against outside attack in the days before it had a permanent standing army, has developed into an unhealthy fetish that brings little but self-harm. In the face of a powerful gun lobby, the political system has proved powerless to stop the unending cycle of senseless deaths wreaked by America's guns. Gun violence is beginning to undermine the very fabric of US society, pitching minority communities against heavily armed law enforcement officers and feeding a sense of fear across the country. If the US cannot enact some form of sensible gun control, it risks the violence spiralling out of control as the political system and economy fail to provide hope and opportunity for millions of young Americans.

The answer to America's scourge is simple too – the banning of all but sporting and hunting rifles. It's a proven model that works in other countries like the UK and Australia. And it would not cut across any sensible interpretation of the constitutional right to bear arms. Such restrictions would be much harder to implement in a country with tens of millions of guns in private ownership and an almost genetically coded attachment to weapons and personal freedom. But Americans have proven time and time again in their rise to becoming the world's superpower, that doing the impossible is possible. American politicians just need to muster the courage to get it done.

Chapter Eight

A World-beating Health System

Myth number 8 – The US has the best healthcare in the world providing access to the most innovative treatments and the highest quality of care.

Most Americans you speak to, or at least the ones with good health insurance, will argue that the US has the best healthcare in the world with high quality services, little waiting time to see family doctors or specialists and access to the most advanced treatments available anywhere. Much of this is true. There's little question that the US has pioneering doctors and some impressive medical facilities. Hospitals often feel more like expensive hotels than health institutions; many clinics and doctors' offices are gleaming and modern complete with all the latest technology. The US is frequently at the forefront of medical advances too through a long-term commitment to investment in research and development backed by world-leading universities, a large and highly profitable pharmaceutical sector and international collaboration. The US still spends far more than any other country on medical research[1] with the UK second or third on the list depending on the data[2]. Many British and American scientists work together on ground breaking medical research in a wide range of fields including cancer, aging and dementia, genetics and obesity[3].

At the same time the US approach to healthcare denies medical services to millions of Americans and massively inflates the cost for those who can afford it. Access to affordable healthcare is arguably the most important safety net in any developed society. Staying fit and well is essential to living a full life, being able to provide for your family, contribute to the economy and have any chance of social mobility – to live the American Dream. But the US healthcare system fails to deliver this to very large numbers of Americans.

While at the Embassy in Washington, I spent endless hours working with our small human resources team to ensure we could continue to provide a decent healthcare package to our 700 American staff around the country. The biggest challenge was maintaining affordability for both the UK government and our employees. The embassy paid the lion's share of staff healthcare costs. But our employees made monthly contributions towards their health coverage and also faced 'co-pays' at the time of treatment. Each year we battled against US healthcare inflation which outstripped general price increases by a factor of three or four, causing our healthcare costs to increase alarmingly quickly[4]. High inflation rates are not unique to the American health sector. New treatments and technologies, and an aging population are all drivers for significant healthcare price increases around the world. But in the US our costs were spiralling, and the proportion we spent on drugs mind boggling.

I knuckled down to learning about the different types of health plans available in the US in the hope that we could continue to offer competitive health benefits to our staff at reasonable cost. I heard about Health Maintenance Organisations – health insurance linked to a specific network of doctors and other providers which could help to keep down costs. Then there were High Deductible Health Plans linked to Health Savings Accounts which were designed to make consumers take more responsibility for their healthcare choices and spending. I tried to get my head around 'co-pays' and 'deductibles' and the different charges for in-network and out-of-network doctors. I soon learned that the American healthcare system is extremely complicated. Trying to make sense of the whole thing was mentally exhausting. Each time I thought I was beginning to understand, I would find another layer of complexity to grapple with. It felt much harder than dealing with some of the most serious and intractable foreign policy issues of the day like the Iran nuclear deal or Syria.

It didn't take long for me to work out that the American healthcare system is hugely bureaucratic too. Every interaction with a healthcare provider triggers an insurance claim which creates a mountain of paperwork through a third party broker. Even as an infrequent individual user, I would receive several different letters whenever I made a simple visit to my doctor or dentist for something quite routine. Each letter was usually incomprehensible with lots of codes to 'explain' the treatment I had received, complete with several pages of small print. Some would have "This is Not a Bill" stamped in large red letters across the top, which was a relief given the price quoted was rarely less than three figures. Others would set out my personal contribution alongside the amount paid by the insurer which usually sent the heart racing as it was much more than I had paid on the day. And then, finally, another letter would arrive almost identical to the first two and saying that my contribution was in fact much less, or even zero.

I never worked out what the different letters were for and why they were sent. The whole thing just seemed to add unnecessary bureaucracy and cost, and caused much confusion. One accurate bill would surely have been enough? Like others I took to throwing the letters in the bottom of a drawer without much of a glance when they arrived in the mail. I knew that my insurer would eventually telephone if an additional payment was required. If a call never came, all the better, and I would assume everything was settled.

All this complexity and bureaucracy adds up. The US spends more than twice as much per capita on healthcare than other Western countries apart from Switzerland and Germany[5]. A bigger proportion of the spending goes on administration not healthcare itself too[6]. More

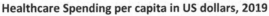

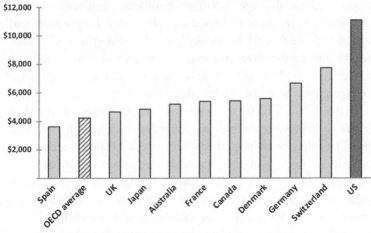

Healthcare Spending per capita in US dollars, 2019

Source: OECD Health Statistics 2020

than one doctor I met in Washington DC told me how they were worn down by the volume of paperwork in the US health insurance system and had to employ several assistants just to keep on top of the requirements. My own brilliant family doctor walked away from her job at one of the big local primary health providers to set up her own practice to try to offer a more old-fashioned, personal and responsive type of care.

Doctors in the US prescribe significantly more tests than their counterparts in other developed countries too, from routine blood tests to more expensive MRI and CT scans which drives up healthcare costs further[7]. This excessive testing is driven in part by patient demand and technological advances bringing new diagnostic tools to market. But it is also the result of financial incentives in a for-profit health system and a 'belt and braces' approach to medicine given the fear of a malpractice lawsuit in a highly litigious society if anything were to go wrong[8].

Despite all this, overall health outcomes in the US are no better than in other developed countries. In fact, they are significantly worse in a number of critical areas[9]. Figures from the National Center for Health Statistics show that, after decades of growth, US life expectancy fell from 2014 to 2017[10] before increasing again slightly to 78.7 years in 2018[11]. But even with this recent improvement, US life expectancy is still two years lower than the average in other advanced economies[12]. It ranks alongside Estonia which spends just over one fifth of the amount Americans do per capita on healthcare[13]. Child mortality is higher in the US than in other developed countries too, and significantly higher in the South and parts of the Midwest[14]. Healthcare coverage is also much worse[15]. The Affordable Care Act and other federal government initiatives have led to significant drops in the number of Americans without medical insurance. But still millions go without coverage and millions more are under-insured[16]. The private sector approach to healthcare should, the proponents say, lead to greater competition and better services for consumers at lower cost – the market will deliver. But that is not what is happening in the US. Something is clearly seriously wrong.

When tendering for a new embassy healthcare provider in 2016, the bids we received from the big American insurance companies including Aetna, Cigna and United Healthcare were almost identical in every detail. Despite each bid stretching to many dozens of pages of bespoke data analysis of our previous medical expenditure to make predictions for future costs, there was nothing to choose between them in terms of the contract price or services offered. And yet, in such a complex industry, differentiation should be pretty straightforward to make a company stand out. Each of the healthcare companies added similar, significant annual fees per employee to cover administrative costs too. Something just didn't feel right.

It turns out that, after years of industry consolidation, just two health insurance companies control the majority of the market in many parts of the US. In some areas, a single insurer has a virtual monopoly[17]. And without genuine competition, prices remain high and tend to increase above the rate of inflation each year to maximise industry profits. In other words, in the embassy's tendering for a new healthcare provider, we had little genuine choice. Not surprisingly, we decided to stick with our existing insurer. Moving to a different company would have created a huge amount of paperwork for little discernible gain. Some of our staff would also have been forced to change their doctors as each insurer works with slightly different groups of medical practitioners. The upheaval would have been unpopular, particularly with those in the middle of pregnancies or treatments for serious illnesses. Ultimately, this lack of a real choice is almost certainly what the big healthcare companies intend. If they pitch an offer that's little different to their competitors, customers will stay because changing provider is too disruptive. The money keeps rolling in.

But that's not even the last of the surprises with the US healthcare system. Americans face higher 'out of pocket' costs for their health services than citizens of any other developed country except Switzerland – and to the tune of more than $1000 per person per year[18]. These out of pocket costs have to be paid direct to a doctor, clinic or pharmacy when receiving health services. They cover insurance shortfalls, as few US insurers will reimburse 100% of all medical costs, and pay for medicines and treatments which are not covered at all. The costs come on top of Americans having to pay hefty annual health insurance premiums and, when in work, contributing 7.6% of their gross salaries to FICA – the US equivalent of national insurance – part of which funds Medicare which provides healthcare coverage to the over 65s[19]. When all this is added together, it's not hard to see how American healthcare spending quickly outstrips anywhere else in the world.

Drug prices are much higher than in most other Western countries too, and often by a factor of three or four[20]. They are one of the main drivers of spiralling US healthcare costs and leave many Americans struggling or even unable to fund life-saving treatments. The US pharmaceutical companies can largely charge what they like for their medicines in an industry that is lightly regulated compared to other countries. In the fragmented, commercial US healthcare system, there is also very little of the collective drug buying which is possible with a universal healthcare system like the NHS to keep prices down and commercial profits reasonable. Rather bizarrely, the federal government's health programme for retirees – Medicare – is even prohibited by law from negotiating prices with drug companies[21] in what can only be a sop to the pharmaceutical industry to protect their profits. It is no coincidence that drugs companies continue to be the top spenders on lobbying in Washington to protect their interests[22].

The majority of American doctors also take payments from pharmaceutical and medical device companies to supplement their incomes[23]. Doctors cannot receive money directly for prescribing a particular drug or following a certain course of treatment. That would be illegal. But the market is the market. Doctors can be paid substantial amounts indirectly for giving speeches, consulting or to cover the costs of fancy meals and travel to conferences. Logic dictates that medical companies would not pay doctors who weren't prescribing their drugs or using their equipment. That would not make financial sense in the profit-driven US market. Not surprisingly, there's increasing evidence that the more US doctors prescribe a particular drug or use a specific medical device, the more money they get from the company concerned[24]. More than half of America's 1.1 million doctors receive payments from pharmaceutical and medical device companies each year. For most, it is relatively small sums of money. But 2,500 doctors received more than $½ million dollars over five years to 2019. More than 700 received at least $1 million[25] which has to raise questions about ethics and propriety. How can Americans ever be sure that the tests and treatments they are prescribed are determined by medical need rather than the extra income they will generate for their doctors?

At the embassy, because of the astronomical cost of drugs in America, we always advised British government staff being posted to jobs in the US to continue to get their prescription medications in the UK if they had regular treatment requirements. The cost savings would be significant. Even some common over-the-counter drugs and supplements like allergy medications and multi-vitamins are considerably cheaper in the UK. A month's supply of the most popular hay fever drug used by millions of people each year – cetirizine hydrochloride – costs no more than £2.00 in a British supermarket, less than half the price of the same drug from the very cheapest US source, and four or five times cheaper than buying the drug from one of the American pharmacy chains. A year's supply of basic multi-vitamins is just over half the price in the UK compared to the US.

Like many other Brits working in America, I would stock up with all sorts of over-the-counter drugs and medical supplies on every trip back to the UK to avoid the high prices in the US. Colleagues often joked about how their suitcases rattled when leaving Heathrow Airport with all the pills they had bought. Before moving to Washington, I had always thought that the large pharmacies at most British airports were for tourists to pick up last minute holiday essentials like sun cream and ibuprofen, or for people going to developing countries where medical supplies were scarce. But that's only part of the story. They are also serving travellers going to the most advanced economy in the world where drugs and medical supplies are massively overpriced. It's not really what you expect.

Some tricky staff cases at the embassy were also made even more difficult to handle because of the profit-driven nature of the American healthcare system. On a couple of occasions, I had to deal with requests from colleagues to change their UK government-provided accommodation on grounds that where they were living was exacerbating a family member's medical condition. Working with the HR team at the embassy, I had to judge whether the member of staff had a genuine case to move to justify the expense involved to the British taxpayer which could amount to several thousand dollars. So, we set out to determine whether the medical conditions were genuine and then whether the embassy-supplied housing could be making the problem worse through pollution, noise or some other factor.

After detailed investigation into both requests, including drawing on the expertise of the Foreign Office's overseas healthcare provider, neither claim appeared to be medically or scientifically based. But, even so, both members of staff were able get their American family doctor to write a letter supporting their case even though the doctors had clearly not assessed the housing or environment where they lived. In one case, the letter was little more than a short, handwritten note from the GP; in another, the language used was clearly cut and pasted from wording previously submitted to the embassy by the member of staff themselves and so, very obviously, not the independent medical assessment of the family doctor.

I was really quite shocked by this. Why would a family doctor, a medical professional, sign such a letter? What had happened to medical ethics? So I checked with a couple of former doctors I knew who confirmed that writing letters like these was common for US medical practitioners for a fee, and certainly didn't mean that the doctor had investigated the environmental impact of where our members of staff were living. It was just another income driven service, and a back-covering exercise in case the patient later claimed they had raised a health concern with their doctor who had done nothing about it. Not surprisingly, until we worked this out, the doctors' letters provided by our staff caused us to reopen the two cases and double check our original assessment. They made our jobs harder and extended the anxiety of our staff – all on the back of profit and a fear of litigation, rather than genuine health concerns.

The same profit-driven behaviours extend to dentistry too. Americans often have fun mocking the British for their 'bad teeth' as we tend to spend much less on cosmetic dental procedures. But teeth straightening, whitening, veneers and implants are big business in the US. Even if you go to an American dentist with perfectly reasonable teeth by US standards, you are likely to come out with a long list of proposed treatments to the tune of thousands of dollars even if they are not clinically necessary. The drive to make profit is front and centre. Not all American dentists are guilty of this, of course. But a few years ago, the British government had to change the way dental treatment was authorised for their staff in the US as tens of thousands of dollars were being racked up each year, particularly in cities like New York, for treatments which were 'prescribed' by dentists but were ostensibly cosmetic and which would ultimately be paid for by the UK taxpayer. The practice was, understandably, quickly stopped.

The opioid crisis in the US – fuelled by the mis-prescription of opioid pain relief over many years[26] – is yet another example of the serious weaknesses of America's profit-driven healthcare system. Almost 47,000 Americans died from overdosing on opioids in 2018, both from prescription medications and, increasingly, synthetic opioids like fentanyl that are obtained on the black market or imported from overseas suppliers[27]. Almost 450,000 Americans have died from overdosing on both prescription and illicit opioids since 1999[28]. An estimated 2 million have substance use disorders related to the mis-prescriptions of the pain-relieving drugs.

When a UK health minister visited Washington DC in autumn 2017, he called on the new Secretary of Health and Human Services. The discussion focused on sharing best practice on current health challenges affecting Britain and America including aging and dementia, anti-microbial resistance and cancer, and encouraging even more research collaboration in these areas. But the most revealing part of the meeting came when the Health and Human Services Secretary asked how the UK was tackling "the opioid addiction crisis in Britain". The Secretary explained that opioids had been massively over-prescribed in America from the late 1990s on the back of industry claims that new drug variants weren't addictive and generous payments to doctors by the drug companies. The more doctors prescribed the more they benefitted, often to the tune of very significant sums of money. The Trump administration had just declared the resulting addiction crisis a Public Health Emergency[29] and was keen to learn from UK experience.

The British minister's reply clearly surprised the Health and Human Services Secretary and his accompanying advisers who looked at each other rather bemused. Britain did not face a serious opioid crisis, the minister explained, because doctors in the UK National Health Service worked within guidelines for prescribing drugs and treatments from the National Institute for Healthcare Excellence. Opiates and opioids had always been strictly controlled given their extremely addictive properties. Unlike the US, the pharmaceutical industry had limited influence over the prescription process.

The minister grasped quickly that this wasn't the answer his US counterpart had expected. Tackling the opioid crisis was a top priority for the Trump administration and they were obviously keen to work with their closest ally on the issue. To find some common ground, the minister turned to a problem we did share – British and American consumers increasingly buying both illegal and potentially fake drugs over the internet largely from China which, in the US case, included synthetic opioids. He suggested a push to tackle this illicit trade could be an area for further cooperation. The Health and Human Services Secretary quickly agreed, evidently relieved that there were some shared challenges which offered the opportunity of working together.

Switch on the TV at any time in the US and you will quickly see evidence of the acutely commercial nature of the prescription drug market which was a major driver of the opioid crisis. Programme breaks are littered with commercials for medications to treat every imaginable condition in the hope that American consumers will ask their doctors to prescribe them. The commercials always show joyful, photogenic Americans enjoying life with their families, against idyllic backdrops, free from any apparent symptoms thanks to whatever drug is being advertised and no matter what the illness might be. The drug companies are obliged to list the potential side effects of their products – which they do, very quickly in monotone towards the end of the advert. If you can catch the details from the hurried recitation, very often the side effects sound like they will exacerbate the very disease the drug is designed to treat – a drug for irritable bowel syndrome that can cause severe stomach pain or one for psoriasis that could trigger an unpleasant rash. Even worse, the side effects are often potentially life-threatening from suicidal thoughts to severe internal bleeding, from a stroke to anaphylactic shock. But they are listed so unremarkably that you have to listen very hard to hear them.

The adverts are not about informing consumers or improving health outcomes. They have one aim – to sell more drugs by encouraging members of the public to press their doctors to prescribe whatever new 'miracle' treatment they have seen on TV. The extent of TV drug advertising suggests this works very effectively, otherwise the drug companies simply wouldn't spend the money; they have shareholders to answer to after all[30]. Not surprisingly, only two countries in the world allow direct prescription drug advertising – the US and New Zealand. It's banned everywhere else to avoid the risk of misinformation and manipulation[31].

I was most shocked by one commercial for a treatment for a particularly aggressive cancer which has no cure. A friend had recently died from the condition, leaving behind a traumatised young family and a devastated husband. The commercial showed a surprisingly healthy looking woman suffering one of the most brutal cancers yet apparently enjoying life with her infant grandchildren as though little was going on, and even though the drug could extend the very end of life by just a few weeks or possibly 3-4 months at best. It felt like a particularly cruel exercise in generating drug sales by implying better results than could ever be achieved to families going through unimaginable trauma.

Yet again, this is not the end of the story of the surprises of US healthcare. The American approach to wider health issues makes it an outlier in a number of other areas too, and not in a good way. On both maternity[32] and sick leave entitlements[33] the US is a global backmarker despite being the richest country on the planet which could easily afford to offer reasonable benefits to American workers. The maternity leave provision under US federal law is 12 weeks *unpaid* time off for the birth and care of a newborn child. In effect, childbirth is treated as a medical condition or 'disability' with a simple clinical assessment of the mother's likely recovery time determining the unpaid leave entitlement under the law. But even then, the provision comes with further restrictions. Forty percent of women in the US aren't even entitled to the unpaid time off because they don't work enough hours, their company is too small to be covered by the requirement under federal law, or they haven't been at their company long enough to qualify for the leave[34].

The approach caused serious headaches in the embassy. The UK Foreign Office sets global minimum standards for the employment terms of all its staff hired locally in British embassies and consulates

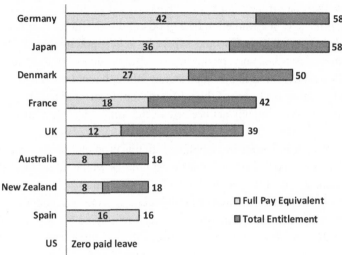

Source: OECD Family Database 2018

around the world. For maternity leave this is three months' paid absence for childbirth and adoption even if local labour law grants less. Not surprisingly, this was hugely popular with our local staff in America. But trying to meet the standard got complicated very quickly. We had somehow to construct a paid entitlement for our staff giving birth or adopting children without falling foul of US anti-discrimination laws which requires men and women to be treated equally. After a lot of legal advice and consulting a few American and international companies who were themselves offering paid maternity leave, we were able to construct a package that met the three month standard. But it was complex and therefore bureaucratic to administer and, even then, probably didn't entirely guarantee against litigation on the grounds of discrimination. It was a bizarre situation to be in for something that is just part of the human condition – having children – and when almost every other country already provides paid maternity leave.

Sick absence entitlements in the US follow a similar model. There's no legal requirement for American employers to provide paid sick leave[35]. In other words, not only does the US fail to provide healthcare for all, but when Americans do get sick they immediately lose their pay if they can't work. This created yet more headaches for the embassy. We wanted to be a good employer and provide benefits in line with what staff would expect from best practice in the UK or Europe. But like any business, we also needed to make sure we followed US law and provided an appealing, but not overly generous and costly, package of benefits in the local market. It was a complicated balancing act because of the limited US legal provisions for sick leave.

We weren't alone in grappling with this problem. Some American companies have leave donation programmes which allow their staff to donate part of their annual holiday entitlement to a colleague going through a serious personal or family medical issue. The colleague can then have extended time off to get well or to care for a sick family member without worrying about losing their income. The programmes are a creative solution to a real problem and show heart-warming levels of generosity from Americans willing to donate some of their very limited annual leave entitlement to help colleagues in need. But it feels like a completely unnecessary problem to have in a wealthy, advanced economy. Wouldn't legislation mandating employers to provide a reasonable level of paid sick leave be a much simpler and more humane solution?

In many ways, the American healthcare system feels broken given it fails so many people and creates untold bureaucracy and cost for others. In the last few years, a few more US politicians have talked about the benefits of a universal healthcare system. But many Americans remain resolutely averse to creating any form of national health service or universal insurance programme. For those who have generous health insurance or can afford the high price of treatments, it's an understandable position in some ways. They get to shop around for the doctors and services they want, and to seek out the leading experts for the particular condition they might have. While the US continues to be a world leader in health innovation, anyone who can afford to pay can have access to the very best care. But the position still feels seriously misguided given the very considerable flaws in the US approach.

At an official dinner I attended in Washington DC in 2017 two of the guests on my table were the Head of the US Department of Veterans Affairs (which provides healthcare and other services to American veterans) and his wife, herself a practicing physician. The conversation quickly turned to healthcare. It wasn't long before I was hearing widely held US perceptions of Britain's National Health Service. It was "socialised medicine" one of the guests said, and adding the word socialism to anything in the US always indicates a negative. The NHS was also "highly bureaucratic", another chipped in, "with long wait times for treatments and little choice". The list of criticisms went on.

As the only Brit at the table, I pushed back on these stereotypes. I acknowledged that patients might wait a bit longer in the UK for treatments for conditions that weren't life-threatening. But that wasn't always the case. Critical care for acute and life-threatening conditions was measured against very clear guidelines, with short targets for each stage of treatment which itself was world class. I acknowledged that the NHS wasn't perfect. But, critically, it ensured that everyone had access to quality health services. The vast majority of British people supported the system. Many would be willing to pay more tax to fund improvements too.

I then went on to describe my own experience of the healthcare system in the US. It was often difficult, I said, to get an appointment with a primary care doctor and so waiting wasn't unusual in America either. There was considerably more paperwork and bureaucracy in the American system too. I didn't necessarily want to have to choose which clinic I would go to for a routine test, then have to make the appointment myself, ensure the clinic had the correct paperwork from my doctor, and chase when things didn't go as planned. And that was without even mentioning the incomprehensible billing and insurance system.

After a little bit of push back on my US experiences from some of the Americans at the table, the conversation took an unexpected turn.

Some started to agree with me. One acknowledged that it was hard to get appointments with a family doctor. Another suggested that connections in the medical industry were useful when trying to see a particular specialist. But even this didn't always help; the person was clearly exasperated that pulling strings wasn't always enough. And yes, another agreed, the paperwork and self-administration required in the US system was stressful and time consuming. We left it at that.

A few months later I was approached by an embassy colleague who was moving to the UK as their partner's job was being transferred to London. The colleague had recovered from a pretty serious health issue and was anxious about the aftercare that might be available in Britain. I tried to be reassuring. The NHS was good, I said, and available to all. And if anyone wanted more choice and sometimes quicker treatment they could opt for private insurance too. I asked whether my colleague's doctor could recommend the centre of excellence in the UK for their condition or perhaps even a particular British consultant? The colleague then disclosed that her specialist had actually been a Brit on a medical exchange to America. The doctor was now back in the UK and possibly able to carry on being the care provider. At that point, I could only scratch my head. My colleague had been anxious not because of any facts, but because of some nightmare-ish myths about universal healthcare no doubt fuelled by American politicians and the drugs lobby suggesting it was some broken, communist-like system that would be bad for America.

The conversation was just more evidence of widespread US misperceptions of what universal healthcare would actually mean. Most countries with national health services or universal insurance programmes also have private healthcare providers for those who want to pay more to choose their doctors or services and to get treatment at the time of their choosing. Establishing some form of universal healthcare in the US would not need to mean less choice. It would almost certainly be considerable cheaper to the US economy and, given the growing evidence of the shortcomings of the current American model, provide better overall health outcomes too.

America already has two large public healthcare systems from which it could draw lessons to create some form of health service for all: the Military Health Service which provides medical services to almost 10 million serving military personnel, retirees and their families[36]; and the Veterans Healthcare Administration[37] which serves a further 9 million veterans in 170 medical centres and more than 1000 outpatient clinics across the country. Both are generally well regarded despite some bad press in recent years about the Veterans Health Administration around waiting times for treatment[38]. Both health services are owned and run by the federal government, just like a national health service, with the Military Health Service being topped up by an insurance plan to allow care to be provided through the private sector to ensure demand can be met. The US has a large public health insurance programme too – Medicare – for retirees. So there are plenty of models to draw on if the US wanted to design a universal healthcare system without starting from scratch.

I can't help feeling that the American approach to healthcare is a form of serious self-harm, fuelled paradoxically by the interests of the pharmaceutical and health insurance industries which are supposed to help make people better. In essence, the American approach amounts to spending considerably more than other developed countries, getting less in return in terms of overall health outcomes and then still leaving a large proportion of US society without even basic health services. It simply doesn't make sense.

In a letter in 1799, George Washington wrote that health is "amongst (if not the most) precious gift of Heaven; without which, we are but little capable of business, or enjoyment"[39]. So it's hard to understand why Americans more than 200 years later would not think that providing affordable healthcare for all is one of the first things a wealthy country should offer as a basic human right. But even if that's not a compelling argument in the 'self-reliant' US, as Washington would understand, not providing healthcare means fewer people are able to contribute fully to the American economy because they are unnecessarily unwell and unable to work or because they are taking unpaid time off to care for sick family members. In other words, the

US approach to healthcare has a negative impact on the potential for wealth generation for the country as a whole. And in a society driven more than most by money, that just doesn't add up.

Chapter Nine

A Thriving Melting Pot

Myth number 9 – America is the world's great melting pot where waves of immigrants over generations have integrated well into society and new arrivals are welcome if they commit to the US way of life.

America's credentials as a country of immigration are not in doubt. Since the first European settlers arrived in North America in the 16th century, US history has been dominated by waves of people arriving first from Britain and northwest Europe, then southern and eastern Europe, the Middle East, Latin America and more recently Asia and Africa. At the National Park Service's Museum of National Immigration on Ellis Island in New York you can delve into the stories of some of the more than 12 million people who arrived through the centre to start new lives in the US over 60 years between 1892 and 1954, often after arduous journeys across the Atlantic with little money and few possessions[1]. With almost no federal restrictions on immigration to the US, Ellis Island was processing an average of 5000 arrivals each day at its peak, opening the doors of the country to more than one million new Americans a year. Numbers dropped considerably when Congress imposed emergency immigration quotas in 1921 and then set up a visa system three years later in response to growing concerns from native born Americans about "undesirables" coming to the country[2]. But the status of Ellis Island as the iconic migrant gateway to the country had already been sealed. Immigration to the US began to grow again in the 1940s. By 1989, more than one million people were again being granted legal permanent residence in the US every year[3].

America's melting pot myth goes much further than just describing sustained immigration into the US over generations from all over the world. It suggests the very success of the country is based on the rapid integration and assimilation of immigrant communities, with new arrivals quickly dropping their own national identities and becoming genuine Americans by embracing the culture and values of their adopted home. But this is where the myth starts to fray at the edges. There is no question that the US is more ethnically diverse than many other Western countries given its long history of immigration. In some areas it has done better at integration too. But in both cases, the picture is nowhere near as clear-cut as the myth would suggest. At more than 44 million, the US has more immigrants in numerical terms

Foreign-born Population by Country, % of total Population

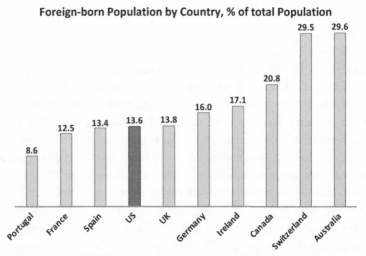

Source: OECD (2020) Foreign-born population indicator, 2018 or latest

than any other country[4]. But America is only in the middle of the pack of countries when it comes to foreign born immigrants as a percentage of total population[5]. And US immigrants are less ethnically diverse than in many other countries including the UK and Canada[6]. The US also continues to face serious challenges integrating some minority communities. More recent arrivals from Latin America face particular barriers to integration[7]. And public hostility towards further immigration is never far from the surface. In other words, despite the myth, America is not so different from other Western countries which also have significant and growing immigrant populations and are grappling with the policy implications of a vocal body of the public demanding tighter immigration control.

The melting pot myth also glosses over the corrosive legacy of slavery in America. Over almost 250 years from 1619, more than 400,000 slaves were kidnapped and forcibly transported from Africa to the American Colonies and, later, to the independent US[8]. In the last census before slavery was abolished by the Thirteenth Amendment to the US Constitution in 1865, there were almost four million slaves in the country[9]. Most of the Founding Fathers were slave owners, as were 12 of the first 18 presidents – a fact that many Americans still like to gloss over when eulogising America's founding credentials[10]. Slavery is indelibly stained into the very fabric of modern America. By definition, it was profoundly racist. It was about subjugation, social domination, exploitation, violence and control in in the search of profit and wealth. Much remains to be done to address the enduring effects of this shameful history. More than 150 years after abolition, the US still faces serious challenges integrating African Americans fully into society. Racial inequality lingers stubbornly in almost every aspect of life.

On a road trip around the deep south in early 2018, I toured the historic sites of the civil rights movement in Alabama, visited plantation homes and national parks in Mississippi and Louisiana and immersed myself in the unique musical history of the region, from the delta blues of Muddy Waters born out of the cotton plantations to the ground-breaking rock and roll of Elvis nurtured in gritty Memphis. It was a wonderful trip to a part of America which I had not previously visited. But it wasn't the rich history, world-famous music or diverse natural landscapes that had most impact. It was the stark and enduring poverty and segregation across the region which imprinted itself on my mind. Despite the South's important role in advancing civil rights in the US more than 50 years ago, in many areas I visited, the white, African American and Hispanic populations still appeared to live in completely separate communities. More often, the whites were in leafy city suburbs or more affluent towns and rural areas in comfortable homes with gardens bordered by picket fences. African Americans and Latinos were concentrated in the inner cities often in decaying housing stock or separate poorer urban communities with poverty rates reaching 40 percent in some areas[11]. White poverty is a serious problem in the south too which remains the poorest region of the US. But it does not reach anywhere near the levels suffered by minority communities who experience particular hardship[12]. The whole thing was shocking to see in one of the richest countries in the world.

In Selma, Alabama – the starting point of civil rights marches in 1965 which played an important role in securing the vote for African Americans – the evidence of continuing segregation was particularly striking. The minority white population lives largely on the west side of the town centre in detached homes with lush lawns surrounded by pine and magnolia trees. The Selma Country Club at the heart of the community was still whites only as late as 2015[13] and may still be segregated today. African Americans who make up two thirds of Selma's population live just a few blocks away in the east of the town in dilapidated and graffitied old properties or sterile social housing on pot-holed and litter-filled streets. Others live in now slum-like former military accommodation across the Alabama River beyond the steel arches of the iconic Edmund Pettus Bridge that has become a symbol of America's civil rights struggle. When the Craig US Air Force base closed near Selma in the 1970s, the military housing was sold off to a private developer who rented units to Selma's civilian residents. The area was grotesquely renamed Nathan Bedford Forrest after a 19th century plantation owner, slave trader and Confederate general during the American Civil War who became the first grand wizard of the Ku Klux Klan[14]. The district is now known more subtly as 'NBF Homes'. But the link to slavery and white supremacy is hardly concealed for the estate's mostly black residents.

But Selma and the South are far from the only parts of the country where the integration and assimilation of minority communities is not as the American melting pot myth suggests. The story is repeated right across the US. In the far west in California, the rich agricultural area of the Salinas valley is majority Hispanic. In towns like Castroville, Watsonville and Salinas the Hispanic population ranges from 76 to 90 percent. Just a few miles away, the affluent coastal communities of Monterey and Carmel are almost entirely white[15]. The two areas have a totally different feel. In the valley, you can see van loads of Hispanic women being dropped off in vast cultivated fields to pick salad crops by hand under a burning sun with little shade, and Latino men operating farm machinery and irrigation systems. In the distance, the crashing waves of the Pacific lure affluent white teenagers in their pastel-coloured, refurbished VW camper vans to test their surfing skills. In the valley towns, fast food joints, cheap general stores and pawn shops abound amongst basic social housing and agricultural suppliers. Household incomes are 30-40 percent lower than on the coast. In Monterey and Carmel, it's fancy boutiques, expensive restaurants and quirky cafes serving both the local white residents and the thousands of tourists who flock to the area for its natural beauty and Spanish history. The two areas feel like different worlds despite being just 20 miles apart.

Even in the largely Democrat-voting, liberal cities on the east coast, minority communities are less integrated than might appear from a brief visit. On a busy working day, the city centres of Washington DC, New York and Philadelphia are visibly multicultural with a diverse mix of people going about their business. But most return home to districts dominated by their own communities. In Washington DC, the affluent north west quadrant of the city is predominantly white with residents living in attractive, detached red brick and clapboard homes along wooded streets. By contrast, the south east of the city is almost entirely African American with large estates of public housing squeezed between industry, rail depots and highways. Hispanic Washingtonians tend to live in pockets together in more affordable suburbs, or outside the city in parts of Virginia and Maryland[16]. And once at home, the different communities don't really mix. In almost five years in Washington, I went to the south east only a handful of times. There was little to draw non-residents to the area. The city didn't really feel very integrated despite the melting pot myth.

The legacy of slavery casts a long shadow over the US and is part of the explanation why some minority communities are less well integrated into American society than the melting pot myth suggests. After a trip to Georgia and the Carolinas in 2015, I stepped innocently into the minefield of American race relations on my return to the embassy. Having visited the beautiful, Antebellum towns of Charleston and Savannah on the southern Atlantic coast, I drove through the back roads of rural Georgia and South Carolina far from the interstate corridor of the I-95 to reach Asheville and the Blue Ridge Mountains, 300 miles to the north east. The journey took me through miles of swamp, forest and marginal farmland of the Georgian interior. Rusting cars and farm machinery decorated the lots of tired wooden homes or trailers, squeezed into damp cuttings out of endless forest along the route. In some of the small towns and villages I passed through, most shops and businesses other than Dollar General and a gas station were boarded up. There was an air of quiet resignation as people whiled away the time sitting on their porches and in the doorways of shops that were no longer open.

On my return to the embassy, I was asked about my trip in our daily staff meeting. I couldn't help but remark on the stark contrast between the visible affluence of the centres of Charleston and Savannah and the deep poverty and deprivation I had seen in many rural communities. Some areas of Georgia and the Carolinas had looked like parts of Africa, I said, trying to capture what I had seen. I immediately noticed some odd, unspoken reactions from American colleagues around the table. But I didn't really get a sense that something was wrong until later in the day when I was walking around the embassy building. As I made my way through different offices, I could feel an unusual chill in the air. Conversations were happening in hushed tones with colleagues quite obviously changing the subject as I approached. I finally worked out that I was the cause of the problem when a delegation of staff asked to see me urgently later that afternoon. I was immediately confronted with anger and outrage at my comment in the morning meeting which, I was told, had been racist.

American colleagues in the embassy had immediately misinterpreted what I had said. To them, it turned out, I had implied that African Americans were responsible for the poverty and economic distress in the rural south and that, of course, wasn't acceptable. I quickly apologised for causing offence and explained what I had been trying to say. Having lived in north Africa and visited other countries on the continent, I had simply been referring to the similarities in the landscapes combined with the marked social deprivation. I genuinely hadn't registered the ethnicity of the people I had seen along the way. I couldn't say now whether they were mostly white, Hispanic or black. I had just been trying to highlight some of the serious challenges America was facing in rural areas which we never saw in the leafy north-west of Washington DC and felt so at odds with the stereotypical image of the wealthy, US economic powerhouse. Suggesting the problems were the fault of one race or another hadn't even crossed my mind.

I am still not sure I fully convinced my embassy colleagues about what I was trying to say. There was a bit of a sense of, 'well you would say that wouldn't you' when challenged over the remarks I had made. But the whole episode was an important lesson in the hyper-sensitivity of race relations in America. Given the country's history of slavery and a century of legal segregation following its abolition in 1865 by the Thirteenth Amendment to the Constitution[17], race relations remain a deep sore that is far from healed. The hyper-sensitivity endures because the US has failed in many respects to address the legacy of the past. Despite the gains of the civil rights movement, America has a long way to go before it can claim to be a fair and equitable society where everyone, no matter what their race or ethnicity, has an equal chance of making a decent living or improving their lives.

The Fair Housing Act of 1968, which was adopted by Congress soon after Martin Luther King's assassination, outlawed racial discrimination in the sale or rental of housing[18]. But it did not mandate specific action to improve integration, nor could it magic away generations of ingrained racism which had been enshrined in law by successive US governments. With little sanction, white Americans often continued to do what they could to prevent integration by making it clear that African Americans were not welcome in their neighbourhoods, and sometimes by pretty unpleasant means[19]. Little was done formally to help communities de-segregate despite decades of government policies that enforced separation.

Most African Americans in any case could not afford the rents or house prices in white districts which were typically more affluent and therefore more expensive. In the ten years immediately after the landmark housing act, integration did gradually improve. But progress then slowed significantly. The average rate of black home ownership in the US is now little higher than it was 50 years ago – virtually all the limited gains made after the passing of the Fair Housing Act were wiped out by the financial crisis in 2007[20]. Some cities in the north east have fared particularly badly. New York and Philadelphia remain almost as racially segregated now as they were in the 1960s[21].

Greater effort was made to integrate the American education system after the Supreme Court ruled in 1954 that school segregation was unconstitutional[22]. The Civil Rights Act of 1964 gave the federal government powers to enforce de-segregation in the face of entrenched resistance from school districts particularly in the South[23]. Considerable progress was made in the 1970s, but this soon ground to a halt in the face of renewed opposition from white communities. School segregation in the US is now on the increase as proactive policies including free cross-district school transport, court supervision of school de-segregation plans and race-based admission systems to ensure better representation have been scrapped or themselves ruled to be discriminatory[24]. In some parts of the country, school segregation is now higher than it was in the 1960s and especially for African American and Latino students[25]. School segregation is compounded by enduring residential separation. Whites, blacks and Latinos mostly still live in different areas, with blacks and Latinos typically in poorer neighbourhoods with greater numbers of students suffering the consequences of poverty and schools with fewer resources. Not surprisingly given the circumstances, African Americans continue to lag behind whites in educational achievement despite considerable gains since the 1960s. They earn less on average than whites by almost 20%. They are twice as likely to be unemployed and six times more likely to be incarcerated[26]. It's a grim reality that is largely ignored by the melting pot myth.

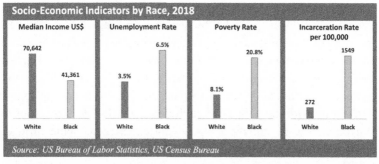

Socio-Economic Indicators by Race, 2018

Median Income US$: White 70,642, Black 41,361
Unemployment Rate: White 3.5%, Black 6.5%
Poverty Rate: White 8.1%, Black 20.8%
Incarceration Rate per 100,000: White 272, Black 1549

Source: US Bureau of Labor Statistics, US Census Bureau

But the legacy of slavery and legal discrimination is not the whole story. Just as in many other Western countries, hostility towards immigration has long been a feature of US history. America's open immigration policy came to an end in the 1920s because native born Americans were alarmed that growing numbers of migrants from southern and eastern Europe along with large numbers of Jews fleeing discrimination would change the traditional northwest-European character of the country and their way of life[27]. Even earlier, Chinese workers had been banned from migrating to the US from 1882 on the back of fears that they were suppressing wages despite making up a tiny fraction of the population[28]. A wider ban on all Asian migration became law in 1917[29]. It was not fully lifted until 1965[30]. There was more than a dose of racism in the belief that Protestant, northern Europeans were somehow superior to other peoples.

Discrimination against immigrant communities in the US has been widespread throughout American history too. When more than a million Irish arrived in the country in less than a decade after the potato famine of the 1840s they were often labelled as drunk and violent, and sometimes explicitly blocked from applying for work with "No Irish Need Apply" slapped on job adverts[31]. In a predominantly Protestant society, many also suffered religious prejudice because they were Catholic. Some particularly pious Americans even feared the arrivals were signs of a Papal conspiracy to take over the US and convert the country to Catholicism.

During World War Two, 120,000 Japanese Americans were interned for years in what were little more than desert prisoner of war camps over fears they would not be loyal to their adopted nation after Japan declared war on the US by its attack on Pearl Harbor. The vast majority of those interned were American citizens who had been born in the country, not recent immigrants[32]. When the numbers of Latinos arriving in the US increased significantly from the 1970s, many suffered discrimination when applying for jobs, seeking housing or interacting with the police or health services[33]. In late 2018, four in ten Latinos were still reporting having experienced some form of discrimination[34].

It's only fair to say that most Americans are not proud of this history and there has been some change in recent years. The US elected its first black President in Barack Obama in 2008. Both government and business have made considerable efforts to improve their diversity and the figures are getting better. But even here, it's a mixed bag. The political appointee system allows US governments to appoint talented leaders from minority communities to senior Cabinet positions as a way of setting an example and driving change from the top. Under President George W Bush in the early 2000s, Colin Powell and Condoleeza Rice became the first and second African-Americans to hold the position of Secretary of State, the most senior secretary role in the US administration. At first glance, the federal government can therefore look more representative of American society or, at least, that serious movement towards greater diversity is being made. But political appointees are temporary positions tied to a particular administration's term in office, not permanent. And progress in increasing diversity across the general workforce in US government departments has been pretty slow. The federal government continues to employ a significantly lower percentage of Latinos than their share of the American workforce. It does employ a greater percentage of African Americans many of whom are attracted by the job security and benefits of government jobs even if they are not particularly well paid. But employees from all minority groups are still disproportionately in lower grades jobs. Less than 21 percent of senior federal government roles are filled by non-whites despite minorities now making up 40 percent of the US population[35].

The 2018 midterms saw American voters elect the most diverse Congress ever. For the first time, more than 20 percent of all members elected were from non-white minorities, an increase of 3 percent over 2016 and continuing a positive trend in Congressional elections over 10 years[36]. But the numbers are still a long way from reflecting the current ethnic makeup of the US[37]. In business, diversity is also increasing, including at board level. But the rate of change is slow and the absolute level small. By 2018, only 16 percent of board members of Fortune 500 companies were from minorities[38]; only four CEOs were black[39]. Not surprisingly, very few businesses have proved willing to publish their diversity statistics given how far many are falling behind American society.

We tried to do our bit in the embassy to improve the diversity of the Americans we employed. Like many other businesses in the north west of Washington, our US staff reflected the local neighbourhood and were largely white with just a few Asians and Africans Americans. We did better on employing Hispanics, but they were largely in more junior, lower paid roles. So we put together a strategy to tackle the problem and set about advertising jobs on websites and in publications more likely to be seen by minority communities as well as the standard recruitment portals. We did outreach too, to encourage applications from minority communities across the city. Our efforts did have some impact over time. But it was frustratingly slow.

When I was putting together our new recruitment strategy, I asked a well-known billionaire entrepreneur how he went about ensuring his employees represented modern US society. His businesses were often celebrated for employing more ethnic minorities and women than many others, including at senior levels. His answer was honest but not entirely helpful. After a brief pause to reflect, the entrepreneur said, "well, if we decide we want someone from a certain ethnic group or a woman in a particular role we just go out and make sure we find one". Turning to me with a somewhat mischievous smile, he added, "but you wouldn't be able to do that as embassies and governments have to follow the rules". The entrepreneur had just admitted positive discrimination to secure his brand's record on diversity. It wasn't entirely what I had expected to hear. But it did help to explain why his businesses were doing considerably better than most in the diversity stakes, and why so many other businesses still had a long way to go.

The cold fact remains that the political and business elites in America are still largely white and most often male too[40]. Prominent leaders from minority groups like Barack Obama are the exception, not the rule. In the 250 year history of the United States, every president other than Barack Obama has been of white, northern European ancestry. Only one has been Catholic. On average, minority communities in the US continue to be poorer, face persistent discrimination and have fewer opportunities than their white compatriots. Both African Americans and Hispanics suffer higher levels of unemployment than whites and Asians and earn considerably lower salaries when in work. Despite the myth, the archetypal American melting pot has not yet produced 'one America' but more of a fragmented and segregated society where inequality and discrimination are commonplace.

A surge in unauthorised immigration into the US over the last 50 years has also acted as a brake on integration. Well-meaning reforms in 1965 to reduce racism and prejudice in the immigration system had the effect of significantly reducing some previously legal routes into the country, triggering a surge in illegal migration[41]. The number of unauthorised immigrants in America has more than tripled over the last thirty years and peaked at more than 12 million just before the economic crisis in 2007-8[42]. Current numbers are around 10.5 million, or a quarter of all foreign born nationals in the country, with the majority of those in the US illegally coming from Mexico and Central and South America[43]. Unauthorised immigrants face even greater challenges than other minorities in American society. They cannot work legally and so find themselves stuck in poorly paid, low-skilled work where no one will ask too many questions about their status. They live in constant fear of deportation even though more than two thirds of illegal immigrants in the US have been living in the country for more than 10 years[44]. And they avoid contact with government authorities when they need help to reduce the risk of being found out and sent back to their countries of origin. In these circumstances, genuine integration into American society is simply not an option.

Successive US Administrations have roundly failed to address the issue of illegal immigrants in the country, expanding the ranks of the struggling American underclass by their inaction. President Obama did introduce a programme that issued renewable, deportation deferrals and work permits to undocumented immigrants who had arrived in the US as children – the so called "Dreamers"[45]. But a number of states then blocked his attempt to extend the programme to undocumented parents of American citizens claiming it was against US immigration law and unconstitutional[46]. Since then, the prospect of immigration reform has diminished as the country has become even more politically polarised. Rather depressingly, some Hispanic members of Congress whose parents themselves were immigrants to America have been most resistant to comprehensive immigration reform on the grounds that regularising undocumented migrants would reward bad behaviour.

After taking office, President Trump quickly set about demonising unauthorised immigrants in the US to try to secure funding for building a wall along the Mexican border, one of his big campaign promises. He also exaggerated the risks of international terrorism to justify excluding certain nationalities from the country on grounds of national security. Within just a few days of moving into the White House in January 2017, he issued an Executive Order temporarily banning nationals from seven predominantly Muslim countries from entering the US until a new system of "extreme vetting" could be introduced to "keep the bad guys out"[47]. The announcement came on a Friday evening just a few hours after the British Prime Minister, Theresa May, had left Washington having been the first foreign leader to meet the new president in the White House after his inauguration. I was on a plane to a conference in Miami.

The President's announcement triggered a flurry of frantic activity around the world trying to work out exactly what the Executive Order meant. No one knew in the Departments of State and Homeland Security or in US Customs and Border Protection even though they would all have a critical part to play in implementing the new measures. The President's policy advisers in the White House had come up with the draft order without consulting the experts. I spent the weekend on my mobile phone coordinating the embassy's work from Florida as we tried to determine whether British dual nationals or permanent residents from the seven named countries would be affected by the ban and no longer able to travel to the US. The Foreign Office in London had started receiving calls from anxious British Muslims concerned they would not be able to take their children on holiday to Disneyland or to accept the student scholarship they had been awarded. The Prime Minister was coming under pressure from the British media for not getting advance notice of the announcement despite having been with the President for talks in the White House just a few hours before it was made. The Saturday morning headlines – *Trump and May. The not-so Special Relationship* – were writing themselves. Downing Street was pressing us hard to find answers to help see off the media onslaught.

After a great deal of working the phones and calls into the White House, including by Foreign Secretary Boris Johnson, we eventually received confirmation that the measures would not apply to British passport holders or anyone with permanent residence in the UK even if they were nationals of the seven countries listed in the ban. In effect, we had secured a carve out for the UK on the grounds of our close relationship with the US and by reminding the White House of the measures we already had in place to prevent suspected terrorists from travelling. But the whole thing had been chaotic. Having not been consulted on the drafting of the Executive Order, US government departments had been forced to make up on the hoof how they would implement the measures. No one knew what "extreme vetting" meant. America already had rigorous procedures in place to make sure known extremists could not travel to the country which were pretty effective. Donald Trump's political team had simply come up with the announcement to show the President was quickly implementing one of his campaign promises to keep America safe, having spent much of the time in his bid for office whipping up fear. It was the first of many plays to Trump's base.

President Trump's 'Muslim ban' was widely condemned as unconstitutional for discriminating against certain visa applicants on the grounds of their nationality and religion. Within a matter of days, the States of Washington and Minnesota took legal action against the President and his administration and successfully stopped the new measures from being implemented. But it was a temporary victory. Over the next few months, the President issued revised orders, the final one of which was ultimately upheld by the Supreme Court. It included many of the original measures, but broadened them to include three non-Muslim countries specifically to undermine the arguments of those claiming the President was illegally targeting a particular religion[48].

The 'Muslim Ban' episode was just the start of a much tougher approach to immigration by the Trump administration. Further action followed to step up the arrest and deportation of unauthorised immigrants in the country. Under revised rules, US immigration enforcement authorities were no longer required to focus on those who were a threat to public safety or had a criminal record. Any illegal immigrant could be picked up whether or not they had lived in the US for decades and had family members who were American citizens[49]. Arrests, detentions and removals all increased significantly in 2018 although arrests then dropped back in 2019[50]. A zero tolerance policy was introduced at the US/Mexico border which meant that all undocumented immigrants would be immediately arrested and prosecuted for criminal offences on trying to cross the frontier. The policy resulted in thousands of children being separated from their parents and held in overcrowded detention centres. In the chaos, some parents were deported without being reunited with their children. The resulting public outcry forced the President to reverse his policy of family separation after just two months. But zero tolerance remained firmly in place[51].

The President also doubled down on trying to secure funding for his promised border wall. He stoked up fears of 'uncontrolled immigration' by exaggerating the numbers of people trying to cross the southern US border illegally and drawing attention to serious crimes committed by a tiny proportion of illegal migrants already in the country. He made wild assertions about the threat posed by unauthorised migrants through gang violence, drugs and terrorism with little evidence to back up his claims[52]. Some Americans lapped up the President's unforgiving approach. Parts of the US appeared to be turning against the very idea that the country should be a well-integrated and tolerant multi-cultural society. Racism was once again not far from the surface.

And yet despite all this, America still manages to pride itself on the diversity of its society and the integration and assimilation of immigrant communities from all over the world. It is a key part of US mythology. America's successful multi-ethnic melting pot is often cited as one of the main reasons for its economic prosperity, and for its pulling power attracting talented people from all over the world to come to its shores to live the American Dream. But the melting pot myth is an oversimplification of a much more complex reality. White immigrants of largely European descent that arrived in the US from many countries over generations integrated effectively into the country. They are Americans by any definition. Even more recent white immigrants have quickly and successfully embedded themselves in the country having not suffered from the race-based discrimination that was written into US law and embedded within so much of society until the 1960s. The story for non-white minority groups is quite different. America's dark past of slavery, the enduring racial and ethnic discrimination in parts of US society and the unresolved issue of millions of undocumented migrants paints a more troubling picture. America was built on the toil of immigrants from all corners of the world. But immigration and integration, diversity and assimilation are quite separate things, and on integration and assimilation the US still has a long way to go.

With an aging population and falling birth rates[53], the US needs a continuing flow of immigrants to help drive continued economic growth. Failing to address ongoing discrimination against minority communities or stirring up fears against future immigration are not the answer. Deporting the millions of unauthorised migrants already in the country would also have a devastating impact on the US economy and split countless American families. No one genuinely expects this to happen. But unless a way can be found for most of those illegally in the US to achieve citizenship, a significant group of people will never be able to integrate fully into American society or contribute all their skills and energy to US success. America's reputation as a haven for those fleeing violence and persecution will also take a hit unless asylum seekers continue to be treated fairly and compassionately.

Without concerted government action to help overcome ingrained segregation and tackle discrimination, it is hard to see significant further progress being made towards greater integration and equality in the US to the point where the melting pot myth could ring true. Continuing to confine some minorities to an underclass from which they cannot escape is not a recipe for future American success. It would go against the very founding principles of the nation for which "all men are created equal" with unalienable rights to life, liberty and the pursuit of happiness. It would further fan the flames of community tensions. The US somehow needs to find a way to push back against those narrowly defining what a 'true American' is and instead work towards a society that respects difference and promotes tolerance and inclusion.

In a speech in 1953, Dwight D Eisenhower said: "I believe as long as we allow conditions to exist that make for second-class citizens, we are making of ourselves less than first-class citizens .... the only way to protect my own rights is to protect the rights of others".[54] Eisenhower was right. Only when every American, no matter what their race or ethnic background, is treated equally and has a fair chance to benefit from US success, will the country be able to reach its full potential.

Chapter Ten

The Threat from Outside

Myth number 10 – The greatest threat to the American way of life comes from outside the US in the form of international terrorism.

Everyone over the age of thirty remembers where they were on 11 September 2001, when they saw the news of planes being crashed deliberately into the twin towers of the World Trade Center on the southern tip of Manhattan Island in New York. The footage of passenger aircraft ploughing silently into the iconic skyscrapers on a perfect autumn morning against vivid blue skies and then exploding into fireballs of searing flames and black smoke were almost impossible to process, but instantly chilling. The coordinated Al Qaeda attacks that morning – in New York, at the Pentagon in Washington DC and in Pennsylvania (where United Airlines flight 93 was deliberately crashed into a field when the passengers and crew tried to take back control of the aircraft) – killed almost 3000 people and injured thousands more from almost 80 countries. It was the deadliest terrorist attack in American history.

On that morning, I was at work as usual in the Foreign Secretary's office in the heart of Whitehall in London. Like every other day in my job as Private Secretary to Jack Straw, I was at my desk preparing an endless in tray of papers for the Secretary of State in a gap between meetings. I was running through policy recommendations being submitted by officials from across the department to make sure they were clear and well argued before putting them to the minister. I was making calls to Downing Street about papers being sent to the Prime Minister. I was checking that letters the Foreign Secretary was being asked to sign were written in plain English in the minister's style and did not contain errors. Jack Straw was eating lunch in his office while reading papers and making a few calls. As usual, the TV on the wall behind me was broadcasting one of the 24 hour news channels.

The minister's Diary Secretary, whose desk faced the TV, was first to notice the reports of something crashing into the north tower of the World Trade Center. She immediately drew the office's attention to the pictures which were being replayed on a constant loop as the news services tried to piece together what was going on. The Principal Private Secretary wandered into the Foreign Secretary's office to tell him that something had happened in New York. But for the first few minutes it wasn't clear whether the incident was a terrible accident or something worse. From the angle of the early video footage, it was difficult to make out what exactly had flown into the building. The media speculated that it was a light aircraft, not a passenger jet. We would only later find out that it was the hijacked American Airlines Flight 11 from Boston which had been bound for Los Angeles. So I continued processing papers while keeping half an eye on the TV. When the second plane crashed into the south tower 17 minutes later in full view of the media cameras, it was clear that we were witnessing something much more significant. America was under serious attack.

For a short period we still tried to carry on the day pretty much as normal; there was little we could do until more concrete news came in and we could make contact with our staff in Washington DC and New York, and the Americans themselves. But before long, the government's crisis machinery clicked into action to coordinate the

UK response. The police and military were put on the highest alert. Airport security was increased and flightpaths into London's airports were changed to stop civilian aircraft overflying the centre of the city[1]. The Foreign Secretary was summoned to a meeting of the COBR Civil Contingencies Committee which coordinates the UK response to national emergencies. After the meeting, the Prime Minister made a brief and solemn statement to the nation from Downing Street expressing his horror at what had happened and pledging to stand shoulder to shoulder with the US in the fight against terrorism[2]. The Queen expressed her disbelief and shock and authorised the Star Spangled Banner to be played at the changing of the guard at Buckingham Palace the next morning[3]. I finally got home around 10pm after a long and exhausting day. I was followed around the house by a nagging sense of anxiety which was impossible to shake off. I sat, shell-shocked in front of the TV news trying, unsuccessfully, to make sense of what had happened before turning in for a largely sleepless night. It had been a bleak day.

Just a few weeks later I travelled to New York with the Foreign Secretary for the annual minister-level meetings of the UN General Assembly. The meetings at the United Nations' Headquarters had been due to take place just days after 9/11 but were postponed to let the city focus on the immediate aftermath of the attacks before having to handle the arrival of dozens of political leaders from around the world. After we landed at John F. Kennedy airport, I went with Jack Straw to the World Trade Center site so he could pay his respects on behalf of the UK government to all those who had died. I remember vividly the horror of the place. Twisted metal remnants of the towers illuminated by floodlights in the autumn afternoon gloom framed an enormous pile of rubble several stories high which was still smouldering from all the energy generated by the collapsing towers several weeks earlier. A cold November drizzle created mist as it landed on the warmer debris. There was an acrid stench of burnt metals and plastics in the air and what seemed like endless amounts of shredded paper from the offices in the building.

I remember hundreds of questions racing through my mind as I took in the awful scene before me. How could this happen? What went wrong at airport security? How had the towers collapsed so precisely doing relatively limited damage to surrounding buildings? Had anyone survived if they were on the floors above where the planes had struck? What would I have done if I had been in the buildings at the time of the attacks? I watched as dozens of workers toiled liked ants over the wreckage of the towers searching for evidence and human remains in the hope of confirming formally who had been killed. A line of empty trucks was waiting to be filled with debris which would then be taken to a site on Staten Island for more detailed forensic investigation. The whole thing was grim.

We paid our respects at the many impromptu shrines around the site to those who had been killed in the attacks, including dozens of firefighters who died as they responded to the incident and were buried in the collapsing towers. Photographs of those missing, presumed dead were pinned to the makeshift fence around the site and pasted on every lamp post and wall nearby with heart wrenching tributes from their families and friends. Young fathers and mothers, brothers and sisters looked down from pictures taken in happier times. The sense of lives unnecessarily cut short and the impact this would have on so many others was sobering. It was impossible not to feel an overwhelming sense of sadness, as well as fear and anger at such an audacious attack. If a complex, coordinated act of terrorism on this scale could happen in America – so far from the Islamic world – it could happen in London or anywhere else. It felt like 9/11 had, in an instant, turned the world into a more dangerous and darker place. The peace we had enjoyed in the West for three generations now seemed to be at serious risk.

The attacks sent shockwaves around the world, immediately changing how the West perceived extremist Islamist terrorism and the threat it posed. For the UK, with 67 dead in New York, it was the single biggest British loss of life in a terrorist attack in history[4]. Much of the world was united in shock and grief. But most of all, 9/11 had a profound impact on the American psyche. Not surprisingly, it changed everything for the US. It was only the second attack on the US homeland in American history since the War of 1812. The first – the Japanese attack on Pearl Harbor 50 years earlier – had triggered America's entry into World War Two. But this time the enemy was shadowy and amorphous, not a nation state with clear territory and visible armed forces which could be targeted. This made the threat from Al Qaeda all the more frightening. Osama bin Laden's modern day guerrilla organisation was diffuse and flexible. It was hard to know how to counter such a twisted ideology and eliminate the threat. Americans were understandably fearful. Their politicians were duty bound to respond to try to keep the country safe.

Just a few days after the attacks, President George W Bush launched the global "War on Terror". In a speech to a joint session of Congress, he described how America would focus initially on Al Qaeda and its base in Afghanistan but then take the war to "every terrorist group of global reach"[5]. Congress quickly passed the USA Patriot Act creating new federal crimes related to terrorism, giving American agencies extra powers to track terrorist finances and, more controversially, significantly extending US government surveillance powers[6]. On 7 October, less than four weeks after 9/11, America with British support launched military action against the Taliban government in Afghanistan to root out Al Qaeda and capture its leader Osama bin Laden. Operation Enduring Freedom had begun.

On that Sunday afternoon, as the airstrikes began, I made my way into the Foreign Office in Whitehall. The Foreign Secretary needed to be kept up to speed with developments on the offensive and fully briefed to make telephone calls to allies in South Asia and around the world to cement their support for the military offensive. We also managed to set up a call to representatives of the Afghan opposition. The line was terrible but Jack Straw was able to underline UK resolve to help them defeat the Taliban and expel Al Qaeda from their country. The Foreign Secretary also checked in regularly with the Prime Minister and Colin Powell.

In the face of a concerted aerial bombing campaign, the Taliban government collapsed within a matter of weeks. Coalition troops from dozens of countries were soon on the ground in Afghanistan in their thousands. But they faced a protracted and bloody guerrilla war alongside local Afghan forces against Taliban fighters who had melted back into their communities or slipped over the border into Pakistan. Osama bin Laden himself was eventually traced to a compound in Pakistan and killed in a raid by American special forces in 2011[7]. But, almost 20 years later, foreign military forces are still in Afghanistan albeit in smaller numbers. The conflict has killed 3,500 coalition military and more than 100,000 Afghans but failed fully to neutralise the Taliban[8].

Only 18 months after 9/11, when the Afghanistan mission was far from over, George W Bush turned his attention to Iraq. A US led coalition invaded the country with the aim of removing Saddam Hossein in the second phase of America's new War on Terror. The campaign in Iraq was sold on grounds that Saddam Hossein's regime had weapons of mass destruction which were an imminent threat to the West as well as links to international terrorism[9]. Both were later proved to be false. But the damage had already been done. America and its allies were no longer focused solely on the Afghan mission to rout the Taliban and destroy Al Qaeda which had broad international support. Instead, they quickly became embroiled in another, much more controversial conflict which turned out to be just as long and even more deadly.

And yet despite the failings of the Afghanistan and Iraq campaigns, there has not been another successful foreign-based terrorist attack on American soil since 9/11[10]. Osama bin Laden and other senior Al Qaeda leaders have also been removed from the picture. But Americans just don't appear to feel much safer. Many continue to believe they are at serious risk from extremist Islamist violence despite everything that has been done in the name of tackling the terrorist threat in the US and overseas over the last 20 years. Polling consistently has terrorism at or close to the top of the list of the biggest issues for voters, and particularly for those on the right of the political spectrum. In 2020, 74% of Americans said defending the country against terrorism should be the top priority for the President and Congress, ranking above the economy, education and healthcare and significantly higher than immigration, crime and climate change[11].

The US media feeds American anxieties through relentless and graphic coverage of terrorist attacks at home and abroad and particularly those committed by Muslims[12]. At the same time, US news outlets downplay the vastly higher number of deaths from American gun violence or other domestic causes. With this continuous stoking of fear, I have lost track of the number of conversations I have had with Americans who remain genuinely worried about another, serious foreign terrorist attack taking place in the US and nervous about travelling to Europe where they perceive the risks from terrorism to be even higher. President Trump himself stirred these anxieties in 2017 when he used Twitter to link a rise in general crime rates in the UK to the "spread of radical Islamic terror"[13]. His audience was domestic, rather than British; his message that only he would take the necessary steps, however politically incorrect, to keep America safe from terrorism by restricting Muslim immigration. It didn't seem to matter that what he said was factually wrong and poorly received in the UK.

Two years earlier, Fox News pundits incorrectly claimed there were "no go" areas in UK and other European cities because they had been taken over by Muslims and Sharia law imposed. The claims were later corrected after a number of formal complaints were made[14]. But Fox News' broad message has remained constant; there are dangers in Europe's immigrant communities and Americans should be fearful about what could happen in the US if too many Muslims were allowed into their country. Donald Trump very adeptly played on these fears in his campaign for the White House in 2016.

America is still unquestionably a target for foreign-based Islamist extremists. Al Qaeda, while much weakened since 2001, has sought to regroup while the international focus has been on the threat from ISIS in Iraq and Syria. On the eve of the controversial move of the US embassy in Israel from Tel Aviv to Jerusalem in 2018, Al Qaeda leader Ayman al Zawahiri issued a video message confirming that

America was the number one enemy of Muslims and calling on the faithful to rise to fight the US[15]. The US Director of National Intelligence told Congress in early 2019 that Al Qaeda was "showing signs of confidence" with its leaders working to strengthen their networks and to encourage attacks against Western interests[16].

The rapid rise of the Islamic State further stoked American fears. As ISIS grabbed large swathes of territory in Iraq in May 2014 including the strategic city of Mosul and declared a caliphate in parts of Iraq and Syria, anxieties rose that a new extremist Islamist organisation could soon replace Al Qaeda as the main global terrorist threat. When thousands from the minority Yazidi community were forced to flee their homes by a vicious ISIS advance in August 2014 leaving them besieged on the inhospitable slopes of Sinjar Mountain in Northern Iraq without food or shelter, the US and its allies were galvanised into action to try to save lives and stop ISIS from making further gains.

We worked around the clock in the embassy with the Obama White House and Pentagon as plans were drawn up to provide air support to anti-ISIS forces in Iraq and to drop humanitarian supplies for the trapped Yazidi community. Within days, British Royal Airforce planes were making airdrops on Sinjar Mountain, but not taking part in airstrikes. Following the UK parliament's shock failure in September 2013 to back airstrikes against Syria after President Assad's use of chemical weapons, Downing Street was nervous about recalling members of parliament from their summer break to vote on direct military action in Iraq. Instead, the UK focused initially on military surveillance flights and dropping aid, neither of which needed parliamentary authorisation[17]. The US Air Force made additional humanitarian drops but also conducted airstrikes against Islamic State targets to help the Yazidis escape to refugee camps in Syria and Iraqi Kurdistan[18]. The British parliament voted to support airstrikes against ISIS in Iraq a few weeks later[19]. RAF jets were soon joining the fight to destroy the Islamic State.

Within a month of these first airstrikes, ISIS spokesman Abu Mohammed al Adnani was urging Islamic State "soldiers" to conduct lone wolf attacks against the West if they could not join the fight in Syria or Iraq[20]. In October, a self-radicalised US citizen who attacked four policemen with a hatchet in New York claimed to have been inspired by ISIS[21]. In November, Islamic State leader Abu Bakr al Baghdadi called on his supporters to "erupt volcanoes of jihad" across the world[22]. Two more ISIS inspired attacks followed in the US in 2015. The most serious – a gun assault on a Department of Public Health Christmas party in San Bernardino, California in December – killed 14 people and seriously injured 21 others[23]. The husband and wife perpetrators both pledged allegiance to Islamic State on Facebook on the day of the attack[24].

America's desirability as a target for radical jihadis is therefore not in doubt. The external threat from Islamist extremists is real even if Al Qaeda has been seriously weakened and ISIS has lost control of its territory in Iraq and Syria. In their twisted ideologies, both have unremitting designs against the US and its Western allies. ISIS is returning to guerrilla war tactics and continues to direct and inspire its supporters around the world[25]. But even with this enduring risk, Americans have a negligible chance of being killed in an act of terrorism, and even less likelihood of being fatally injured in an attack by foreign-based Islamist extremists inside their country[26]. US geography helps; the American mainland is separated from the likely sources of foreign Islamist terrorists by two oceans. More importantly, the work the US has done to tackle the international terrorist threat since 2001 has paid dividends, including better joined up domestic intelligence activities, much greater cooperation with international allies and a range of programmes to counter violent extremism at home and abroad.

Since 9/11 in 2001, 240 people have been killed in terrorist attacks in the US – 107 by violent Islamists; 112 by far right extremists; and 21 by perpetrators with other ideologies. Except for three years between 2016 and 2019, the numbers killed each year by far right terrorism has been higher than those killed by Islamist extremists[27]. All but one of the jihadi attackers were US citizens or legal residents; the other was a visiting US-Saudi military exchange officer who

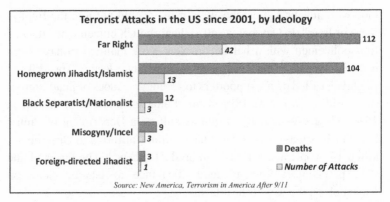

Source: New America, Terrorism in America After 9/11

killed three people at the Naval Air Station in Pensacola in December 2019 and may have been supported by Al Qaeda in the Arabian Peninsula[28]. In other words, Americans are more likely to be caught up in a terrorist attack committed by white supremacists than violent Islamists. And the most likely profile of an extremist Islamist terrorist in the US is a homegrown American or legal resident who has been radicalised through the internet and social media, not a foreign jihadi directly coordinated by Al Qaeda or ISIS. But this is still not how many Americans tend to see the problem.

The enduring impact on the US of the shocking and deadly events of 9/11 should not be underplayed. No country could fail to be changed profoundly by such an act of terrorism. Nor could any government fail to pursue those responsible or to do everything it could to try to reduce the risk of future attacks. But after almost 20 years, the threat picture for America and the West has changed significantly. In 2018, for the first time since 9/11, the Pentagon's National Defence Strategy did not list international terrorism as the US military's primary focus. The Department of Defense committed to continuing its efforts to combat terrorism. But it argued that the re-emergence of strategic competition from "revisionist powers", China and Russia, was now the principal challenge for US national security. It also listed a range of emerging threats to be countered including nuclear proliferation, political subversion and cyber attacks by state and non-state actors – and all in a world where the international order which has underpinned global stability and security since World War

Two was increasingly being challenged[29]. In other words, as far as the Pentagon was concerned, international terrorism was now just one of a much broader range of risks facing the US. Public perceptions, however, are proving harder to change.

Americans are not alone in misjudging the threat from foreign Islamist extremists having suffered from a deadly attack. Terrorism, which is unpredictable and arbitrary, is designed to instil a heightened level of fear. Its guerrilla nature raises anxiety further; it prompts concerns that extremists with the intent to do harm could be living below the radar within the communities they are preparing to attack – an invisible and deadly enemy. So, it is very easy to come to the conclusion that the terrorist threat is greater and more widespread than it actually is. Maintaining perspective is often the first victim of fear.

But the US does have a history of exaggerating external threats to justify certain policies and actions at home and abroad. The relatively new phenomenon of international terrorism is not the first time America has misjudged the perils it actually faces. It was probably reasonable in 1789 for the Second Amendment to the US Constitution to guarantee the right of the American people to keep and bear arms on the grounds that a "well regulated militia" could be necessary for the security of country[30]. After the Revolutionary War, much of the US army had been disbanded. The Founding Fathers feared that a permanent, professional army could be misused against its own citizens if they were unarmed. But as the War of 1812 later proved, the US would still need to defend itself against external threats. So being able to draw on militias of American citizens with their own weapons was an essential part of the defence strategy of the new nation and a means of avoiding potential oppression from within the country[31]. Two hundred and thirty years later, when the US has the largest military in the world and spends more on defence than the next 10 countries combined, the same logic no longer applies[32]. But even so, the right to bear increasingly powerful weapons continues to be vigorously defended on the grounds of individual and national defence.

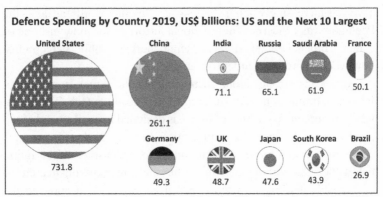

Source: *Stockholm International Peace Research Institute, Military Expenditure Database 2020*

The anti-communist witch hunts in the 1940s and 1950s symbolised by Senator Joseph McCarthy also stemmed from over exaggerated fears of an external enemy which then distorted American policy with grim consequences. McCarthy capitalised on growing alarm about communism in the US after World War Two to bolster his own political career by stirring up hysteria in the guise of American patriotism[33]. In the late 1940s, Moscow had detonated its first atomic bomb and Chairman Mao had proclaimed the People's Republic of China after leading the communists to victory in a three year civil war against the Nationalist Kuomintang. Not long afterwards, Soviet-backed North Korean communist forces invaded the West's ally, South Korea, triggering the Korean War. These communist advances over a matter of months shook America and its allies. Fear of the spread of communism to the US itself reached new heights. The hysteria of the 'Red Scare' was about to reach its peak.

In a speech in 1950, Senator McCarthy waved a piece of paper containing the names of more than 200 US State Department officials who he claimed were members of the Communist Party at the heart of American foreign policy making[34]. What followed were public investigations into many thousands of government employees on the back of scant evidence. McCarthy used his chairmanship of the Senate Permanent Subcommittee on Investigations to try to uncover subversion and espionage. He laced his questioning of suspected

"Reds" with innuendo and false allegations and threatened, intimidated and insulted his witnesses.

McCarthy was not alone, or the first, in his zeal to expose communist infiltration. The House of Representatives had established a Committee on Un-American Activities in 1938 to investigate individuals or groups with links to communism and fascism. It pursued its investigations with added gusto from the late 1940s, including into alleged communist influence in Hollywood[35]. Well known stars like Orson Wells, Arthur Miller and Leonard Bernstein were accused of communist sympathies. Charlie Chaplin was forced into exile following unsubstantiated allegations against him[36].

J Edgar Hoover's FBI opened files on thousands of Americans, putting many under surveillance with little cause[37]. Many were intimidated into resigning their careers, thousands were sacked. Others committed suicide under the pressure of public scrutiny. Even Albert Einstein came under the 'Red Scare' spotlight[38]. In the end, Senator McCarthy was censured by the Senate for his behaviour as concerns grew about a breach of US civil liberties[39]. His political influence quickly waned. But many lives had already been irreparably damaged by the anti-communist crusade stirred by McCarthy and others.

Later in the Cold War, inflated estimates of the Soviet Union's military strength fuelled ever increasing American defence spending. The money funded an arms race which resulted in the US and Soviet Union having the nuclear capability to destroy each other many hundreds of times over[40]. I remember being pretty scared as a teenager in the 1980s by the UK government's advice, Protect and Survive, on how best to prepare for a nuclear attack[41]. The suggestions seemed ludicrous even to a young adult including: unscrew lots of doors off their hinges to create a 'lean-to' shelter in your home; fill the bath and sinks for a supply of drinking water; seal the windows and doors against fallout; and stock up on lots of tinned food to survive for at least two weeks until help might arrive. None of this seemed likely to mitigate against the detonation of a devastating nuclear bomb. At school, we would joke rather macabrely about how we were supposed to make all these preparations within the four minute warning we might get before the impact of incoming Soviet nuclear missiles. We came up with increasingly outlandish ideas for what we might do instead in our last minutes before nuclear evaporation. But it didn't take away the fear. The whole horror of a nuclear war was graphically captured by a BBC drama, Threads, which depicted the consequences of a US/Soviet confrontation on the city of Sheffield[42]. It made alarming

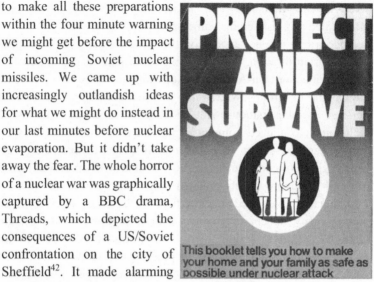

PROTECT AND SURVIVE

This booklet tells you how to make your home and your family as safe as possible under nuclear attack

viewing and gave me nightmares for several days. The risk of a nuclear conflagration seemed terrifyingly real.

A similar ABC TV film – The Day After – told the story of a nuclear strike on Kansas in equally chilling terms[43]. So it isn't really surprisingly that many people on both sides of the Atlantic bought into the idea that the US and NATO should have even greater destructive firepower than the Soviets in the hope of deterring an attack which could only be catastrophic. I certainly did. On my exchange program to California later in the 1980s I was asked by school friends why women protesting at Greenham Common airbase were so against the presence of American cruise missiles in England when they were being deployed for our defence against the Soviets. My reply wasn't very flattering. I was pretty scathing about the 'far left' motivations of the protesters and was more than happy to support the US contributing to Britain and Europe's defence. I had bought the government's narrative on how best to combat the Soviet threat.

The arms race may have contributed to the collapse of the Soviet Union by putting extra strain on its struggling economy. But there has to be a serious question over whether it was really necessary to go to such extremes as Mutually Assured Destruction; of being able to bring human civilisation to an end through a global nuclear holocaust, to win the Cold War. US military spending supported a massive defence industry which enriched American businesses and their executives, supporting thousands of American jobs in the process. But the existence of enormous arsenals of nuclear weapons also increased the risk of a catastrophic accident or miscalculation by both sides which could have imperilled humanity. An exaggerated fear of the Soviet Union's military capability had distorted American, and wider NATO, policy to the edge of absurdity.

Roll forward more than 30 years and exaggerating external threats is still part of US politics. President Trump wilfully inflated the impact of illegal migration over the southern US border to try to win support for the wall he promised to build along the 2000 mile-long frontier with Mexico[44]. In its desperation to deliver a signature campaign pledge, the Trump administration brushed aside the risks of creating a backlash against America's existing immigrant communities and of throwing billions of US dollars away on a policy which was unlikely to solve the genuine immigration issues the US is facing or stop many new migrants. Truth was again thrown into the fire of political opportunism.

In all these cases over US history, the risks to America were real. The Soviets were trying to infiltrate the US and its allies in the fight to emerge victorious from the Cold War. Moscow did have a terrifying arsenal of weapons pointed at America and the West, and still does. America does need serious immigration reform after the issue has languished in Congress' too difficult tray for decades. But misperceptions of the real scale of these external threats – often fuelled by politicians in search of re-election or political advantage – have skewed American actions at home and abroad with unexpected and sometimes undesirable consequences. Some of the policy decisions arguably left the US at even greater risk.

The pressures on political leaders to act can be enormous when national security and public safety are under threat. It is not surprising then that politicians on both sides of the Atlantic can have a tendency to oversimplify complex challenges in the search for solutions that can meet the public's demand for quick and effective action. In the wake of recent terrorist attacks in the UK, some mainstream politicians unhelpfully pointed the finger at British Muslims for 'failing' to self-police their communities. The allegations implied that Islam itself was a cause of the terrorist problem, rather than wider drivers of alienation that can leave people susceptible to extremist propaganda and radicalisation. The approach promised a quick solution that didn't really exist; just getting the Muslim community somehow to identify all those at risk and set them back on track before they could be radicalised. If only it were that simple.

In the US case, the enduring fear of international terrorism has driven support for extreme policies which have risked making the problem worse. The use of "enhanced" interrogation techniques and the continued incarceration of "enemy combatants" in Guantanamo Bay without due process both strained relations with the US' allies and arguably contributed to further radicalisation in Muslim communities around the world incensed by American behaviour. Two long wars in Afghanistan and Iraq which brought death and suffering to large civilian communities are unlikely to have reduced the pool of those open to radicalisation. Greater US surveillance powers enacted immediately after 9/11, although now partially rolled back or put on a stronger legal footing, continue to raise concerns about privacy and civil liberties.

The perception of international terrorism as the greatest threat to the American way of life has also left more serious and pressing issues largely neglected. Americans are far more likely to suffer violence from the prevalence of guns in US culture, far right extremism and the radicalisation of American citizens through a largely unregulated internet and social media. But none of these receive the level of resources devoted to tackling international terrorism, even if the US government is slowly rebalancing its efforts across a range of threats.

Americans should be wary of politicians stoking up fears of external threats and promising simple or quick solutions. History has shown that fear can be an effective tool of political manipulation. In a letter to Thomas Jefferson in 1798, James Madison wrote: "Perhaps it is a universal truth that the loss of liberty at home is to be charged to provisions against danger, real or pretended, from abroad"[45]. As Madison recognised, it is often easier to talk up an external threat – something remote and unknown – and to promise measures to fix it than to address complicated, societal issues at home that would take a concerted effort over years to put right. But most of the serious challenges facing the US and other Western countries have their roots in domestic issues – in enduring poverty, growing inequality and discrimination and the failure of governments to find effective responses to them – not external threats. Policies based on fear are also fraught with risk. In the clamour to respond to an exaggerated threat, they tend to drive excessive and indiscriminate action which can have grave consequences.

In the aftermath of 9/11, the policy choices were not easy as Americans rightly demanded a major response to a deadly assault on US soil by a new type of enemy. Nor should the US government take its eye off the ball now. International terrorism still poses a threat. But Americans would be better served by trying to consider the risk posed by international terrorism in its wider context, alongside other threats which could and do have a greater real impact on US lives, even if they are sometimes less visible or newsworthy than an act of foreign jihadi violence. Only then can Americans hope to see policy responses which begin genuinely to address the homegrown threats that pose the most serious risk to the US way of life.

Part Two

THE RISKS

"If destruction be our lot, we must ourselves be its author and finisher. As a nation of freemen, we must live through all time, or die by suicide". Abraham Lincoln, 1838[1]

Chapter Eleven

The Perils of Myth Blindness

A merica is not alone in having national myths which gloss over imperfections in its society. In essence, that's exactly what national myths do – they paint a simplified picture of what a country believes its defining characteristics to be, or what a nation's leaders wants its citizens to aspire towards. Nor is the US alone in its myths influencing the behaviour of its people with sometimes unpredictable or damaging consequences. The UK's vote in 2016 to leave the EU, which is likely to turn out to be the biggest act of political and economic self-harm in modern British history, was based on a romantic notion of the country's past as a largely ethnically homogeneous, independent nation and global superpower before World War Two.

The possibility of a return to something like that mythical 'golden age' as promised by pro-Brexit campaigners gave many Britons the courage to vote to leave the EU. It didn't seem to matter how unlikely the outcome would be in any fact-based analysis of the possible consequences of Brexit in a very different world to that of the 1940s. Experts' warnings about the dangers of leaving the EU were roundly rejected as politically motivated 'Project Fear'. In essence, Brexiteers won the argument on the back of a vague promise to 'make Britain great again'. Donald Trump's surprise victory in the US presidential election in November 2016 was similarly secured through broad promises to return the country to some mythical former heyday which would deliver greater prosperity for 'real' Americans, despite disturbing undertones for the country's many immigrant communities and unarticulated implications for its approach to the world.

Where the US is unique, however, is in how strongly Americans continue to believe in their national myths despite the growing political, economic and social challenges facing the country on which Donald Trump capitalised to win the 2016 election. Americans seem to buy into their national myths more than people from other Western countries. American exceptionalism is still alive and well. Perceptions have been shaped by decades of political rhetoric exhorting unique strengths which set the country apart from all others. Broader social bravado glorifying America has played its part too. For many, the US is still unquestionably *the* exceptional nation even if the political and economic environment is increasingly difficult. Some Americans of faith even argue that the US has a God-given purpose to lead the world as the exemplary Western society – something that's even more difficult to challenge when it's wrapped up in religious beliefs. The myths are further reinforced by America's continued economic success and military power. Why wouldn't Americans be convinced of their own exceptionalism when the US is still the biggest global economy with wealth that many other countries can only dream of, and while it continues to be the world's military superpower, even if its relative wealth and power are falling and its wealth increasingly inequitably shared?

But a firmly ingrained sense of exceptionalism in US society is not the same as the myths being true or an argument that they should be free from scrutiny and challenge. There is little doubt that many of the America's national myths no longer reflect reality for large numbers of Americans in the early 21st century. The aspirations some of the myths describe are out of reach for all but a small fraction of US society. In other words, an almost blind belief in America's myths is obscuring growing weaknesses in the very fabric of the US system or – at best – significantly underplaying how serious they are. And yet the weaknesses, if not addressed, could have grave consequences for the future.

The first and arguably biggest risk to America's enduring success is the conviction that the US continues to be the standard bearer for Western democracy despite significant flaws in its political system. Excessive amounts of money in politics now buy undue influence for big corporations, wealthy interest groups and religious organisations, leaving most American citizens with little real chance of influencing political decision making. Corrupt practices by the political parties prevent genuine competition in many elections and fuel ever more partisan gridlock. The Electoral College system distorts the votes of the US electorate when they choose their most important political leader – the President of the United States. And the increasing politicisation of judicial appointments skews some of the most important decisions that are taken for the future of US society, including how the Constitution should be interpreted in the modern world. Unless these flaws can be addressed, they risk undermining the framework which holds American society together. No nation can continue to prosper if its political system ceases to enjoy the trust of its people.

The second risk to future US success is the continuing belief that simple hard work, with perhaps just a little bit of luck thrown in, is the ticket to the American Dream despite irrefutable evidence of declining social mobility. This conviction limits public support for government action which could help to ensure that genuine opportunity for all survives for future generations. And it sees politicians that advocate a more interventionist approach to help people move up the socio-economic ladder being defined as 'socialists', on the extreme progressive fringes of US politics. It creates the sense that those Americans who struggle to make it only have themselves to blame; if only they worked harder or took the opportunities that came their way, they would improve their lot. In reality, however, many other factors are now at play in determining who is likely to be successful in modern America. It's not just about toil and pioneering spirit but includes social and ethnic background, access to affordable healthcare and good schooling, and even where in their country Americans are born.

The persistent faith in the superiority of the US economic model and the instinctive aversion to any form of regulation also brings risks for the country's future success. Despite Americans' attachment to laissez-faire economics, it is pretty clear now that the market doesn't always deliver for the American people and with damaging consequences. The approach has allowed powerful companies to build excessive market power and then exploit American consumers, reducing choice, competition and innovation. Sharp practices also go unchecked, with legal action to seek redress out of reach for many given the eye-watering costs and risks involved. At the same time, the super-rich have continued to get ever richer and more powerful at the expense of America's middle and working classes sounding alarm bells for social cohesion and sustainable economic growth. No democratic country can expect to maintain its success if its wealth and the levers of power are controlled by an increasingly small minority of individuals and corporations.

The conviction that the US continues to be a secular state as established by the Founding Fathers sees many Americans underestimating the dangers of the growing attempts by the evangelical right to redefine the US as a Christian nation. Politicians keen to secure the votes of Americans of faith increasingly pander to the evangelical community even though their demands, if followed through, would have negative consequences for tolerance and diversity and would see other American communities increasingly marginalised.

The sense of individualism so ingrained in the US psyche increasingly manifests itself as a knee-jerk and unquestioning antipathy towards government with damaging consequences for American society. It limits investment in federal, state and local authorities even though many critical services could be delivered more effectively, fairly and cheaply by government, rather than by the private sector or civil society. It reduces scrutiny and oversight of government too which slows modernisation and reform. Ultimately, it leads to Americans getting fewer or poorer services for their tax dollars due to underinvestment, inefficiency and poor spending decisions or over reliance on expensive, profit-taking private companies. It also places undue weight on philanthropy to fill gaps in provision for those most in need although this creates significant disparities across the country and leaves many struggling Americans without critical support.

A dogmatic and purist approach to the freedom of speech combined with limited government oversight of the increasingly partisan US media leaves Americans without easy access to balanced, factual information on which to make sensible and rational choices. This has helped to create a febrile environment which is stoking ever-growing division in society and being exploited by America's enemies. At the same time, the growing internet and social media giants, with their activities largely unregulated by federal or state governments, are turbo-charging the dissemination of extreme views, fake news and foreign propaganda which is further widening fissures in American society with disturbing consequences. The compromises so essential to effective government and a functioning society are all the more difficult to make.

The mythological attachment to guns as an intrinsic part of what it means to be American perpetuates excessive gun ownership and a cycle of violence that destroys untold lives each year, undermining the very fabric of society in many cities and rural communities. Despite growing support for change, the powerful gun lobby and US arms industry malevolently play on the American gun myth to resist any reform of US gun laws even though this could see so many lives saved each year and communities no longer living in fear. The actions of the gun lobby and arms industry are all the more indefensible when other countries have successfully reformed their gun laws and seen significant reductions in violence without cutting across the right to bear arms.

The conviction that America's commercial healthcare system provides the best care in the world despite its obvious shortcomings leaves Americans paying more than almost anyone else for their health services, but also getting less in terms of overall health outcomes. The widespread antipathy towards universal healthcare as some form of failed experiment of the communist system leaves millions of Americans without medical coverage and many others underinsured with obvious implications for individual wellbeing and US economic performance. If a nation's people are not healthy, the country as a whole will never be able to achieve its full potential. That just doesn't make sense in the wealthiest country on the planet.

The assumption that America is a vibrant and successful melting pot where immigrants arriving over generations have been well integrated into US society overlooks the continuing discrimination and ingrained segregation faced by many minority communities across the country. Without concerted action to build a more inclusive society, America will face growing inequality and increased poverty with even more of the societal problems they create including higher rates of crime, poorer health and lower educational achievement – none of which are a recipe for continued success in an increasingly competitive world. The US will never reach its peak economically if it fails to capitalise on the talents and energies of all its people.

The continued focus on international terrorism as the greatest threat to American safety and national security drives US authorities to spend more on the problem than the risk warrants as the threat picture changes. It fuels hostility towards immigrant communities, particularly Muslims, with all that means for fracturing American society. And it leaves serious domestic challenges like poverty, discrimination and gun crime given lower priority and fewer resources even though they kill so many more Americans.

If the American people continue to be blinded by their national myths, to swallow the political rhetoric about their country's exceptionalism, they risk failing to grasp the gravity of these growing flaws in the US system before it is too late. And yet the flaws are already having a serious and damaging impact on many American lives as they weaken the very foundations on which the US' economic success and global superpower status were built.

America was able to dominate the globe over the last century because of its greater wealth, its military might and the influence of its soft power. But that global dominance was only possible because of sustained economic success and political stability at home delivered through the promise of an ever improving way of life for the American people. A less prosperous US would not have had the resources to build and then to project its hard power to defend the Western system from outside threats. An America distracted by persistent political challenges at home would not have developed the soft power to influence the world as a beacon of the Western democratic system or had the space to look beyond its borders and make its mark around the world.

If the US cannot continue to deliver progress for all Americans, to sustain the hope of a better life for those less well off, its enduring success and standing in the world will be at risk. Until recently, America's contract with its people saw most working and middle class Americans able to improve their standard of living if they worked hard; children in the US had a good chance of being more prosperous than their parents[1]. The contract also included a political system which allowed Americans to feel they had a genuine say in the future direction of their country through their democratic vote and the ability to influence change if they were unhappy with the results.

But that promise of a better life for all Americans has been under severe strain for years. Since the economic crisis of 2007-8 wages have been stagnating and real growth rates weak and uneven. Social mobility has been declining since the 1940s[2]. At the same time, the political element of the deal – the promise of being able to bring about change by electing new leaders – has been undermined by intensifying political gridlock whoever wins power. Even when America's elected representatives do propose solutions to the challenges facing the country, they are rarely implemented because the compromises necessary to secure agreement on what to do are too difficult to reach in an increasingly confrontational political

American Children Earning more than their Parents, by Year of Birth

Source: *Opportunity Insights, Harvard University*

environment. It's no surprise that increasing numbers of Americans now feel the system is no longer delivering for them[3].

The flaws in the American system being obscured by its national myths are not new; they have developed slowly over decades. Some were arguably not weaknesses when the US was a younger, pioneering country, taming a great continent in a simpler and less competitive global environment. The Declaration of Independence, which laid down the founding principles of the new American nation, drew on the latest Enlightenment thinking in establishing that government derived its power from the consent of the governed and could be altered or abolished by the people, and a new government established, if that consent were betrayed[4]. It set the stage for the creation of a more responsive and adaptable form of government in the US than the distant and autocratic 18th century British monarchy. Along with the US Constitution, it would – for the most part – serve the country well for two centuries.

When America was expanding west across the continent, conquering land and finding abundant natural resources, the American Dream proved real to many. The growing country supported its existing population and waves of immigration, with citizens old and new offered land and opportunity in return for hard work and commitment to the American way of life. Not everyone succeeded and life for many was tough. But the opportunity to build a much better life was real. Millions of people were willing to take the risk of trying to make it in a young, growing country as the rewards could be significant. American wealth grew quickly, surpassing Britain somewhere between 1870 and 1900, further reinforcing the draw of the US way of life[5]. America's superpower status was all but assured.

But after fewer than 100 years as the dominant global power, America has arguably reached an inflection point in its history. Some of the systems which worked for a young, pioneering nation are no longer right for the US in the early 21st century in a more complex, interconnected world. In declaring independence from Great Britain in 1776, the first leaders of the United States established that change was the natural step if a government could no longer secure the unalienable rights of its people – the right to life, liberty and the pursuit of happiness[6]. The US has now reached a level of maturity as a nation where significant change is necessary if it is to continue to prosper and stay at the top of the global tree. With a large and aging population, its territory fixed, natural resources identified, and growing competition from rising powers around the world, America needs to adapt if it is to continue to thrive. And yet change seems persistently beyond reach.

The real life consequences of the flaws in the US political and economic system for many Americans helped to create the environment where Donald Trump could win the presidential election in 2016; where a brash and unvarnished outsider with no political experience could defeat a hugely experienced political insider on the back of 'sound bite' promises playing on Americans' fears for the future. But Trump is not the cause of the problems the US is facing. He is a symptom of the failure to tackle them. Americans were willing to take a punt on a political novice because he promised to shake up the US system that many believed was beginning to fail them.

Donald Trump was elected with a promise to put "America First", an acknowledgement that the US had problems to fix at home if it was to continue to be economically successful and the dominant global power. But rather than pursuing policies that would create new opportunities for all Americans and ultimately strengthen the US system by bringing people together, the Trump administration weaponised the flaws concealed by America's national myths to sow further division, spread anger and distrust between communities and create alternative truths in order to stay in power.

After his election victory, Trump skilfully played the increasingly partisan US media to pitch conservatives and liberals ever more against each other and cleverly used social media to distort facts, divert attention from damaging stories and erode public trust in his opponents, the media and public institutions. Despite the constitutional separation of church and state, he drew religious conservatives ever more into politics by stirring up their fears, however unfounded, that liberals would take away their religious freedom. He amplified the economic challenges facing many Americans, blaming them on immigrant communities and foreign trading powers taking advantage of America. Anyone who dared criticise Trump's approach was immediately branded as part of the establishment – the swamp – that Trump promised to drain, although he did nothing of the sort. On the international stage, Trump weakened alliances like NATO that have kept the West safe since World War Two. He questioned key elements of the rules based international system that have helped to secure wider peace and prosperity. And he let the West's enemies off the hook with worrying consequences. America and the world woke up to a dangerous and uncompromising new American approach.

In the short term, given its existing power and wealth, America may well be able to fare better than others in a Trumpian-style dystopian and isolationist world. But until the fundamental flaws in the US system are addressed, the economy will continue to struggle to provide a decent standard of living for all Americans and maintain sufficient growth rates to deliver greater prosperity for society as a whole. On the global stage, if the world's authoritarian leaders conclude that they can more easily push back against America with few real consequences they will be emboldened. They will expand the boundaries of their illegal actions, whether developing nuclear weapons, threatening or invading neighbouring countries or interfering politically in others. The role the US has played for decades as a brake on bad behaviour around the world where it threatens Western interests would cease to be effective. Oppressive leaders and dictators who chose to advance their positions by the tools of force and manipulation would be less constrained in their actions, bringing instability to greater parts of the world.

A divisive, fear-mongering Trump approach could never be the answer to the challenges the US is facing, nor enhance America's place in the world. It simply compounded the problems at home and encouraged further and more sophisticated external attempts to interfere in Western politics to keep America and its allies on the back foot. We are unlikely ever to know definitively whether Russian interference in the 2016 US presidential election influenced the outcome of the vote in Trump's favour – whether it made the difference between victory and defeat. But Russia will undoubtedly have concluded that its efforts were successful. Divisions in American society were amplified, distrust in official institutions and the media increased and the US machine was destabilised by the Trump victory. America's allies also had to begin asking themselves whether Washington still had their backs. In other words, leaders in Moscow will have been rubbing their hands in glee. It had successfully rocked the Western system by interfering in the 2016 US election and with few significant consequences, bar a limited number of sanctions. Russian, Iranian and North Korean cyber warriors were given a major boost in their efforts to keep the West off balance.

In essence, once in the White House, Trump was soon approaching government like a Wild West gambler played the tables. It was unconventional, high adrenalin and high risk driven by gut instinct. Trump might have believed in a few big lucky wins along the way.

But the approach was ultimately doomed to fail. The gambler never wins in the end.

In the circumstances, the temptation for many Americans to want simply to ride out this period in their history was understandable. America had bounced back from serious challenges before, so why not again? Similarly, it would be easy to blame all America's problems on Donald Trump and to conclude that once he was out of office they would be resolved simply by the election of a new president. But it would be a mistake for Americans to bury their heads in the sand in this way. Donald Trump will always be just a painful novelty act; a destructive sideshow. Whatever the consequences of his administration, Donald Trump is not the cause of the flaws in the American system. He simply exacerbated them with his angry and reckless style of government. His departure from office might reduce the noise and melodrama in American politics. But it is not the solution to America's problems which are more profound.

The most significant threats to America's future come from fundamental weaknesses in the US system that have developed over many years and which are being compounded by growing global competition, politically, militarily and economically. A simple change of government, even from one so unconventional as Trump, will not overcome them. Deep fault lines have emerged in the bedrock of America which cannot be papered over or wished away. If Americans continue to cling blindly to their national myths and these fault lines are not addressed, the consequences will be unpredictable, but undeniably serious, for the US itself and for the wider Western world.

Without change, working Americans are unlikely to swallow indefinitely the ever-growing wealth of a tiny minority of the population while basic jobs no longer pay wages that allow a reasonable standard of living, and while housing, a good education and healthcare are increasingly unaffordable for the majority. Nor are Americans likely to continue to accept a political system that gives them so little voice while allowing the super-rich, large corporations and wealthy interest groups to call the shots. Unless something is done to tackle the fundamental challenges the US is facing, extremists on the fringes of American politics will gain strength as their populist solutions curry greater favour with an increasingly frustrated and angry underclass. Intolerance will rise as Americans look for scapegoats to blame, causing growing tension between different minority communities. Immigrants whose hard work has been central to US success will fight back against the growing hostility and violence towards them, or simply vote with their feet and move to somewhere else where they can thrive. Other minorities who feel excluded by an increasingly religiously conservative America borne out of an unholy alliance between politicians and the evangelical community will resist the growing constraints on their freedoms.

Without change, crime and violence will also rise on the back of growing economic stress, with ugly consequences given the number of high powered weapons in US society. The pace of technological change will add fuel to the fire as further industries close on the back of innovation and automation, leaving more Americans without jobs and hope, and with a limited social safety net to protect them. Just as after the Great Depression, the very fabric of American society will be at risk unless the US takes concerted action to address the flaws at the heart of its system and the growing political, economic and social challenges which flow from them.

If America fails to act, the consequences for the Western world would be profound too. Ever more distracted by its own problems, the US would be less able to push back against those countries seeking to challenge and weaken the West. Americans would increasingly demand that their leaders focus on issues at home, not overseas. Isolationism would gain the upper hand over global engagement. America's allies would then face ever tougher choices about their alliances as rising powers like China look to expand their influence, and powerful dictators seek to deter their neighbours from moving towards the West. Those on the outer edges of the Western world would be particularly exposed. Global security and stability would be at risk.

America might not quickly lose its position as the dominant global military power as it spends so much more on defence than other countries. But with growing issues at home, it would have less political space to deploy its armed forces to solve 'other people's problems'. And ultimately, as its prosperity declined, the US would not be able to maintain its defence spending at world-leading levels, reducing its relative military power as countries like China and Russia increase their own expenditure.

In the Asia-Pacific, a weaker and less present America would see China flexing its muscles even more in the South China Sea. Smaller regional countries, without a bankable insurance policy of US support, would have little option but to fall into line with Chinese aspirations. Western allies like Australia, South Korea and New Zealand would be more isolated and exposed. In the Middle East, age-long rivalries between Iran and the Gulf States which have been tempered by an overwhelming American military presence in the region since World War Two could be reignited with consequences for regional stability and global oil supplies. In Europe, the NATO alliance and its mutual defence guarantee would be weakened leaving many countries with hard choices about where their best interests lie between a resurgent Russia and distracted America.

The global economy would also be hit by falling American demand for goods and services and a weaker dollar as the US economy struggled to maintain growth. Many of America's trading partners would face significant job losses, falling income, lower investment and rising poverty. The US' reputation would be tarnished by the deteriorating political, economic and social situation inside America. Its soft power would no longer be the envy of the world. The draw of the Western model for those countries aspiring towards greater freedom would be diminished. The liberal international order that has helped to expand freedom, security and prosperity around the globe for the last century could itself be under threat.

No one should underestimate the challenges for the West from rising powers like China or hostile regimes intent on undermining the Western world view. But first and foremost, the US must get its own house in order if it is not to precipitate its own decline and the fall of the West as the dominant world system. The effect of a declining and distracted America on its neighbours and closest allies, including the UK, would be particularly profound. But no one in the West can afford the US to fail. Every Western nation would see their values and way of life at risk in a new emerging world order. Most of all, the US itself would find its wealth, global position and associated privileges in rapid decline. With so much to lose, no one, least of all Americans, should want that outcome.

Part Three

THE SOLUTIONS

"If we succeed, it will not be because of what we have, but it will be because of what we are; not because of what we own, but, rather because of what we believe". Lyndon B Johnson, 1965[1]

Chapter Twelve

A Path to American Renewal

M any Americans do see the underlying problems their country is facing. Not all are blinded by the myths of US exceptionalism or hoodwinked by politicians eulogising the nation in a bid somehow to prove their credentials as true American patriots deserving of support at the ballot box. Nor are the solutions to get the US back on track rocket science. Many good ideas are being debated at dinner tables across the country and analysed in parts of the media, albeit usually with a particular, partisan political slant. But with very many Americans still taken in by their national myths and growing political division in the country making the myths all the more appealing as a source of comfort in a rapidly changing world, building a consensus for change will be far from easy.

America needs to look beyond the immediate rough and tumble of party politics, beyond the internecine warfare of President Trump, to the real causes of the challenges the country is facing in a very different world to that of the Founding Fathers. It should take a renewed look at its founding documents to ensure they remain fit for purpose in the 21st century and come up with a new set of policies that begin to tackle the growing social and economic problems many

Americans are facing. The approach needs to bring the American people together rather than fuelling greater division. And it must provide solutions which counter the efforts of extremists and populists aiming to capitalise on the current stresses within American society with the promise of simplistic and sometimes racially driven answers to America's problems.

In essence, three things are needed to chart a genuine path towards American renewal: amendments to the Constitution; a number of important political reforms; and considerable social and economic policy change. Not all of these would be easily achievable even in the most benign of political environments and certainly not quickly. In a particularly toxic period in US history, America's leaders face an arduous task in bringing people together to build support for action. But this should not deter Americans from pressing for change. It is essential if the US is to get back on track, if it is to continue to deliver prosperity to all its people and if it is to safeguard its leading place in the world. There is no time to waste.

The US Constitution remains remarkably relevant despite being amended just 27 times in its 230 year history. Even with so few changes, only around half the 27 were major amendments to reflect significant political and social progress in the country which saw the abolition of slavery, giving non-whites and women the right to vote and introducing the direct election of US senators rather than them being selected by State legislatures. The first 10 amendments were agreed almost immediately after the Constitution was originally signed in the form of the Bill of Rights. In essence, they were part of the original constitutional drafting process. Two more were to introduce and later repeal prohibition[1]. In other words, the Constitution has proved impressively durable even if the country has changed enormously. When the Constitution was agreed in 1787, America was just 13 states covering the eastern coastal strip of what is now the country. Its economy was based on agriculture and its population less than 4 million people of largely British and other northern European stock with 700,000 slaves[2]. Today, the US is a highly industrialised economy of 50 states covering half the North

American continent with a multi-ethnic population of almost 330 million in a highly competitive world[3]. It couldn't be more different from the America of the Founding Fathers.

On the back of such profound change in the US over more than two centuries, a number of articles of the Constitution do now warrant revision to ensure they continue to serve America effectively in very different times. The Electoral College system (Article 2, Section 1) distorts the value of votes in the selection of the most important office in the land – the President of the United States. It should be replaced by a direct election model; one person, one vote should mean one person, one vote. The Constitution should also be amended to establish an independent process for making senior federal judicial appointments. The growing politicisation of these critical roles has to end. The current system (Article 2, Section 2) is simply exacerbating divisions in US society and producing increasingly partisan legal judgements rather than objective decisions in the best interests of America as a whole. The frequency of elections to the House of Representatives (Article 1, Section 2) should also be reduced to help tackle the political fatigue that drives voter apathy and to remove one of the drivers of the ever increasing amounts of money in American politics.

Changing the US Constitution is hard. The Founding Fathers rightly ensured that such a critical political document could not be amended on a whim to avoid building instability into the American system. The most common route to an amendment is agreement by a two thirds majority in both the Senate and the House of Representatives which must then be ratified by three quarters of all states, or 38 out of 50 – an increasingly tall order in the current febrile political environment in the US[4]. It is not hard, therefore, to understand why the Constitution has not been amended since 1992. But however difficult the process, this cannot be an argument against working towards constitutional change when elements of the most important founding document of the United States are no longer fit for purpose. The need for revision is neither a criticism of the original document nor of the Founding Fathers who are held in high esteem.

The Founding Fathers themselves foresaw the Constitution being updated from time to time to keep pace with change when they defined the process for making amendments.

Alongside these essential constitutional amendments, the second priority to get America back on track is serious political reform to reduce significantly the amount of money in US politics – to prevent wealthy individuals, powerful corporations and well-financed interest groups unduly distorting US elections and government decision making. The consequences of the current model are all too clear, with governments from both parties turning a blind eye to pseudo-cartels controlling critical sectors of the American economy and exploiting consumers with high prices and poor service or damaging the environment due to a lack of regulation ensuring protection. The failure to reach agreement on sensible gun control has its roots in interest group and industry money skewing political decisions, despite growing public calls for action. The opioid crisis which is devastating communities across America would not have emerged, or would have been much less serious, if there had been sensible regulation of one of the sectors that spends most on political lobbying, the pharmaceutical industry. In essence, the rules of lobbying and campaign finance including super PACs must be rewritten to ensure all American voices have a chance of being heard in the political debate in the US, not just those backed by the most money. The revolving door between political office and industry should also be better regulated and oversight made more effective to reduce the very real risk of conflict of interest.

Gerrymandering must be quickly stamped out. It is almost incomprehensible that such an overtly corrupt practice still goes on in the US in the 21st century and despite numerous judicial challenges over the years. It undermines America's very credentials as a modern democracy. By reducing political competition, the gerrymandering of districts stifles healthy political debate, fuels the growing partisan divide and makes it even more unlikely that politicians will be able to come together and reach agreement on how to tackle the problems the US is facing. An independent district boundary commission should be established to stop future gerrymandering by both political parties in their desperate efforts to weaken their opponents and stay in power. All existing districts where gerrymandering is suspected should be reviewed and boundaries redrawn when evidence of political manipulation is found.

Voter suppression must be stamped out too. It is yet another way that US election outcomes are distorted to suppress the will of the people. It is very often racially, as well as politically, motivated and means that millions of Americans, particularly those from black and other minority communities do not have a voice in their own country. Voter suppression further ekes away at America's democratic legitimacy and its claims of being a leading Western democracy. Key provisions of the Voting Rights Act of 1965 must be restored. They were one the major achievements of the US civil rights movement and yet were overturned by the Supreme Court in 2013 on spurious grounds that the US no longer needed federal intervention to prevent discrimination[5]. Regular nationwide campaigns to encourage voter participation should also become mandatory.

The oversight of all elections in the US should similarly be taken out of the hands of political parties and given to independent or bipartisan bodies. In most US states, senior elected officials have responsibility for overseeing elections[6]. The risk of a serious conflict of interest is obvious. It's the political equivalent of players from one football team providing the referee in a critical championship match. No one would tolerate this in sport and so it makes no sense that it is the model applied to American elections. The potential conflict of interest becomes even more acute when the elected official presiding over elections in a state is also a candidate for office. In the 2018 midterm elections, this happened at least three times – in Florida, Georgia and Kansas – leading to calls for the officials to step back from their election responsibilities while standing for office[7]. Most did not. States should therefore pass legislation to ensure politicians on the ballot cannot skew the mechanics of elections to their own advantage. If states will not, the federal government should step in to impose change.

Amending the Constitution and achieving these wider political reforms could take many years. Neither may be achievable in the near term given growing ideological differences across the political divide. It might just be too hard to find the compromises necessary to reach the demanding threshold required for constitutional change or to build a consensus around reform of the political system. And yet, however challenging, both are critical to getting the US back on track. They would address the root causes of much of the growing dysfunction and divisions in the American system: the excessive influence of money in politics; the corrosive impact of political corruption; and the injustice of voter discrimination. The reforms cannot be placed in the 'too difficult' tray and left to fester without serious consequences for America's future.

At the same time, while these reforms are being pursued, a great deal could be done more quickly through policy change to begin addressing the growing social and economic challenges confronting the US. Agreement won't be easy here either in the current political climate. Successive recent Presidents have seen their agendas frustrated by a Congress partly or wholly controlled by the other party and a 'resist at whatever cost' mentality. When a single party holds the White House and controls Congress, more can be achieved. But these moments are usually fleeting; the President's party has controlled both the Senate and the House of Representatives in only 14 of the last 50 years[8]. The US political system was purposefully constructed around checks and balances to prevent a president wielding too much power. So if US administrations are to implement meaningful policy change, they must be willing to work across the political aisle and seek compromise. Change in the US can therefore be frustratingly slow. It is more often achieved through persistence and grind than the speedy passage of bills that garner widespread support. The results are often imperfect and incremental too. But it is still change, and can make a huge difference to American lives.

The policy reforms needed to get the US back on track are significant. They would mean Americans accepting a bit less individualism, more investment in government and community, and

US Presidents and Control of Congress

Year	President	Senate	House	Years
1977-81	*Jimmy Carter (D)*	*Democrats*	*Democrats*	*4*
1981-87	Ronald Reagan (R)	Republicans	Democrats	
1987-89	Ronald Reagan (R)	Democrats	Democrats	
1989-93	George H W Bush (R)	Democrats	Democrats	
1993-5	*Bill Clinton (D)*	*Democrats*	*Democrats*	*2*
1995-2001	Bill Clinton (D)	Republicans	Republicans	
2001-03	George W Bush (R)	Democrats	Republicans	
2003-7	*George W Bush (R)*	*Republicans*	*Republicans*	*4*
2007-09	George W Bush (R)	Democrats	Democrats	
2009-11	*Barack Obama (D)*	*Democrats*	*Democrats*	*2*
2011-15	Barack Obama (D)	Democrats	Republicans	
2015-17	Barack Obama (D)	Republicans	Republicans	
2017-19	*Donald Trump (R)*	*Republicans*	*Republicans*	*2*
2019-21	Donald Trump (R)	Republicans	Democrats	

Source: US Senate, US House of Representatives

an expanded social safety net for those who inevitably get left behind in a capitalist economic system. In other words, America needs to adjust the balance between personal freedoms and social responsibility and agree on a fairer distribution of wealth so all Americans have the opportunity to benefit from its economic success. It's about levelling the playing field to give every American a reasonable start in life – pushing back against the reality that future success in the US is now increasingly linked to zip code, class or ethnicity. There is much the US could do.

To kick start the stalling American Dream, there should be greater investment in struggling communities across the US to tackle inequality, unemployment, poverty and crime, including offering more social support and retraining when industries close. The enduring racial divide must be tackled head on, with more programmes to help minorities move up the socio-economic ladder and greater effort to integrate every part of America's diverse society. A concerted effort must be made to tackle institutionalised racism – in business, in law enforcement and in the wider public sector. The tide of increasing segregation in some parts of the country must be turned and instead a new wave formed to drive greater integration across all parts of US society.

Businesses and industries should be encouraged through better government incentives to invest across the whole country rather than concentrating their activities in a small number of more affluent states. Many rural areas of the US are largely reliant on a single industry or the government for jobs which suppresses wages, reduces opportunity and increases the risk of being left without work should the industry close[9]. Ultimately, a mature and established nation cannot leave its people to fend for themselves when left behind, and watch the rich become richer and the poor become poorer on the back of unbridled capitalism and the unchecked power of money. That is a recipe for societal breakdown, not continued prosperity.

In the 1960s, Lyndon Baines Johnson launched the Great Society, a far-reaching set of programmes to try to improve Americans' lives[10]. It included the first major federal investment in elementary and high school education with programmes specifically targeted to help underprivileged children. Sixty years later, the US needs a similar programme backed by substantial government investment to ensure all American children have access to a good school wherever they live. Providing a quality education to every child would help to unleash the potential of all Americans not just those from more privileged backgrounds whose parents can afford to pay for a private school or those who just happened to be fortunate enough to grow up in an area with a good public school. Put simply, failing to invest sufficiently and equitably in schools is an act of grievous self harm. Access to higher education needs to be improved for all Americans too. With tuition costs significantly higher than almost every other country, going to college or university in the US is often a direct route to considerable debt for those without wealthy parents or a generous scholarship. The system undoubtedly deters those from lower income families from going into higher education and improving their economic prospects.

A root and branch review of government services at federal, state and local level is needed to drive modernisation and improve efficiency and service delivery. The 9/11 Commission, the inquiry into the 2001 terrorist attacks on the US, found that the multiple law enforcement and intelligence agencies in the US system had failed to work collaboratively and share information with grave consequences for US national security. It also found a duplication of effort which America could ill afford[11]. Other parts of the US government still suffer from a similar lack of cooperation, duplication and waste. The government should be overhauled to provide better, more consistent services to the American public at reasonable cost. The extensive use of private contractors by government agencies to deliver services should also be investigated to ensure US taxpayers are getting value for money and not simply contributing to significant corporate profit at the expense of the range of services governments can afford to provide.

A New Deal-like programme of major investment in US infrastructure should be launched to modernise America's creaking road and rail networks, its failing airports and its aging water and energy systems. At the same time, much greater investment is needed in the critical new infrastructure for the digital age to ensure all Americans have access to high speed broadband and nationwide mobile communications at reasonable cost, ensuring the country continues to have the edge over its rivals. The US has been slipping down the global infrastructure rankings for a number of years as its investment levels have fallen significantly behind other advanced economies and as developing countries invest heavily in catching up. Much of American infrastructure has been little more than patched up since it was built in the 1950s and 60s[12]. The US needs urgently to retake the infrastructure top spot if it is to protect its position as the most successful global economy in an increasingly competitive world.

Major US tax reform should be a priority to simplify a mind-blowingly complex system which adds considerable cost to individuals and businesses and creates untold bureaucracy and opportunities for tax avoidance. Any tax reform should ensure corporations and wealthy individuals pay a fair share of the tax burden, not proportionately less than average Americans. It should work to control US debt, not increase it. Donald Trump's reforms of late 2017, while being the biggest overhaul of the US tax system for more than 30 years, only scratched the surface. They did little to simplify the US tax code which still amounts to several thousand pages. The new bill gave a temporary tax cut to most Americans, but disproportionately benefited higher earners. US corporations made the biggest gains with substantial and permanent rate cuts. At the same time, the reforms looked set to increase the federal budget deficit by $1 trillion over 10 years[13]. Congress' passing of the bill was more to do with Republican fears of being punished in the 2018 midterms for failing to pass any significant legislation in Trump's first year in office than the tax reforms themselves. Many Republicans had to swallow hard on their life-long belief in fiscal conservatism and balancing the federal budget to have something to give to the American electorate. Trump's new bill was a missed opportunity that leaves the way open for more substantial and equitable tax reforms that could put the US economy back on a more sustainable footing.

Reform of the American social security system is also long overdue but essential to ensure future benefit recipients have a liveable income at an affordable cost to the American taxpayer. US Social Security provides retirement pensions for the majority of Americans and income for those with disabilities. It is the main source of funds for many – so it's an important part of the US safety net. The last changes to Social Security were made in 1983. But since 2010, with people living longer and lower birth rates, more money has been paid out of the Social Security Trust Fund in terms of benefits than was paid in from taxes. Without reform, the Trust Fund will be exhausted by the early 2030s[14]. Some argue that economic growth will solve the problem. But that seems unlikely given sluggish average growth rates over the last few years and the fact that payroll contributions to social security are capped. Higher earners only pay social security contributions on salaries up to $132,900 (2019)[15]. In other words social security taxation is regressive, not progressive. Unless the system can be reformed quickly, Americans will face significant benefit cuts or large tax rises to fill the hole in the budget within 10-15 years. Both would be a significant negative shock to the US economy.

The policy reforms needed to get the US back on track should also include the provision of affordable healthcare to all Americans through a national US health service or a universal insurance programme. Access to health services should not be a privilege for the wealthy in a modern, advanced democratic economy. Failing to provide healthcare to all Americans is tantamount to the country shooting itself in the foot repeatedly, and implies a callousness in US culture that most Americans would hotly dispute. It doesn't just go against a fundamental human right – the right to life – but also stops many Americans from being as economically active as they could be if they were able to afford the treatment and drugs needed for their medical conditions. The impact on US prosperity is obvious.

Existing Medicare coverage for retirees should be expanded to all until a genuine universal healthcare system could be established. The current Medicare programme should also be revised for retirees. It excludes essential services like dental, vision and hearing care. An American pensioner needing a simple hearing aid is faced with a bill of thousands of dollars which many cannot afford. And yet not treating hearing loss or correcting sight problems adds to the social exclusion and loneliness already experienced by many old people by making it harder for them to function in society. The American healthcare system is well and truly broken and needs to be fixed.

More effective regulation of the media and greater oversight of the large internet companies are essential to protect American democracy. A 21st century Fairness Doctrine applied to all national broadcast media would ensure that all Americans have easy access to genuinely factual and balanced news reporting, not increasingly partisan opinion that distorts American thinking and fuels ever greater rifts in society. The new Fairness Doctrine would not need to cover all broadcast media, but only those companies that had a certain, defined national reach and therefore considerable power to influence the perspectives of millions of Americans.

The US Public Broadcasting Service and National Public Radio should be built into a more sustainably funded, single media organisation that reaches all the US and can compete with the commercial giants across TV, radio and digital media. Such a transformed national public broadcaster could provide a critical service to the American people in a world of increasing fake news and media manipulation. Many democratic countries have good examples of national public broadcasters which are editorially independent of government and required by their charter to provide unbiased news and information to the public and balanced wider programming for the greater good. The US could draw on these examples as a way of underpinning American freedoms, society and culture which are increasingly under threat.

The big technology companies like Facebook and Google should be required by law to take responsibility for the content on their platforms. They must work to prevent users, including malign foreign powers, from sowing hatred, amplifying divisions and distorting the truth on a mass scale which risks undermining the very fabric of American democracy and society. Further regulation should also be considered if the technology companies don't begin to take a more reasonable approach to national security issues. Claims that the personal data of their customers is sacrosanct when government authorities have a legitimate requirement, confirmed by a legal warrant, to access data to prevent or investigate serious crime is indefensible and a misuse of corporate power. Many of the companies have built their success on the collection and manipulation of personal data, sometimes in an opaque and sinister manner. It cannot be right for those same companies to be the arbiters of whether governments agencies can have access to data for law enforcement and national security reasons while they freely mine personal data for commercial gain.

The US should press ahead with substantial gun control to take large numbers of firearms out of American society while permitting limited, registered gun ownership of specialised weapons for hunting and sporting purposes. This would not cut across any sensible interpretation of the constitutional right to bear arms. But, in an ideal world, the Second Amendment would be rewritten too to clarify exactly what "the right of the people to keep and bear arms" means in a 21st century context. Only by substantially reducing the number and power of weapons in personal ownership can America hope to cut its shocking levels of gun violence and bring safety and security back to many depressed communities across the country.

With many fewer weapons in circulation, policing in America would also become less dangerous. Over time, US law enforcement officers would not need to be so heavily armed or to use their weapons so frequently. That in turn could help to rebuild confidence in the US police, confidence that has been falling among minority communities on the back of alarmingly frequent killings of unarmed black and Hispanic men by armed law enforcement officers in disputed circumstances[16]. It is hard to see what America would genuinely lose from greater gun control other than some twisted interpretation of personal freedom that perversely romanticises the ownership of weapons of mass killing. Americans having nothing to be proud of in their attachment to personal gun ownership.

Finally, Americans should work hard to ensure the continuing separation of church and state as envisioned by the Founding Fathers when they crafted the Constitution. Campaigns by evangelical organisations to loosen the restrictions on religious groups being active politically should be rebuffed. Efforts to replace the Johnson Amendment, which prevents non-profit organisations including churches from supporting political candidates, should be blocked[17]. Claims by evangelicals that the current restrictions amount to censorship or the targeting of pastors are bogus. A church steering its followers to support a particular political candidate should be no more acceptable than corporations telling their employees how to vote or anyone else unduly influencing the free choice of the American people. It would amount to a misuse of power and a manipulation of US democracy. American politicians should focus on ensuring the continued tolerance of all religions, rather than aiding and abetting one influential religious group to impose its beliefs on the American people.

Some Americans will shriek in opposition to these proposals for a path to American renewal. Many on the right are likely to claim it is a dog whistle call to some dangerous European form of socialism that would undermine the very fabric of American society. But that would just confirm how the polarisation of US politics and society has created an environment where it is increasingly difficult to have genuine debate and where reasonable compromise is almost impossible to achieve. Americans need to break out of this destructive cycle and work to coalesce around pragmatic solutions to the challenges the country is facing; solutions which won't necessarily fit within the traditional confines of right and left or alongside mythical ideals about what America is or should be. Only then will America have a chance of getting back on track.

The reforms the US needs to make are not about changing the fundamental essence of America or imposing some ill-fitting foreign model on the country. The many essential American traits which helped to propel the country to superpower status over the last century will be just as important to America's future success. Change will not weaken the strong US work ethic driven by a clear link between individual effort and personal reward. It will not undermine the powerful sense of drive and the belief that anything is possible. Nor should it affect the confidence to take risks and to tolerate failure which have been critical to America's world-leading innovation.

But substantial reforms are now essential if America is to get back on track and continue to thrive. The US is no longer the new kid on the block; that young, pioneering nation making its mark on the world. It is a mature and established country in an increasingly dangerous and competitive global environment, where the challenges it faces are very different to those which confronted the Founding Fathers. America must adapt to survive. It can change without cutting across the essence of what it means to be American. The much greater risk would come from a failure to act.

Epilogue

Can America Save itself and the West?

During World War Two, President Roosevelt and Winston Churchill forged a bond that helped overcome what appeared to be an insurmountable enemy in Nazi Germany and the Axis powers. Working together and with other allies they helped to free the world from violent fascism which risked consuming much of the globe and smothering out Western democracy. In his eulogy in the House of Commons to the President after his death in April 1945, Churchill said, "in FDR there died the greatest American friend we have ever known and the greatest champion of freedom who has ever brought help and comfort from the new world to the old"[1].

Will a Western leader be able to say this again about a future US president? Can the US mobilise once more as it did on an enormous scale in the 1940s, but this time to *fix itself* so it can continue to thrive politically, economically and socially; so it can reinforce its position as the world's leading superpower; and so it can continue to be a beacon of the Western system through the power of its example, backed by its economic strength, its soft power and military might?

The current political climate in the US does not give immediate cause for optimism. Fractures in American society are growing, not healing. The Trump administration, while not the cause of America's problems, amplified divisions by pitching communities against each other rather than working to bring Americans together. It demonised its opponents rather than reaching out to seek common ground on which to build solutions to the challenges facing the country and which could benefit all Americans. The Trump administration's woeful response to the coronavirus pandemic made matters worse, not better.

Even before Trump, the gap between mainstream Republicans and Democrats had been widening for more than 20 years[2], making compromise ever more difficult. Republicans and Democrats no longer just disagree on policy solutions, but basic facts too[3]. To make matters worse, these facts are then twisted and distorted by politicians themselves and amplified by an aggressively partisan media which makes reaching agreement even harder. In America's hyper-polarised environment, fewer politicians are willing to reach across the aisle, fearing career suicide from trying to find common cause with their opponents. But seeking agreement across the political divide is essential if the US is to address the growing political, social and economic challenges it now faces.

Within the Republican and Democratic Parties themselves, differences between right wing and moderate conservatives and centrists and progressives are more entrenched than ever. And in the absence of unambiguous party agreement on the direction of policy, the American public are left without a clear agenda around which to rally or genuine leaders to inspire action, reinforcing the tendency for elections to become little more than personality contests. Instead, US politics has descended into a dark and wretched place ruled by a political version of Newton's Third Law where every action by one party automatically triggers an equal and opposite reaction from the other even if it is not reasonable or sensible. Whatever Democrats propose has immediately to be condemned by Republicans as 'dangerous progressivism' or even worse, 'socialism' that could threaten the very essence of what it means to be American, at least to them. The opposite proposition has then to be put forward as the only viable solution to whatever problem is being considered. Whatever the Republicans suggest has to be slammed by Democrats as 'discriminatory, unreconstructed or uninformed' and the reverse suggested as the solution America really needs. Sensible debate is ever more rare; the chances of American political forces working together minimal. US politicians, and politically active Americans more generally, increasingly see their political adversaries as sworn enemies rather than just someone with a different perspective with whom they should work in the best interests of their country[4]. Not surprisingly, little gets done.

Even if some US politicians can find a way to come together, the scale of the reforms required to get America back on track could appear daunting. The changes needed would be controversial even in a more benign political environment, let alone one that is increasingly hostile to opposing views and becoming more dysfunctional by the day. Any significant reforms are likely to be appealed all the way to the Supreme Court by opposing political forces or wealthy interest groups. New federal laws that might try to limit the amount of money in politics, to regulate the media more effectively or to implement more sensible gun control would undoubtedly be challenged. Endless legal wrangling and delay could be inevitable. The growing politicisation of Supreme Court appointments could also make change even harder to achieve. Unless the Supreme Court Justices can find the courage once again to stand above the political beliefs that secured their appointments, any court rulings on new legislation or revised interpretations of the Constitution would likely be made on partisan lines and simply reinforce the divisions in US society rather than confirm the reforms necessary to secure the future of the country.

In many ways, it would be disturbingly easy for America to continue along the path of even greater polarisation. Growing political tribalism provides a clear enemy – the 'socialist' left or 'extremist' right – for Americans feeling left behind economically or culturally by rapid global change. It offers the comfort of someone else to blame, however misplaced. By continuing on this path, the right and left would exist ever more within their own comfortable echo chambers of endorsement and reinforcement, with progressively more extreme views rarely questioned. Neither side would take responsibility for the problems confronting their country or for addressing them. Instead, they would launch increasingly vitriolic political attacks on their opponents, aided and abetted by the partisan US media, forcing ever more Americans to pick sides to avoid being ostracised or attacked themselves. Even less would get done and America's fault lines would grow deeper.

The US would not be the first country to play out this scenario. We've seen it before in other parts of the world, where traditional systems break down, where opponents are demonised and dehumanised, and where seemingly stable and prosperous countries descend into serious political crises and worse. The US may be some way from this sort of breakdown. But moving further down the path of polarisation would not be in the interests of the US itself or the wider Western world which would quickly feel the cold wind of a distracted and declining America.

Americans would not be alone amongst people in developed countries if they somehow reached the conclusion that the freedoms, prosperity and peace we enjoy in the West are the natural state of human affairs in our advanced societies. The passing of time dims the lessons of history. Ever increasing automation, which makes tasks that were once onerous or even impossible now invisible or easy, also tends to reinforce a sense that the levels of development we have reached in Western democracies are locked in. Complexity is concealed by slick software applications that make almost anything possible at the click of a button or touch of a finger. Modern life in the West seems so far removed from the societies that prevented women from voting, that legally endorsed racial segregation, and that were embroiled in brutal conflicts with their neighbours or themselves.

But Americans would be foolish to conclude that the privileged position they have reached as a stable, prosperous and democratic society is irreversible. That would belie the lessons of history where advanced societies have risen and fallen over millennia and where seemingly civilised countries have oppressed and violated their own people. Of all the myths by which America could be blinded, this would be the most dangerous. Apathy would win the day as inaction would appear to hold little risk to the American way of life. But apathy and inaction would simply leave the US on a path to even greater fracture and decline.

Could the Coronavirus pandemic serve as a timely wake-up call for America? Sooner or later, the US was going to face a grave test if it failed to challenge its own myths and to begin addressing the systemic weaknesses afflicting the country. America is not alone in being hit hard by the Coronavirus pandemic. Many other countries, including the UK, have been badly affected too. But Covid-19 has laid bare the growing flaws in the American system. It has shown, in vivid technicolor, how parts of the system are no longer fit for purpose and must be reformed if America is to continue to prosper. The US might not yet be at breaking point. But the virus is putting the growing fault lines in the bedrock of America under increasing strain. And unless the pressure is released, they will break.

The pandemic is arguably one of the biggest challenges the US has faced in decades. It has tested almost every government around the world. But America has fared worse than most despite being the wealthiest and most technically advanced nation on earth. Donald Trump's early downplaying of the virus and his chaotic leadership thereafter is a part of the explanation. But even with a different president in the White House, America would have struggled to respond as well as others. A comparatively bad pandemic was almost inevitable.

A healthcare system which leaves so many millions of Americans without medical cover and others desperately underinsured was always going to struggle to respond to a novel virus and keep the death rate down when faced with a widespread health emergency. A highly polarised and fragmented political system so tainted by money and corruption was inevitably going to make a coordinated, national response difficult to achieve when faced with a virus that disregards state and county lines and political persuasion. A media environment where many powerful players place political partisanship above fact would, unsurprisingly, undermine efforts to control a disease which needed clear, science-based public messaging to reach all Americans quickly and without spin. A highly flexible 'gig' economy that relies more than others on low paid, zero hours contracts with few employment benefits was always going to see more jobs lost than other Western economies where workers have greater rights. The lack of a robust social safety net could only make matters worse by driving more Americans quickly into poverty when losing their jobs. The enduring impact of racism and inequality would inevitably be amplified by a disease that wreaks most harm on those with the very underlying health conditions so often made worse by poverty and exclusion. And the evangelical Christian right, followed by millions of believers and with increasing political clout, could only compound the problem with its trust in faith over science and its leaders' taste for power and money over godliness.

The strength and resilience of the American people so central to the country's myths has also been clear during the Coronavirus pandemic. Many communities have come together in the face of adversity, offering support to neighbours at most risk, expanding the reach of food banks to those newly in need and coming up with innovative ways to support local businesses throughout the crisis. But Americans' over-developed sense of individualism, which manifests itself in a bloody-minded resistance to government in any form, has been on display too even when it meant ignoring science-based health advice. This has undoubtedly contributed to the high level of deaths in the US and the struggle to bring the virus under control. For some, freedom in America appears to mean the freedom to infect others, or to die unnecessarily, too.

So what does America need to do? The priority has to be for politicians and the public to acknowledge that their country is not always what its national myths suggest. It should be to challenge those myths rigorously, to see that while the US has very many strengths, there are growing, underlying problems which need to be addressed given America is now a mature, established nation facing markedly different challenges from when it was a young pioneering country more than two centuries ago. In essence, the US needs to question what it previously believed to be truths about being American, to redefine Americanism for the 21st century, to find again what de Tocqueville called the "greatness of America" – "her ability to repair her faults"[5].

In many ways the US continues to operate like a start-up company which has grown rapidly on the back of its original idea, systems and culture. It has delivered untold success and wealth for its founders and investors, the American people. But just as a start-up must transform the way it operates if it is to develop into a bigger and more successful global business, the US now needs to adapt if it is to continue to prosper and even survive in a changed domestic environment and with growing international competition. Political and civic leaders need somehow to find the courage to rise above political partisanship and build coalitions for change across party lines, and despite the risks of political suicide if their attempts initially fail in a particularly unforgiving environment. They need to sideline the extremists by coming together in the middle ground. America once again needs leaders who put country before self and party, who focus on factors that unite Americans not divide them, and who will work to build alliances for the greater good, not simply for the vested interests that might have financed their election campaigns. In other words, the US needs to apply its world renowned drive and innovation to itself to build a consensus for change.

Despite the many obstacles to reform, there are a number of reasons to be optimistic that Americans will ultimately come together and address the problems the country is facing. The US was built on doing the impossible and never shying away from challenge whether that was taming the west, mobilising a sceptical country to help win World War Two or putting men on the moon in a race against the Soviet Union. America has survived grave threats in its past from the Civil War to the Great Depression, so it has a track record of overcoming upheaval and re-emerging stronger. The US tradition of political protest seen in the civil rights movement and anti-Vietnam demonstrations in the second half of the 20th century is also alive and well. Large numbers of Americans still regularly take to the streets to demand everything from greater human rights, increased gun control or to resist new oil and gas pipelines which risk polluting the environment. And while it seems that little changes after these protests, particularly as social media amplifies the noise around demonstrations raising unrealistic expectations of immediate impact, those taking action are persisting in their efforts to bring about genuine changes to US society.

An increasing number of grass roots movements are also emerging across the country which are working to find common ground across the political divide, to collaborate on finding solutions to local problems and to improve government. Americans on the left and right are beginning to see the perils the US is facing and want to bring about change. The Bridge Alliance links more than 100 civic action organisations working individually and together across the ideological spectrum to reinvigorate US democracy[6]; Unite America invests in non-partisan election reforms and supports the election of unity candidates from both parties who are "pragmatic, pro-reform, and put people over party"[7]; Braver Angels[8] and Living Room Conversations[9] aim to bring together people from different backgrounds and with profoundly opposing political views in conversations across the country to increase understanding, build trust and respect and find areas of agreement which can then be applied to shared problems.

These grassroots movements and many others across the country are pushing at an open door. While more than half of all Americans believe democracy is working at least somewhat well in the US, more than 60 percent think significant changes are needed in the design and structure of government to make it work for America in the 21st century[10]. Frustration is growing that America's political dysfunction is leaving serious problems unresolved. More Americans are concluding that they must take action personally if there is to be change. Those on the extreme fringes of American politics, right or left, may currently feel emboldened, but they could easily find themselves on the wrong side of history. The tide will turn again towards political, economic and social progress if moderates on both sides of the political spectrum can mobilise in sufficient numbers to reinforce the middle ground and re-establish ways of working together to address the challenges now confronting the US.

America can regroup and re-emerge stronger from this fraught period in its history. But it should not delay; time is short. Extreme voices will continue to find greater resonance in communities across the country until the weaknesses in the political system and the growing social and economic problems are addressed. And the further Americans move to the extremes, the harder it will be to bring people back together. Other nations which do not share Western beliefs and values are also rising rapidly and flexing their muscles. They will not miss an opportunity to gain advantage from a distracted and weakened America, or to help keep the country off balance. If the US cannot come together quickly and repair its faults, it could miss the opportunity to adapt and reform before destructive political currents take greater hold at home or emerging nations like China are in a stronger position to challenge its place in the world.

America is resilient, with significant wealth and intellectual resources to draw on and a drive that many other nations can only hope to emulate. Over its history, it has shown an impressive ability to innovate and reinvent itself, and almost unbending self-belief. So if the American people put their minds to it, they can bring about significant change to address their problems at home and to reinforce America's place as the global superpower.

All empires have risen and fallen throughout human history. But a new American approach would mean the US could look forward to many more years of growing prosperity, political stability and global influence. America's national myths would be reinforced and again provide inspiration to the American people and others around the world seeking a better life. Successful change would also help to ensure that when the tide of history did eventually deliver a new global power, the US would have retained sufficient strength and wealth to continue to be a significant global player and with that an enduring beacon of the Western democratic system. In other words, effective change in the US is critical for America itself and for the future of the Western world. The Great American Delusion must end, before it's too late.

Acknowledgements

This book – my first – would not have been written without the support and generosity of many family, friends and colleagues. I remain grateful to the whole team at Saddle Mountain Ranch in Carmel, California where I started my writing journey and who showed great flexibility when I almost certainly overstayed my welcome. I am indebted too to friends from Stevenson School in Pebble Beach, particularly the Petersons and Elmores, who treated me like family in those first weeks when I jumped into the unknown. A number of people gave me a roof over my head while writing – Chloë Somers, the Bates family, the Hunts and the ever-patient Richard Jones – who were all valuable sounding boards for my ideas too. I am grateful for their generous support. To my family, who never questioned quite a significant change in career direction, thank you.

I am particularly indebted to Kathryn and Douglas Lindsay for their unfailing encouragement and sage advice over the last two years including about the world of book publishing. To my old university friends – Mandy and Roy, Liz and Neil and Sarah and Rich – I have appreciated your patient advice and encouragement more than you know. Elliot Canning was also generous with his professional advice when I was grappling with the cover design. To others who read early versions of the book, gave me feedback and acted as a focus group on choosing the title – thank you. I know many of you thought the project would never end. You weren't alone.

Writing has been a jump into the unknown for me. I will always be grateful to those who came on the journey.

About the Author

Patrick Davies is an author, consultant and company adviser. He was a British diplomat for 25 years, wrapping up his career in Washington DC as the UK's Deputy Ambassador to the United States from 2013-18 where he worked alongside the Obama and Trump White Houses for 5 years. Earlier in his career, he served in the British embassies in Morocco, Poland and Iran. During periods at the Foreign and Commonwealth Office in London he was Private Secretary to two consecutive Foreign Secretaries, Robin Cook and Jack Straw (2000-3) and, later, led the UK's response to the Arab Spring (2010-12).

Patrick's first experience of the US was on an English Speaking Union student exchange programme to California in 1987 when he spent a semester at a high school in Pebble Beach. America has been an important part of both his professional and personal life since then. He has more than 30 years' experience of the country, its people and politics and has travelled to more than 40 US states.

End Notes

Introduction

[1] Richard Gott, 'Let's end the myths of Britain's imperial past', *The Guardian,* 19 October 2011, https://www.theguardian.com/books/2011/oct/19/end-myths-britains-imperial-past

[2] John Elledge, 'Britain has built a national myth on winning the Second World War, but it's distorting our politics', *The New Statesman*, 18 August 2017, https://www.newstatesman.com/politics/brexit/2017/08/britain-has-built-national-myth-winning-second-world-war-it-s-distorting-our

[3] Max Hastings, 'Privately Churchill called them 'bloody Yankees' - but with a lover's ardour he fawned, flattered and flirted to woo the U.S', *The Daily Mail,* 20 August 2009, https://www.dailymail.co.uk/debate/article-1207763/Privately-Churchill-called-bloody-Yankees--lovers-ardour-fawned-flattered-flirted-woo-U-S.html

[4] US Library of Congress exhibition, 'Churchill and the Great Republic: The Finest Hour', 2004, https://www.loc.gov/exhibits/churchill/wc-hour.html

[5] Pew Research Center report, 'Public Trust in Government: 1958-2019', 11 April 2019, https://www.people-press.org/2019/04/11/public-trust-in-government-1958-2019/

[6] Alexis de Tocqueville, 'Democracy in America: And two essays on America', *Penguin Classics,* October 2003

[7] UK Prime Minister Theresa May and US President Donald Trump, Press Conference during President Trump's State Visit to the UK, recording on *PBS News Hour,* 4 June 2019, https://www.youtube.com/watch?v=0HDbH8hLx2k&feature=youtu.be&t=585

[8] Daniel S Hamilton and Joseph P Quinlan, Report for the US Chamber of Commerce, 'The Transatlantic Economy 2019: Annual Survey of Jobs, Trade and Investment between

the United States and Europe', page 150, 20 March 2019, https://www.uschamber.com /report/the-transatlantic-economy-2019

[9] Report by UK Research and Innovation, The Impact of UK-US research collaboration, 2019, https://www.ukri.org/files/international/usa/uk-us-impact-brochure/

[10] Report by Full Fact, 'How many Nobel Prizes has the UK won?', 6 September 2017, https://fullfact.org/news/how-many-nobel-prizes-has-uk-won/

The Myths

[1] Thomas Jefferson, Letter to Nathaniel Macon, *Library of Congress,* 12 January 1819 https://www.loc.gov/item/mtjbib021070/

Chapter One: A Model Democracy

An abridged version of this chapter appeared in Tortoise Media in November 2019, https://members.tortoisemedia.com/2019/10/30/democracy-in-name-only/content.html

[1] Report by the Electoral Commission, UK Parliamentary General Election 2015: Campaign spending report, February 2016, p 19, https://www.electoralcommission.org.uk /media/4179

[2] Center for Responsive Politics, Most Expenses Races: 2016 Election Cycle, based on data from the Federal Election Commission in May 2017, https://www.opensecrets.org/ overview/ topraces.php?cycle=2016&display=allcandsout

[3] Niv M Sultan, 'Election 2016: Trump's free media helped keep cost down, but fewer donors provided more of the cash', *Center for Responsive Politics,* 13 April 2017, https://www.opensecrets.org/news/2017/04/election-2016-trump-fewer-donors-provided-more-of-the-cash/

[4] Center for Responsive Politics, 2016 Outside Spending by Group, *OpenSecrets.org*, https://www.opensecrets.org/outsidespending/summ.php?cycle=2016&chrt=V&disp=O&t ype=I

[5] US Supreme Court ruling, Citizens United v. Federal Election Committee, 558 US 310, 21 January 2010, https://www.supremecourt.gov/opinions/09pdf/08-205.pdf

[6] US Court of Appeals ruling, SpeechNow.org v. Federal Election Committee, No. 08-5223, 26 March 2010, https://campaignlegal.org/sites/default/files/SpeechNow_ Circuit_Court_ Decision_3.26.10.pdf

[7] The Forbes 400: The Definitive Ranking Of The Wealthiest Americans, *Forbes.com*, 2 October 2019, https://www.forbes.com/forbes-400/#2db176b17e2f

[8] Ashley Balcerzak, 'Richest billionaires are also top political spenders', *Center for Responsive Politics,* 31 March 2017, https://www.opensecrets.org/news/2017/ 03/richest-billionaires-are-top-political-spenders/

[9] Statement by President Trump on Jerusalem, White House, 6 December 2017, https:// www.whitehouse.gov/briefings-statements/statement-president-trump-jerusalem/

[10] Opcit Ashley Balcerzak, 'Richest billionaires ..'

[11] Opcit Center for Responsive Politics, 2016 Outside Spending

[12] Igor Bobic, 'The Most Memorable Political Ads of the 2016 Election'. *Huffington Post US*, 3 November 2016, https://www.huffingtonpost.co.uk/entry/political-ads-2016_n_5811fff4e4b064e1b4b0a700?ri18n=true&guccounter=1

[13] Ed Pilkington and Sabrina Siddiqui, 'Democrats go after political 'dark money' with anti-corruption measure', *The Guardian*, 14 February 2019, https://www.theguardian.com/us-news/2019/feb/13/political-funding-dark-money-anti-corruption-trump

[14] Review for the UK parliament by The Lord Hodgson of Astley Abbotts CBE, 'Third Party Election Campaigning – Getting the Balance Right', March 2016, pp 46 (section 6.4) and 49 (section 6.16), https://assets.publishing.service.gov.uk/government/uploads/system/uploads/attachment_data/file/507954/2904969_Cm_9205_Accessible_v0.4.pdf

[15] Opcit Report by the UK Electoral Commission, February 2016, p 16, section 2.19

[16] Center for Responsive Politics, Lobbying Data Summary and Ranked Sectors, *OpenSecrets.org*, http://www.opensecrets.org/federal-lobbying/summary

[17] Kimberly Kindy, 'In Trump era, lobbyists boldly take credit for writing a bill to protect their industry', *The Washington Post*, 1 August 2017, https://www.washingtonpost.com/powerpost/in-trump-era-lobbyists-boldly-take-credit-for-writing-a-bill-to-protect-their-industry/2017/07/31/eb299a7c-5c34-11e7-9fc6-c7ef4bc58d13_story.html

[18] Women's March, Annual Report 2017, via Women's March website, https://static1.squarespace.com/static/5c3feb79fcf7fdce5a3c790b/t/5c422af80e2e725f8f0ea8f8/1547840252450/2017%2BWM%2BAnnual%2BReport_LoRes.pdf

[19] Tamasin Cave and Andy Rowell, 'The truth about lobbying: 10 ways big business controls government', *The Guardian*, 12 March 2014, https://www.theguardian.com/politics/2014/mar/12/lobbying-10-ways-corprations-influence-government

[20] Jim Pickard and Lindsay Fortado, 'Political lobbying register criticised as 'feeble'', *The Financial Times*, 27 January 2016, https://www.ft.com/content/6a1e6f14-c420-11e5-b3b1-7b2481276e45

[21] Christopher Ingraham, 'America's most gerrymandered congressional districts', *The Washington Post*, 15 May 2014, https://www.washingtonpost.com/news/wonk/wp/2014/05/15/americas-most-gerrymandered-congressional-districts/?noredirect=on

[22] F.H, 'How Britain draws its electoral boundaries', *The Economist*, 20 September 2018, https://www.economist.com/the-economist-explains/2018/09/20/how-britain-draws-its-electoral-boundaries

[23] Elections Canada website, 2012 Redistribution of Federal Election Districts, FAQs, https://www.elections.ca/content.aspx?section=res&dir=cir/red/faq&document=index&lang=e

[24] Australian Election Commission website, Federal Redistributions, https://www.aec.gov.au/Electorates/Redistributions/

[25] Adam Liptak, 'Justices reject 2 gerrymandered North Carolina districts, citing racial bias', *The New York Times*, 22 May 2017, https://www.nytimes.com/2017/05/22/us/politics/supreme-court-north-carolina-congressional-districts.html

[26] BBC News website: 'Supreme Court: Federal judges cannot block gerrymandering', 27 June 2019, https://www.bbc.co.uk/news/world-us-canada-48789838

[27] BBC News website: 'US mid-terms: what are the claims of voter suppression', 1 November 2018, https://www.bbc.co.uk/news/world-us-canada-45986329

[28] The Brennan Center for Justice, 'Project: The Myth of Voter Fraud', Brennan Center website, https://www.brennancenter.org/issues/ensure-every-american-can-vote/vote-suppression/myth-voter-fraud

[29] US National Archives, 'What is the Electoral College?', National Archives website, https://www.archives.gov/electoral-college/about

[30] Nate Cohn, 'The Electoral College's Real Problem: It's Biased Toward the Big Battlegrounds', *The New York Times*, 23 March 2019, https://www.nytimes.com/2019/03/22/upshot/electoral-college-votes-states.html

[31] Drew Desilver, 'Trump's victory another example of how Electoral College wins are bigger than popular vote ones', *Pew Research Center*, 20 December 2016, https://www.pew research.org/fact-tank/2016/12/20/why-electoral-college-landslides-are-easier-to-win-than-popular-vote-ones/

[32] Ibid

[33] Philip Bump, 'Donald Trump will be president thanks to 80000 people in three states', *The Washington Post*, 1 December 2016, https://www.washingtonpost.com/news/the-fix/wp/2016/12/01/donald-trump-will-be-president-thanks-to-80000-people-in-three-states/

[34] Ron Elving , 'The Florida recount of 2000: A nightmare that goes on haunting', National Public Radio, 12 November 2018, https://www.npr.org/2018/11/12/666812854/the-florida-recount-of-2000-a-nightmare-that-goes-on-haunting?t=1583771892957

[35] Ibid

[36] Alana Abramson, 'Brett Kavanaugh confirmed to Supreme Court after fight that divided America', *Time*, 7 October 2018, https://time.com/5417538/bett-kavanaugh-confirmed-senate-supreme-court/

[37] BBC News report, 'What did the FBI inquiry into Kavanaugh result in?', 4 October 2018, https://www.bbc.co.uk/news/world-us-canada-45693211

[38] United States Courts website, Judgeship Appointments by President (up to 31 December 2019), https://www.uscourts.gov/judges-judgeships/authorized-judgeships/judgeship-appointments-president

[39] Democracy Index 2019: A year of democratic setbacks and popular protest, pp40-42, *The Economist Intelligence Unit Limited*, 2020, http://www.eiu.com/topic/democracy-index

[40] Letter from John Adams to John Taylor, 17 December 1814, *Founders Online*, US National Archives, https://founders.archives.gov/documents/Adams/99-02-02-6371

[41] John F Kennedy, Inaugural address, 20 January 1961, *John F Kennedy library*, https://www.jfklibrary.org/learn/about-jfk/historic-speeches/inaugural-address

Chapter Two: You can Make it. Just work Hard

[1] Ronald Reagan, Farewell address, 11 January 1989, *Ronald Reagan Foundation and Institute website*, https://www.reaganfoundation.org/media/128652/ farewell.pdf

[2] Georgetown University Center on Education and the Workforce, *Born to Win, Schooled to Lose: Why Equally Talented Students Don't Get Equal Chances to Be All They Can Be*, 2019, https://cew.georgetown.edu/cew-reports/schooled2lose/

[3] Alexis de Tocqueville, 'Democracy in America: And two essays on America', *Penguin Classics,* October 2003

[4] Baltimore Homicides data, *Baltimore Sun*, accessed January 2020, https://homicides.news. baltimoresun.com/?range=2019

[5] City of Baltimore, 'Baltimore Police Department (BPD) Part 1Victim Based Crime Data', *Open Baltimore website* https://data.baltimorecity.gov/Public-Safety/BPD-Part-1-Victim-Based-Crime-Data/wsfq-mvij#

[6] US Federal Bureau of Investigation report, '2018 Crime in the United States', *FBI website,* https://ucr.fbi.gov/crime-in-the-u.s/2018/crime-in-the-u.s.-2018/tables/table-16

[7] Maryland Alliance for the Poor report, '2018 Maryland Poverty Profiles', page 8, *Maryland.gov website,* https://mda.maryland.gov/about_mda/Documents/SNAB/Maryland-Poverty-Profiles_2018_1-15-2018_T.pdf

[8] Olga Khazan, 'Being Black in America Can be Hazardous to your Health', *The Atlantic*, July/August 2018, https://www.theatlantic.com/magazine/archive/2018/07/being-black-in-america-can-be-hazardous-to-your-health/561740/

[9] Maryland Department of Labor, 'Local Area Unemployment Statistics - Workforce Information & Performance', January 2020, https://www.dllr.state.md.us/lmi/laus/

[10] Jordan Malter, 'Baltimore's economy in black and white', 29 April 2015, cnn.com, https://money.cnn.com/2015/04/29/news/economy/baltimore-economy/index.html

[11] Prosperity Now, 'Racial Wealth Divide in Baltimore, January 2017, https://prosperitynow.org/files/resources/Racial_Wealth_Divide_in_Baltimore_RWDI.pdf

[12] Baltimore City Health Department, 'White Paper: State of Health in Baltimore', May 2018, pages 5 and 10, https://health.baltimorecity.gov/sites/default/files/BCHD%20White%20 Paper%20May%202018.pdf

[13] US National Park Service, Selma to Montgomery March, *nps.gov,* https://www.nps.gov/articles/selmatomongtomerymarch.htm?utm_source=article&utm_medium=website&utm_campaign=experience_more&utm_content=small

[14] US Census Bureau, Quickfacts: Selma City, Alabama, *census.gov,* https://www.census.gov/quickfacts/selmacityalabama

[15] Adam Dodson, 'Charlie's Place to close later this month', *The Selma Times-Journal,* 11 May 2018, https://www.selmatimesjournal.com/2018/05/11/charlies-place-to-close-later-this-month/

[16] Alberto Alesina, Stefanie Stantcheva and Edoardo Teso, 'How Closely Do Our Beliefs About Social Mobility Match Reality?', *KellogInsight,* 6 November 2018, https://insight.kellogg.northwestern.edu/article/how-closely-do-our-beliefs-about-social-mobility-match-reality

[17] International Student House, 'Our History', *ishdc.org*, https://www.ishdc.org/about-ish/our-history/

[18] Richard V Reeves and Eleanor Krause, 'Raj Chetty in 14 charts: Big findings on opportunity and mobility we should all know', *brookings.edu*, 11 January 2018, https://www.brookings.edu/blog/social-mobility-memos/2018/01/11/raj-chetty-in-14-charts-big-findings-on-opportunity-and-mobility-we-should-know/

[19] World Economic Forum, 'The Global Social Mobility Report 2020: Equality, Opportunity and a New Economic Imperative', *weforum.org*, January 2020, http://www3.weforum.org/ docs/Global_Social_Mobility_Report.pdf

[20] Taylor Kate Brown, 'How US welfare compares around the globe', *BBC News*, 26 August 2016, https://www.bbc.co.uk/news/world-us-canada-37159686

[21] Linda Darling-Hammond, America's School Funding Struggle: How we're Robbing our Future by Under-Investing in our Children', *Forbes.com*, 5 August 2019, https://www.forbes.com/sites/lindadarlinghammond/2019/08/05/americas-school-funding-struggle-how-were-robbing-our-future-by-under-investing-in-our-children/#74229dfb5eaf

[22] US Census Bureau, '2017 Public Elementary-Secondary Education Finance Data – Table 20', *census.gov*, 21 May 2019, https://www.census.gov/data/tables/2017/econ/school-finances/secondary-education-finance.html

[23] 2020 Best High Schools in the Washington, D.C. Area, *niche.com*, https://www.niche.com/k12/search/best-high-schools/m/washington-dc-metro-area/

[24] Dwight D Eisenhower, Address in Convention Hall, Philadelphia, 1 November 1956, *The American Presidency Project, UC Santa Barbara*, https://www.presidency.ucsb.edu/documents/address-convention-hall-philadelphia-pennsylvania

Chapter Three: The Most Successful Capitalist Economy

[1] Prableen Bajpal, 'The 5 Largest Economies in the World and their Growth in 2020', *Nasdaq.com*, 22 Jan 2020, https://www.nasdaq.com/articles/the-5-largest-economies-in-the-world-and-their-growth-in-2020-2020-01-22

[2] World Bank Open Data, 'GDP Per Capita (current US$), *worldbank.org*, https://data.worldbank.org/indicator/NY.GDP.PCAP.CD

[3] Edward Luce, 'Corporate tie binds US to a slow internet', *Financial Times*, 24 February 2013, https://www.ft.com/content/98e2a5fc-7c54-11e2-99f0-00144feabdc0

[4] Worldwide Price Comparison: The cost of fixed-line broadband in 206 countries, *cable.co.uk*, accessed 18 August 2020, https://www.cable.co.uk/broadband/pricing/worldwide-comparison/

[5] World Bank Open Data, 'GDP Per Capita, PPP', *worldbank.org*, https://data.worldbank.org/indicator/NY.GDP.PCAP.PP.CD?most_recent_value_desc=true

[6] OECD, Broadband Portal, 'Fixed and mobile broadband subscriptions per 100 habitants', *oecd.org*, June 2019, https://www.oecd.org/sti/broadband/broadband-statistics/

[7] Joseph E Stiglitz, 'America has a Monopoly Problem and it's Huge', *The Nation*, 23 October 2017, https://www.thenation.com/article/archive/america-has-a-monopoly-problem-and-its-huge/

[8] Allan Holmes and Chris Zubak-Skees, 'These maps show why internet is way more expensive in the US than Europe', *The Verge*, 1 April 2015, https://www.theverge.com/2015/ 4/1/8321437/maps-show-why-internet-is-more-expensive-us-europe-competition

[9] Center for Responsive Politics, Lobbing Top Spenders 2019, *OpenSecrets.org,* https://www.opensecrets.org/federal-lobbying/top-spenders?cycle=2019

[10] David Crow, 'Verizon and AT&T accused of hurting rivals', *Financial Times,* 23 August 2015, https://www.ft.com/content/135a2162-4853-11e5-b3b2-1672f710807b

[11] AT&T Blog Team, 'The British are Coming (and This Time They Want Pricing Regulation)', *attpublicpolicy.com,* 10 September 2015, https://www.attpublicpolicy.com/business-broadband/the-british-are-coming-and-this-time-they-want-pricing-regulation/

[12] Worldwide Mobile Data Pricing: The cost of 1GB of Mobile Data in 228 countries, *cable.co.uk,* accessed 18 August 2020, https://www.cable.co.uk/mobiles/worldwide-data-pricing/

[13] Wikipedia, 'Comparison between US States and sovereign states by GDP', *https://en.wikipedia.org/wiki/Comparison_between_U.S._states_and_sovereign_states_by_GDP*

[14] David Leonhardt, 'Big Business is Overcharging you $5000 a year', *The New York Times,* 10 November 2019, https://www.nytimes.com/2019/11/10/opinion/big-business-consumer-prices.html

[15] The Nilson Report, 'Card Fraud Losses Reach $27.85 billion', *nilsonreport.com,* 18 November 2019, https://nilsonreport.com/mention/407/1link/

[16] US Federal Reserve, 'The 2019 Federal Reserve Payments Study', *federalreserve.gov,* 6 January 2020, https://www.federalreserve.gov/paymentsystems/2019-December-The-Federal-Reserve-Payments-Study.htm

[17] Banking Strategist, 'Trends in Bank Charters, Q4 2019, *bankingstrategist.com,* https://www.bankingstrategist.com/community-bank-trends

[18] Bill Medley (Federal Reserve Bank of Kansas City), 'Riegle-Neal Interstate Banking and Branching Efficiency Act of 1994', *Federal Reserve History website,* September 1994, https://www.federalreservehistory.org/essays/riegle_neal_act_of_1994

[19] James Dean et al, 'Buy America: An Analysis of US Domestic Preference Legislation for the North American Strategy for Competitiveness', *Texas A&M University,* May 2016, https://papers.ssrn.com/sol3/papers.cfm?abstract_id=2780156

[20] Scott A Freling and Sandy Hoe, 'Key Takeaways from the "New York Buy American Act" and Beyond', *Inside Government Contracts Blog – Covington and Burling LLP,* 4 April 2018, https://www.insidegovernmentcontracts.com/2018/04/7529/

[21] Nicholas Clairmont, 'The Many Ways 'Buy American' Can Harm The Economy', *The Atlantic,* 19 April 2017, https://www.theatlantic.com/business/archive/2017/04/buy-american-trump/523584/

[22] American Society of Civil Engineers, '2017 Infrastructure Report Card', https://www.infrastructurereportcard.org

[23] Congressional Research Service, 'Effects of Buy America on Transportation Infrastructure and US Manufacturing', *crsreports.congress.gov*, 2 July 2019, https://crsreports.congress .gov/product/pdf/R/R44266

[24] Lauren Debter, 'Why Virgin America Will Soon Cease To Exist', *forbes.com*, 23 March 2017, https://www.forbes.com/sites/laurengensler/2017/03/23/virgin-america-brand-retired-following-alaska-airlines-merger/#76a1a71e28a6

[25] Melanie Zanona, 'Lawmakers urge feds to block Norwegian Air from flying to US', *The Hill*, 27 April 2016, https://thehill.com/policy/transportation/277951-lawmakers-urge-feds-to-block-norwegian-air-from-flying-to-us

[26] Bill Carey, 'US Transportation Agency Favors Norwegian Air Carrier Permit', *AINonline.com*, 15 April 2016, https://www.ainonline.com/aviation-news/air-transport/2016-04-15/us-transportation-agency-favors-norwegian-air-carrier-permit#

[27] John Mulligan and Donal O'Donovan, 'Trump team backs Norwegian Air in row over US flights', *independent.ie*, 10 July 2017, https://www.independent.ie/business/world/trump-team-backs-norwegian-air-in-row-over-us-flights-35911958.html

[28] HM Treasury handbook, 'Managing public money', *gov.uk*, July 2013, https://assets.publishing.service.gov.uk/government/uploads/system/uploads/attachment_data/file/742188/Managing_Public_Money__MPM__2018.pdf

[29] The US Fair Labor Standards Act of 1938, as amended, https://www.dol.gov/sites/dolgov/files/WHD/legacy/files/FairLaborStandAct.pdf

[30] Rebecca Baird-Remba, 'How Scabby the Inflatable Rat became the Ultimate Union Symbol', *Commercial Observer*, 14 June 2017, https://commercialobserver.com/2017/06/history-of-scabby-the-rat/

[31] Susan Adams, 'Why should Stage Hands at Carnegie Hall make $400,000', *forbes.com*, 4 October 2013, https://www.forbes.com/sites/susanadams/2013/10/04/why-should-stage-hands-at-carnegie-hall-make-400000/#3eec0c5c6807

[32] Franklin D Roosevelt, Second Inaugural Address, Washington DC, 20 January 1937, *The American Presidency Project, UC Santa Barbara*, https://www.presidency.ucsb.edu/documents/inaugural-address-7

Chapter Four: Separation of Church and State

[1] Kenneth C Davis, 'America's True History of Religious Tolerance', *Smithsonian Magazine*, October 2010, https://www.smithsonianmag.com/history/americas-true-history-of-religious-tolerance-61312684/

[2] The Constitution of the United States, Article VI, 1787, *US National Archives*, https://www.archives.gov/founding-docs/constitution-transcript

[3] The Bill of Rights of the United States, Amendment I, 1789, *US National Archives*, https://www.archives.gov/founding-docs/bill-of-rights-transcript

[4] Pew Research Center, 'In US, Decline of Christianity Continues at Rapid Pace', *pewforum.org*, 17 October 2019, https://www.pewforum.org/2019/10/17/in-u-s-decline-of-christianity-continues-at-rapid-pace/

[5] Ibid

[6] Pew Research Center, 'The Age Gap in Religion around the World, Section 3 – How religious commitment varies by country among people of all ages', *pewforum.org*, 13

June 2018, https://www.pewforum.org/2018/06/13/how-religious-commitment-varies-by-country-among-people-of-all-ages/

[7] David Masci and Gregory A Smith, '5 Facts about US Evangelical Protestants', *Pew Research Center FacTank*, 1 March 2018, https://www.pewresearch.org/fact-tank/2018 /03/ 01/5-facts-about-u-s-evangelical-protestants/

[8] Opcit Pew Research Center, 'In US, Decline of Christianity Continues ..'

[9] John Fea, 'Evangelical Fear Elected Trump', *The Atlantic*, 24 June 2018, https://www.theatlantic.com/ideas/archive/2018/06/a-history-of-evangelical-fear/563558/

[10] Ed Stetzer, 'Why Evangelicals Dislike and Distrust Hillary Clinton so Much', *Christianity Today*, 31 October 2016, https://www.christianitytoday.com/edstetzer/2016/ october/why-evangelicals-dislike-and-distrust-hillary-clinton-so-mu.html

[11] Jordan Steffen, 'Colorado Supreme Court won't hear Lakewood Baker Discrimination Case', *The Denver Post*, 25 April 2106, https://www.denverpost.com/2016/04/25/ colorado-supreme-court-wont-hear-lakewood-baker-discrimination-case/

[12] Focus on the Family website, Our Vision page, accessed, May 2020, https:// www.focusonthefamily.com/about/foundational-values/#mission

[13] The Family Policy Alliance website, About Us and Issues pages, accessed July 2020, https://familypolicyalliance.com/about/about-us/, https://familypolicyalliance.com/issues/

[14] Pew Research Center, 'Lobbying for the Faithful', *pewforum.org*, 15 May 2012, https:// www.pewforum.org/2011/11/21/lobbying-for-the-faithful-exec/#expenditures

[15] US Election 2016: Exit Polls, *cnn.com*, https://edition.cnn.com/election/2016/results/ exit-polls

[16] Sarah Posner, 'Amazing Disgrace: How did Donald Trump hijack the Religious Right?', *The New Republic*, 20 March 2017, https://newrepublic.com/article/140961/ amazing-disgrace -donald-trump-hijacked-religious-right

[17] Alexis de Tocqueville, 'Democracy in America', *Penguin Classics*, October 2003

[18] National Public Radio website, NPR Stations and Public Media, *npr.org*, https://www.npr .org/about-npr/178640915/npr-stations-and-public-media?t=1586521352695

[19] Inside Radio, 'While you weren't watching, Christian radio turned into a Goliath', *insideradio.com*, 12 February 2018, http://www.insideradio.com/while-you-weren-t-watching -christian-radio-grew-into-a/article_4b0feef8-0fc4-11e8-9ac6-cfe74883b60e.html

[20] Pew Research Center, 'Religion and Electronic Media', *pewforum.org*, 6 November 2014, https://www.pewforum.org/2014/11/06/religion-and-electronic-media/

[21] Heath W Carter, 'The Cautionary Tale of Jim and Tammy Faye Bakker', *Christianity Today*, 19 September 2017, https://www.christianitytoday.com/ct/2017/september-web-only/cautionary-tale-of-jim-and-tammy-faye-bakker.html

[22] Robert L Jackson, 'Ministry Makes $150 Million a Year: Rich Life Style Reflects Swaggart Empire's Wealth', *LA Times*, 14 March 1988, https://www.latimes.com /archives/la-xpm-1988-03-14-mn-715-story.html

[23] Marlow Stern, 'John Oliver Exposes Shady Televangelists Fleecing Americans for Millions', *The Daily Beast,* https://www.thedailybeast.com/john-oliver-exposes-shady-televangelists-fleecing-americans-for-millions

[24] Ruth Graham, 'Church of the Donald. Never mind Fox. Trump's most reliable media mouthpiece is now Christian TV, *Politico Magazine,* May/June 2018, https://www.politico.com/magazine/story/2018/04/22/trump-christian-evangelical-conservatives-television-tbn-cbn-218008

[25] Ben Finlay, 'Christian TV network enters world of 24-hours news',1 October 2018, *Associated Press,* https://apnews.com/699d6134306e4933a890b441adab7124/Christian-TV-network-enters-world-of-24-hour-news

[26] Letter from James Madison to Edward Livingston, 10 July 1822, *Founders Online,* https://founders.archives.gov/documents/Madison/04-02-02-0471

Chapter Five: Good Government is Small Government

[1] Ronald Reagan, Farewell address to the Nation, 11 January 1989, *reaganfoundation.org,* https://www.reaganfoundation.org/media/128655/farewell.pdf

[2] D Bank et al, 'National Sources of Law Enforcement Data', *US Department of Justice, Bureau of Justice Statistics,* 4 October 2016, www.bjs.gov/content/pub/pdf/nsleed.pdf

[3] Wikipedia, "List of law enforcement agencies in the United Kingdom, Crown dependencies and British Overseas Territories, *wikipedia.org,* https://en.wikipedia.org/wiki/List_of_law_enforcement_agencies_in_the_United_Kingdom,_Crown_dependencies_and_British_Overseas_Territories#Miscellaneous_police_forces

[4] Jess Bidgood, 'On a field at MIT, 10000 Remember an officer who was Killed', *New York Times,* 24 April 2013, https://www.nytimes.com/2013/04/25/us/boston-marathon-bombings-developments.html

[5] Tyler Rogoway, 'The Fascinating Anatomy of the Presidential Motorcade', *The Drive,* 22 July 2016, https://www.thedrive.com/the-war-zone/4518/the-fascinating-anatomy-of-the-presidential-motorcade

[6] OECD Data: General Government Spending (2015-18), *data.oecd.org,* https://data.oecd.org/gga/general-government-spending.htm

[7] Manhattan Institute for Public Policy, Economic Policies for the 21st Century (E21 portal), 'The US and Europe: Governments of Equal Size', *economics21.org,* 8 February 2012, https://economics21.org/html/us-and-europe-governments-equal-size-409.html

[8] Professor Klaus Schwab, 'The Global Competitiveness Report 2019', *World Economic Forum,* http://www3.weforum.org/docs/WEF_TheGlobalCompetitivenessReport2019.pdf

[9] Amy Goldstein, 'HHS failed to heed many warnings that Healthcare.gov was in trouble', *The Washington Post,* 23 February, 2016, https://www.washingtonpost.com/national/health-science/hhs-failed-to-heed-many-warnings-that-healthcaregov-was-in-trouble/2016/02/22/ dd344e7c-d67e-11e5-9823-02b905009f99_story.html

[10] Devin Coldewey, 'Matt Cutts on solving big problems with lean solutions at the US Digital Service', *techcrunch.com,* 12 April 2019, https://techcrunch.com/2019/04/12/matt-cutts-on-solving-big-problems-with-lean-solutions-at-the-us-digital-service/

[11] United Nations Department of Economic and Social Affairs, 'United Nations E-Government Survey 2018', p89, https://publicadministration.un.org/Portals/1/Images/E-Government%20Survey%202018_FINAL%20for%20web.pdf

[12] Jamiles Lartey, 'Will the 35-day government shutdown lead to privatizing government functions?', *The Guardian,* 29 January 2019, https://www.theguardian.com/us-news/2019/jan/27/shutdown-government-functions-will-they-be-privatized

[13] Jonathan Weisman and Jeremy W Peters, 'Government Shuts Down in Budget Impasse', *New York Times,* 30 September 2013, https://www.nytimes.com/2013/10/01/us/politics/ congress-shutdown-debate.html

[14] Kim Gittleson, 'What's the economic impact of a US government shutdown?', *BBC News,* 17 October 2013, https://www.bbc.co.uk/news/business-24341406

[15] Andrew Restuccia, Burgess Everett and Heather Caygle, 'Longest shutdown in history ends after Trump relents on the wall', *Politico,* 25 January 2019, https://www.politico.com/story/2019/01/25/trump-shutdown-announcement-1125529

[16] James Fallows, 'What 35 Days of Shutdown Accomplished: Nothing', *The Atlantic,* 26 January 2019, https://www.theatlantic.com/notes/2019/01/what-35-days-shutdown-accomplished-nothing/581392/

[17] Paul C Light, 'The True Size of Government', *The Volcker Alliance*, 5 October 2017, https://www.volckeralliance.org/publications/true-size-government

[18] Heidi M Peters, 'Defense Primer: Department of Defense Contractors', *Congressional Research Service,* 31 January 2020, https://fas.org/sgp/crs/natsec/IF10600.pdf

[19] Steven Pearlstein, 'The federal outsourcing boom and why its failing Americans' *The Washington Post,* 31 January 2014, https://www.washingtonpost.com/business/the-federal-outsourcing-boom-and-why-its-failing-americans/2014/01/31/21d03c40-8914-11e3-833c-33098f9e5267_story.html

[20] Theodore Roosevelt speech, 'Citizenship in a Republic', The Sorbonne, Paris, 23 April 1910, *leadershipnow.com,* https://www.leadershipnow.com/tr-citizenship.html

Chapter Six: Free Speech Fortifies American Democracy

[1] Mission Statement, Alliance for Securing Democracy, https://securingdemocracy.gmfus.org /about-us/

[2] Dylan Matthews, 'Everything you need to know about the Fairness Doctrine in one post', *The Washington Post,* 23 August 2011, https://www.washingtonpost.com/blogs/ezra-klein/post/everything-you-need-to-know-about-the-fairness-doctrine-in-one-post/2011/08/23/ gIQAN8CXZJ_blog.html

[3] Penny Pagano, 'Reagan veto kills Fairness Doctrine Bill', *The Los Angeles Times,* 21 June 1987, https://www.latimes.com/archives/la-xpm-1987-06-21-mn-8908-story.html

[4] Robert D Hershey Jr, 'FCC votes down Fairness Doctrine in a 4-0 decision', *New York Times,* 5 August 1987, https://www.nytimes.com/1987/08/05/arts/fcc-votes-down-fairness-doctrine-in-a-4-0-decision.html

[5] Victor Pickard, 'The Strange Life and Death of the Fairness Doctrine: Tracing the Decline of Positive Freedoms in American Policy Discourse', *International Journal of Communication,* 2018, https://repository.upenn.edu/asc_papers/745

[6] Kevin M Kruse and Julian Zelizer, 'How policy decisions spawned today's hyperpolarised media', *The Washington Post,* 17 January 2019, https://www.washingtonpost.com/outlook/ 2019/01/17/how-policy-decisions-spawned-todays-hyperpolarized-media/

[7] Hélène Mulholland and agencies, 'Shock jock banned from UK vows to sue Jacqui Smith', *The Guardian,* 6 May 2009, https://www.theguardian.com/politics/2009/may/06/michael-savage-sue-jacqui-smith

[8] Guy Adams, 'Shock Jocks: Voice of Unreason', *The Independent,* 28 May 2009, https://www.independent.co.uk/news/world/americas/shock-jocks-voice-of-unreason-1691792.html

[9] Joe Concha, 'Fox News prime-time lineup delivers highest ratings in network history', *The Hill,* 25 February 2020, https://thehill.com/homenews/media/484592-fox-news-primetime-lineup-delivers-highest-ratings-in-network-history

[10] Public Broadcasting Act 1967, Subpart D: Corporation for Public Broadcasting, Section 396 g(1)(A), https://www.cpb.org/aboutpb/act/

[11] Pew Research Center, Journalism & Media: PBS Newshour viewership (2016-18), 23 July 2019, https://www.journalism.org/chart/sotnm-public-media-pbs-newshour-viewership/

[12] John Nichols, 'With his Assault on PBS and NPR, Trump seeks to Eliminate Real News', *The Nation,* 14 February 2018, https://www.thenation.com/article/archive/with-his-assault-on-pbs-and-npr-trump-seeks-to-eliminate-real-news/

[13] Pew Research Center, 'Key findings about the online news landscape in America', *pewresearch.org,* 11 September 2019, https://www.pewresearch.org/fact-tank/2019/09/11/key-findings-about-the-online-news-landscape-in-america/

[14] BBC News website, US & Canada, 'Edward Snowden: Leaks that exposed US spy programme', *bbc.co.uk/news,* 17 January 2014, https://www.bbc.co.uk/news/world-us-canada-23123964

[15] Deb Riechmann, 'US expects fallout from Snowden leaks for years to come', *Associated Press,* 14 June 2018, https://apnews.com/f8424471585f44da95918c0e784e83af/US-expects-fallout-from-Snowden-leaks-for-years-to-come

[16] Facebook Newsroom, Press release by Nathanial Gleicher, Head of Cyber Security Policy, 'Removing more Coordinated Inauthentic Behavior from Iran and Russia', *fb.com,* 21 October 2019, https://about.fb.com/news/2019/10/removing-more-coordinated-inauthentic-behavior-from-iran-and-russia/

[17] Sheryl Sandberg, Facebook COO, Testimony to US Senate Select Committee on Intelligence, *intelligence.senate.gov,* 5 September 2018, https://www.intelligence.senate.gov/sites/default/files/documents/os-ssandberg-090518.pdf

[18] Nuala O'Connor, 'Reforming the US approach to data protection and privacy', *Council on Foreign Relations,* 30 January 2018, https://www.cfr.org/report/reforming-us-approach-data-protection

[19] Sheera Frenkel, Davey Alba and Raymond Zhong, 'Surge of Virus Misinformation Stumps Facebook and Twitter', *New York Times,* 8 March 2020, https://www.nytimes.com/2020/03/ 08/technology/coronavirus-misinformation-social-media.html

[20] Tony Romm, 'Tech giants led by Amazon, Facebook and Google spent nearly half a billion on lobbying over the past decade, new data shows', *Washington Post,* 22 January 2020, https://www.washingtonpost.com/technology/2020/01/22/amazon-facebook-google-lobbying-2019/

[21] Reuters Factbox: 'When can Free Speech be restricted in the United States', *reuters.com,* 14 August 2017, https://www.reuters.com/article/us-virginia-protests-speech-factbox/ factbox-when-can-free-speech-be-restricted-in-the-united-states-idUSKCN1AU2E0

[22] US Supreme Court ruling: Schenck v. United States, 249 US 47 (1919), via Cornell Law School, https://www.law.cornell.edu/supremecourt/text/249/47

[23] Letter from Thomas Jefferson to John Norvell, 11 June 1807, *Library of Congress,* https://www.loc.gov/resource/mtj1.038_0592_0594/?sp=1&st=text

Chapter Seven: Our Guns Keep us Safe

[1] Gallup Polls In Depth, 'Guns', *gallup.com,* https://news.gallup.com/poll/1645/guns.aspx

[2] Leanna Garfield, 'There are 50,000 more gun shops than McDonalds in the US'. *Business Insider,* 6 October 2017, https://www.businessinsider.com/gun-dealers-stores-mcdonalds-las-vegas-shooting-2017-10?r=US&IR=T

[3] John Gramlich, '5 facts about crime in the U.S.', *Pew Research Center*, 2019, https://www.pewresearch.org/fact-tank/2019/10/17/facts-about-crime-in-the-u-s/

[4] Wayne LaPierre, Executive Director of the National Rifle Association: Statement in response to the Newtown shootings, via *The Guardian*, 21 December 2012, https://www.theguardian.com/world/2012/dec/21/nra-full-statement-lapierre-newtown

[5] Report by US Department of Justice, Office for Victims of Crime: 'Urban and Rural Victimization', *via ovc.gov,* 21 August 2018, https://ovc.ncjrs.gov/ncvrw2018/info_flyers/fact_sheets/2018NCVRW_UrbanRural_508_QC.pdf

[6] Report by the Centre for American Progress: 'Myth vs. Fact: Debunking the Gun Lobby's Favorite Talking Points', 5 October 2017, https://www.americanprogress.org/issues/guns-crime/reports/2017/10/05/440373/myth-vs-fact-debunking-gun-lobbys-favorite-talking-points/

[7] Emanuella Grinberg and Steve Almasy, 'Students at town hall to Washington, NRA: Guns are the problem, do something', *CNN.com,* 22 February 2018, https://edition.cnn.com/2018/ 02/21/politics/cnn-town-hall-florida-shooting/index.html

[8] Jon Swaine and Amanda Holpuch, 'Ferguson police: a stark illustration of newly militarised US law enforcement', *The Guardian,* 14 August 2014, https://www.theguardian.com/world/ 2014/aug/14/ferguson-police-military-restraints-violence-weaponry-missouri

[9] US Defense Logistics Agency website: DLA Disposition Services, 1033 Program FAQs, accessed 7 August 2020, https://www.dla.mil/DispositionServices/Offers/Reutilization/LawEnforcement/ProgramFAQs.aspx

[10] Matt Apuzzo, 'War Gear Flows to Police Departments', *New York Times,* 8 June 2014, www.nytimes.com/2014/06/09/us/war-gear-flows-to-police-departments.html?_r=1

[11] Opcit US Defense Logistics Agency FAQs

[12] Ryan Welch and Josh Mewhirter, 'Does military equipment lead police offices to be more violent? We did the research', *The Washington Post, 30 June* 2017, https://www.washingtonpost.com/news/monkey-cage/wp/2017/06/30/does-military-equipment-lead-police-officers-to-be-more-violent-we-did-the-research/

[13] US Department of Homeland Security booklet: Active Shooter, How to Respond, 28 May 2019, https://www.cisa.gov/sites/default/files/publications/active-shooter-how-to-respond-2017-508.pdf

[14] Michael D Shear and Michael S Schmidt, 'Gunman and 12 Victims Killed in Shooting at D.C. Navy Yard', *The New York Times,* 16 September 2013, https://www.nytimes.com/2013/ 09/17/us/shooting-reported-at-washington-navy-yard.html

[15] Jade F Smith and Emma G Fitzsimmons, '3 Dead in Shooting at Maryland Mall: Police Call the Episode Isolated', *The New York Times,* 25 January 2014, https://www.nytimes.com/2014/01/26/us/3-reported-dead-in-maryland-mall-shooting.html?login=email&auth=login-email

[16] F Gani, JV Sakran and JK Canner, 'Emergency Department Visits for Firearm-Related Injuries in the United States, 2006-14', *Health Affairs, Vol 36, No 10,* October 2017, https://www.healthaffairs.org/doi/full/10.1377/hlthaff.2017.0625

[17] Report by US Congress Joint Economic Committee Democratic Staff, 'A State-by-State Examination of the Economic Costs of Gun Violence, *jec.senate.gov,* 18 September 2019, https://www.jec.senate.gov/public/_cache/files/b2ee3158-aff4-4563-8c3b-0183ba4a8135/economic-costs-of-gun-violence.pdf

[18] US Centers for Disease Control & Prevention: 'Fatal Injury Reports, National, Regional and State', 1981-2018, *cdc.gov,* https://webappa.cdc.gov/sasweb/ncipc/mortrate.html

[19] UK Office of National Statistics: 'Homicide in England and Wales: year ending March 2019', *ons.gov.uk,* 13 February 2020, https://www.ons.gov.uk/peoplepopulationand community/crimeandjustice/articles/homicideinenglandandwales/yearendingmarch2019# what-were-the-most-common-methods-of-killing

[20] Scottish Government Publications, 'Homicide in Scotland: 2018-19 statistics', *gov.scot,* 29 October 2019, https://www.gov.scot/publications/homicide-scotland-2018-19/pages/1/

[21] Australian Bureau of Statistics: 'Victims of Crime, Australia 2019', *abs.gov.au,* 9 July 2020, https://www.abs.gov.au/AUSSTATS/abs@.nsf/DetailsPage/4510.02019? OpenDocument

[22] Aaron Karp, 'Estimating Global Civilian-Held Firearms Numbers', *Small Arms Survey briefing paper,* June 2018, http://www.smallarmssurvey.org/fileadmin/docs/T-Briefing-Papers/SAS-BP-Civilian-Firearms-Numbers.pdf

[23] US Bureau of Alcohol, Tobacco, Firearms and Explosives: 'Annual Firearms Manufacturing and Export Report', *atf.gov,* 28 January 2020, https://www.atf.gov/file/142946/download

[24] Nick Wing, 'NRA Spending Approached Half a Billion Dollars in 2016', *Huffington Post,* 16 November 2017, https://www.huffingtonpost.co.uk/entry/nra-2016-spending_n_5a0dd3e6e4b0b17e5e14e636?ri18n=true&guccounter=1

[25] US National Archives, 'The Bill of Rights, A Transcription', *archives.gov,* https://www.archives.gov/founding-docs/bill-of-rights-transcript

Chapter Eight: A World-beating Health System

[1] Research America report, Fall 2019: 'U.S. Investments in Medical and Health Research and Development 2013-2018', *researchamerica.org,* www.researchamerica.org/sites/default/files/Publications/InvestmentReport2019_Fnl.pdf

[2] UK Office for Life Sciences report, June 2019: 'Life Sciences Competitiveness Indicators', *gov.uk,* https://assets.publishing.service.gov.uk/government/uploads/system/uploads/ attachment_data/file/811347/life-sciences-competitiveness-data-2019.pdf

[3] UK Research and Innovation brochure: 'The Impact of UK-US Research Collaboration, *ukri.org,* February 2020, https://www.ukri.org/files/international/usa/uk-us-impact-brochure/

[4] Rabah Kamal et al, 'How has U.S. spending on healthcare changed over time', *Peterson Center on Healthcare and Henry J Kaiser Family Foundation, Health System Tracker, healthsystemtracker.org,* 20 December 2019, https://www.healthsystemtracker.org/chart-collection/u-s-spending-healthcare-changed-time/#item-start

[5] OECD Health Statistics 2020: 'Key Indicators – Current expenditure on health, per capita, US $, purchasing power parities', *oecd.org,* updated 1 July 2020, http://www.oecd.org/els/ health-systems/health-data.htm

[6] Karen Feldscher, 'What's behind high U.S. health care costs', *The Harvard Gazette,* 13 March 2018, https://news.harvard.edu/gazette/story/2018/03/u-s-pays-more-for-health-care-with-worse-population-health-outcomes/

[7] Marshall Allen, 'Wasted Medicine: Unnecessary Medical Care is More Common than you Think' *ProPublica,* 1 February 2018, https://www.propublica.org/article/unnecessary-medical-care-is-more-common-than-you-think

[8] A Bhardwaj, 'Excessive Ancillary Testing by Healthcare Providers: Reasons and Proposed Solutions', *Journal of Hospital and Medical Management Vol.5 No.1:1,* 18 March 2019, https://hospital-medical-management.imedpub.com/excessive-ancillary-testing-by-healthcareproviders-reasons-and-proposed-solutions.php?aid=24249

[9] Roosa Tikkanen and Melinda K Abrams, 'US Health Care from a Global Perspective, 2019: Higher Spending, Worse Outcomes?', *The Commonwealth Fund,* 20 January 2020, https://www.commonwealthfund.org/publications/issue-briefs/2020/jan/us-health-care-global-perspective-2019

[10] B Bastian, Vera B Tejada, E Arias et al, 'Mortality Trends in the United States, 1900-2017', *National Center for Health Statistics,* 2019, https://www.cdc.gov/nchs/data-visualization/mortality-trends/index.htm

[11] US National Center for Health Statistics, Factsheet April 2020, *cdc.gov/nchs,* https://www.cdc.gov/nchs/data/factsheets/factsheet_NVSS.pdf

[12] OECD 'Health at a Glance 2019: United States', *oecd.org,* published 7 November 2019, http://www.oecd.org/unitedstates/health-at-a-glance-united-states-EN.pdf

[13] OECD, 'Health at a Glance 2019, OECD Indicators', pp33 & 67, *OECD Publishing,* 2019, https://www.oecd-ilibrary.org/social-issues-migration-health/health-at-a-glance-2019_4dd50c09-en

[14] R Kamal et al, 'What do we know about infant mortality in the U.S. and comparable countries?', *Peterson-KFF Health System Tracker, healthsystemtracker.org,* 18 October 2019, https://www.healthsystemtracker.org/chart-collection/infant-mortality-u-s-compare-countries/#item-the-u-s-infant-mortality-rate-has-improved-over-time

[15] Opcit OECD, 'Health at a Glance 2019, OECD Indicators', p 81

[16] SR Collins, HK Bhupal and MM Doty, 'Health Insurance Coverage Eight Years After the ACA', *The Commonwealth Fund,* 7 February 2019, https://www.commonwealthfund.org/publications/issue-briefs/2019/feb/health-insurance-coverage-eight-years-after-aca

[17] Open Markets Institute report: 'Health Insurance & Monopoly', *openmarketsinstitute.org,* https://openmarketsinstitute.org/explainer/health-insurance-and-monopoly/

[18] Peterson-KFF Health System Tracker: Health System Dashboard, Affordability, Out of Pocket Spending, https://www.healthsystemtracker.org/indicator/access-affordability/out-of-pocket-spending/

[19] US Social Security Administration factsheet: 'What is FICA?', *ssa.gov,* March 2017, https://www.ssa.gov/thirdparty/materials/pdfs/educators/What-is-FICA-Infographic-EN-05-10297.pdf

[20] Hannah Kuchler, 'Why prescription drugs cost so much more in America', *The Financial Times,* 19 September 2019, https://www.ft.com/content/e92dbf94-d9a2-11e9-8f9b-77216ebe1f17

[21] Juliette Cubanski et al, 'What's the latest on Medicare Drug Price Negotiations', *The Kaiser Family Foundation,* 17 October 2019, https://www.kff.org/medicare/issue-brief/whats-the-latest-on-medicare-drug-price-negotiations/

[22] Karl Evers-Hillstrom, 'Big Pharma continues to top lobbying spending', *Center for Responsive Politics,* 25 October 2019, https://www.opensecrets.org/news/ 2019/10/big-pharma-continues-to-top-lobbying-spending/

[23] Mike Tigas et al, 'Dollars for Docs: How Industry Reached Your Doctors', *ProPublica,* updated 17 October 2019, https://projects.propublica.org/docdollars/

[24] Hannah Fresques, 'Doctors Prescribe More of a Drug if they Receive Money from a Pharma Company Tied to It', *ProPublica,* 20 December 2019, https://www.propublica.org article/doctors-prescribe-more-of-a-drug-if-they-receive-money-from-a-pharma-company-tied-to-it

[25] Charles Ornstein, et al, 'We Found Over 700 Doctors Who Were Paid More Than a Million Dollars by Drug and Medical Device Companies', *ProPublica,* 17 October 2019,

https://www.propublica.org/article/we-found-over-700-doctors-who-were-paid-more-than-a-million-dollars-by-drug-and-medical-device-companies

[26] Jessie Hellmann, 'What caused the opioid crisis?', *The Hill,* 3 March 2018, https://thehill.com/homenews/politics-101/376508-what-caused-the-opioid-crisis

[27] US Centers for Disease Control: Opioid Overdose, Drug Overdose Deaths, *cdc.gov,* updated 19 March 2020, https://www.cdc.gov/drugoverdose/data/ statedeaths.html

[28] US Centers for Disease Control: Opioid Overdose, Understanding the Epidemic, *cdc.gov,* updated 19 March 2020, https://www.cdc.gov/drugoverdose/epidemic/index.html

[29] Julie Hirschfeld David, 'Trump Declares Opioid Crisis a 'Health Emergency' but Requests No Funds', 26 October 2017, https://www.nytimes.com/2017/10/26/us/politics/trump-opioid-crisis.html?login=email&auth=login-email

[30] Robert H Shmerling MD, 'Harvard Health Ad Watch: What you should know about direct-to-consumer ads', *Harvard Health Publishing,* 20 September 2019, https://www.health. harvard.edu/blog/harvard-health-ad-watch-what-you-should-know-about-direct-to-consumer-ads-2019092017848

[31] David Lazarus, 'TV commercials for prescription drugs 'doing more harm than good', *Los Angeles Times,* 20 April 2018, https://www.latimes.com/business/lazarus/la-fi-lazarus-direct-to-consumer-drug-ads-20180410-story.html

[32] Christopher Ingraham, 'The world's richest countries guarantee mothers more than a year of paid maternity leave. The U.S. guarantees them nothing', *The Washington Post,* 5 February 2018, https://www.washingtonpost.com/news/wonk/wp/2018/02/05/the-worlds-richest-countries-guarantee-mothers-more-than-a-year-of-paid-maternity-leave-the-u-s-guarantees-them-nothing/

[33] Amy Raub et al, 'Paid Leave for Personal Illness: A Detailed Look at Approaches Across OECD Countries', *World Policy Analysis Center, UCLA,* 2018, https://www.worldpolicy center.org/sites/default/files/WORLD%20Report%20-%20Personal%20Medical%20Leave %20OECD%20Country%20Approaches_0.pdf

[34] Miranda Bryant, 'The US doesn't offer paid family leave – but will that change in 2020', *The Guardian,* 28 October 2019, https://www.theguardian.com/us-news/2019/oct/28/us-paid-family-leave-2020-election

[35] US Department of Labor website: Sick Leave, *dol.gov,* www.dol.gov/general/topic/workhours/sickleave

[36] US Military Health System website: About the MHS, *health.mil,* https://www.health.mil/ About-MHS

[37] US Department of Veteran Affairs website: Veterans Health Administration, About the VHA, *va.gov,* https://www.va.gov/health/aboutvha.asp

[38] Patricia Kime, '5 Years After Nationwide Scandal, VA Still Struggles to Track Wait Times, *Military.com,* 26 July 2019, https://www.military.com/daily-news/2019/07/26/5-years-after-nationwide-scandal-va-still-struggles-track-wait-times.html

[39] Letter from George Washington to James Anderson, 16 September 1799, *founders.archive.gov,* https://founders.archives.gov/documents/Washington/06-04-02-0258

Chapter Nine: A Thriving Melting Pot

[1] The Statue of Liberty-Ellis Island Foundation website, Ellis Island History, *libertyellisfoundation.org,* https://www.libertyellisfoundation.org/ellis-island-history

[2] US National Park Service website article, 'Closing the Door on Immigration', *nps.gov,* updated 18 July 2017, https://www.nps.gov/articles/closing-the-door-on-immigration.htm

[3] US Department of Homeland Security, 2018 Yearbook of Immigration Statistics, 'Table 1: Persons Obtaining Lawful Permanent Resident Status: Fiscal Years 1820 to 2018', *dhs.gov,* 6 January 2020, www.dhs.gov/immigration-statistics/yearbook/2018/table1

[4] Jynnah Radford, 'Key Findings about U.S. Immigrants', *Pew Research Center,* 17 June 2019, https://www.pewresearch.org/fact-tank/2019/06/17/key-findings-about-u-s-immigrants/

[5] OECD Data: Foreign-born Population (2015-18), *data.oecd.org,* https://data.oecd.org/migration/foreign-born-population.htm

[6] Phillip Connor and Gustavo López, '5 facts about the U.S. rank in worldwide migration', *Pew Research Center,* 18 May 2016, https://www.pewresearch.org/fact-tank/2016/05/18/5-facts-about-the-u-s-rank-in-worldwide-migration/

[7] MC Waters and M Gerstein Pineau, Editors, 'The Integration of Immigrants into American Society', *The National Academies of Sciences, Engineering and Medicine,* The National Academies Press 2015, https://www.nap.edu/catalog/21746/the-integration-of-immigrants-into-american-society

[8] Nina Strochlic, 'How slavery flourished in the United States', *National Geographic,* 23 August 2019, https://www.nationalgeographic.com/culture/2019/08/how-slavery-flourished-united-states-chart-maps/

[9] New York Times archive: 'Census of 1860 Population–Effect on the Representation of the Free and the Slave States', 5 April 1860, https://www.nytimes.com/1860/04/05/archives/census-of-1860-populationeffect-on-the-representation-of-the-free.html

[10] Evan Andrews, 'How Many U.S. Presidents Owned Slaves?', *History.com,* 3 September 2019, https://www.history.com/news/how-many-u-s-presidents-owned-slaves

[11] Catholic Campaign for Human Development, Poverty USA, Maps and Data 2018, Poverty by state/county/race, https://www.povertyusa.org/data/2018/AL/perry-county

[12] Center for American Progress, TalkPoverty Project, Poverty data by state, 2019, https://talkpoverty.org/poverty

[13] Colleen S Good, 'The (Still) All-White Country Club', *Bridging Selma,* 30 April 2015, https://www.bridgingselma.com/long-time-selma-resident-reflects-on-the-all-white-country-club/

[14] Greg Jaffe, 'Decayed, uninhabitable homes will be Obama's first view of Selma', *The Washington Post,* 7 March 2015, https://www.washingtonpost.com/politics/decayed-uninhabitable-homes-will-be-obamas-first-view-of-selma/2015/03/07/6d412282-c489-11e4-9271-610273846239_story.html

[15] Data USA website, City Profiles - demographics, *datausa.io, accessed June 2020,* https://datausa.io/profile/geo/castroville-ca/#demographics, https://datausa.io/profile/geo/ watsonville-ca/#demographics, https://datausa.io/profile/geo/salinas-ca/#demographics, https://datausa.io/profile/geo/carmel-by-the-sea-ca#demographics, https://datausa.io/profile/ geo/monterey-ca#demographics

[16] Aaron Williams and Armand Emamdjomeh, 'America is more diverse than even – but still segregated', *The Washington Post,* 10 May 2018, https://www.washingtonpost.com/ graphics/2018/national/segregation-us-cities/

[17] US National Archives website: America's Historic Documents, 13th Amendment to the U.S. Constitution: Abolition of Slavery, 6 December 1865, https://www.archives.gov/ historical-docs/13th-amendment

[18] US Department of Justice, Civil Rights Division: The Fair Housing Act, *justice.gov,* updated 21 December 2017, https://www.justice.gov/crt/fair-housing-act-1

[19] Michelle Adams, 'The Unfulfilled Promise of the Fair Housing Act', *The New Yorker,* 11 April 2018, https://www.newyorker.com/news/news-desk/the-unfulfilled-promise-of-the-fair-housing-act

[20] The Urban Institute: Gaps in Black-White Homeownership & Wealth, *urban.org,* 2019, http://www.urban.org/sites/default/files/black_homeownership_data_talk_slides.pdf

[21] Daily Chart, 'Segregation in America', *The Economist,* https://www.economist.com/ graphic-detail/2018/04/04/segregation-in-america

[22] US Supreme Court ruling 347 U.S. 483 (1954), Brown v. Board of Education of Topeka, *supreme.justia.com,* accessed 6 May 2020, https://supreme.justia.com/cases/ federal/us/ 347/483/

[23] US National Park Service website article, 'Civil Rights Act of 1964', *nps.gov,* updated 22 March 2016, https://www.nps.gov/articles/civil-rights-act.htm

[24] P R Lockhart, '65 years after Brown v Board of Education, school segregation is getting worse', *Vox,* 10 May 2019, https://www.vox.com/identities/2019/5/10/18566052/school-segregation-brown-board-education-report

[25] Fred Harris and Alan Curtis, 'The Unmet Promise of Equality', *The New York Times,* 28 February 2018, https://www.nytimes.com/interactive/2018/02/28/opinion/the-unmet-promise-of-equality.html?smid=fb-share

[26] Janelle Jones, John Schmitt and Valerie Wilson, '50 years after the Kerner Commission', *Economic Policy Institute,* 26 February 2018, https://www.epi.org/ publication/50-years-after-the-kerner-commission/

[27] US National Park Service website article, 'Closing the Door on Immigration', *nps.gov,* updated 18 July 2017, https://www.nps.gov/articles/closing-the-door-on-immigration.htm

[28] Irene Hsu, 'The Echoes of Chinese Exclusion', *The New Republic,* 28 June 2018, https://newrepublic.com/article/149437/echoes-chinese-exclusion

[29] Lily Rothman and Liz Ronk, 'Congress Tightened Immigration Laws 100 Years Ago. Here's Who They Turned Away', *Time,* 2 February 2017, https://time.com/4645728/ 1917-immigration-law-photos/

[30] Mindy Weisberger, 'Immigration Act of 2017 turns 100: America's Long History of Immigration Prejudice', *Live Science,* 5 February 2017, https://www.livescience.com/57756-1917-immigration-act-100th-anniversary.html

[31] Julia Higgins, 'The Rise and Fall of the American Melting Pot', *The Wilson Quarterly,* 5 December 2015, https://www.wilsonquarterly.com/stories/the-rise-and-fall-of-the-american-melting-pot/

[32] T A Frail, 'The Injustice of Japanese-American Internment Camps Resonates Strongly to this Day', *Smithsonian Magazine,* January 2017, https://www.smithsonianmag.com/history/injustice-japanese-americans-internment-camps-resonates-strongly-180961422/

[33] Discrimination in America poll 2017, 'Experience and Views of Latinos', *NPR, Harvard TH Chan School of Public Health and the Robert Wood Johnson Foundation,* https://cdn1.sph.harvard.edu/wp-content/uploads/sites/94/2017/10/NPR-RWJF-HSPH-Discrimination-Latinos-Final-Report.pdf

[34] M H Lopez, A Gonzalez-Barrera and J M Krogstad, 'Latinos and Discrimination', *Pew Research Center,* 25 October 2018, https://www.pewresearch.org/hispanic/2018/10/25/latinos-and-discrimination/

[35] US Office of Personnel Management, Federal Equal Opportunity Recruitment Program Report, Fiscal Year 2017, *opm.gov,* October 2019, https://www.opm.gov/policy-data-oversight/diversity-and-inclusion/reports/feorp-2017.pdf

[36] A W Geiger, K Bialik and J Gramlich, 'The changing face of Congress in 6 charts', *Pew Research Center,* 15 February 2019, https://www.pewresearch.org/fact-tank/2019/02/15/the-changing-face-of-congress/

[37] US Census Bureau Quick Facts: United States, accessed 6 May 2020, https://www.census.gov/quickfacts/fact/table/US/PST045219#PST045219

[38] The Alliance for Board Diversity/Deloitte, Missing Pieces Report: The 2018 Board Diversity Census of Women and Minorities on Fortune 500 Boards, *deloitte.com,* https://www2.deloitte.com/us/en/pages/center-for-board-effectiveness/articles/missing-pieces-fortune-500-board-diversity-study-2018.html#

[39] Ruth Umoh, 'The Dearth of Black CEOs: How Corporate Diversity Initiatives Ignore People of Color', *Forbes.com,* 10 December 2019, https://www.forbes.com/sites/ruthumoh/2019/12/10/the-dearth-of-black-ceos-how-corporate-diversity-initiatives-ignore-people-of-color/#3dc103934983

[40] Pamela Newkirk, 'No room at the top: why are US boardrooms still so white?', *The Guardian,* 5 November 2019, https://www.theguardian.com/news/2019/nov/05/us-boardrooms-still-so-white-corporate-business-diversity

[41] Douglas S Massey, 'How a 1965 immigration reform created illegal immigration', *The Washington Post,* 25 September 2015, https://www.washingtonpost.com/posteverything/wp/2015/09/25/how-a-1965-immigration-reform-created-illegal-immigration/

[42] JM Krogstad, JS Passel and D'Vera Cohn, '5 facts about illegal immigration in the U.S.', *Pew Research Center,* 12 June 2019, https://www.pewresearch.org/fact-tank/2019/06/12/5-facts-about-illegal-immigration-in-the-u-s/

[43] JS Passel and D'Vera Cohn, 'Mexicans decline to less than half the US unauthorized population for the first time', *Pew Research Center,* 12 June 2019, https://www.pewresearch.org/fact-tank/2019/06/12/us-unauthorized-immigrant-population-2017/

[44] Ibid Passel and Cohn, Pew Research Center

[45] Center for Immigration Studies website: Historical Overview of Immigration Policy, *cis.org,* accessed 7 May 2020, https://cis.org/Historical-Overview-Immigration-Policy

[46] Adam Liptak and Michael D Shear, 'Supreme Court Ties Blocks Obama Immigration Plan', *The New York Times,* 23 June 2016, https://www.nytimes.com/2016/06/24/us/supreme-court-immigration-obama-dapa.html

[47] Liam Stack, 'Trump's Executive Order on Immigration: What we Know and What we Don't', *The New York Times,* 29 January 2017, https://www.nytimes.com/2017/01/29/us/trump-refugee-ban-muslim-executive-order.html

[48] Josh Gerstein and Ted Hesson, 'US Supreme Court upholds Trump Travel Ban', *Politico,* 26 June 2018, https://www.politico.eu/article/us-supreme-court-upholds-donald-trump-travel-ban/

[49] Tal Kopan, How Trump changed the rules to arrest more non-criminal immigrants', *CNN.com,* 2 March 2018, https://edition.cnn.com/2018/03/02/politics/ice-immigration-deportations/index.html

[50] US Immigrations and Customs Enforcement, Fiscal Year 2019 Enforcement and Removal Operations Report, *ice.gov,* 24 February 2020, https://www.ice.gov/sites/default/files/ documents/Document/2019/eroReportFY2019.pdf

[51] Congressional Research Service report, 'The Trump Administration's "Zero Tolerance" Immigration Enforcement Policy', *fas.org,* updated 26 February 2019, https://fas.org/sgp/crs/homesec/R45266.pdf

[52] Salvador Rizzo, 'Fact checking President Trump's Oval Office address on Immigration', *The Washington Post,* 9 January 2019, https://www.washingtonpost.com/politics/2019/ 01/09/fact-checking-president-trumps-oval-office-address-immigration/

[53] BE Hamilton, JA Martin and MJK Osterman, 'Births: Provisional data for 2019. Vital Statistics Rapid Release No. 8', *National Center for Health Statistics*, May 2020, https://www.cdc.gov/nchs/data/vsrr/vsrr-8-508.pdf

[54] Dwight D Eisenhower, Remarks at United Negro College Fund Luncheon, 19 May 1953, *The American Presidency Project, UC Santa Barbara,* https://www.presidency.ucsb.edu/ documents/remarks-the-united-negro-college-fund-luncheon

Chapter Ten: The Threat from Outside

[1] Daily Mail news archive, 11 September 2001, 'Blair puts Britain on high security alert', *Mail Online,* accessed 12 May 2020, https://www.dailymail.co.uk/news/article-71896/Blair-puts-Britain-high-security-alert.html

[2] Michael White and Patrick Wintour, 'Blair calls for world fight against terror', *The Guardian*, 12 September 2001, https://www.theguardian.com/politics/2001/sep/12/uk.september11

[3] Paul Kelso, 'US anthem played at changing of the guard', *The Guardian*, 14 September 2001, https://www.theguardian.com/uk/2001/sep/14/september11.usa3

[4] Lecture by Eliza Manningham-Buller, Director General of the Security Service, 'Countering Terrorism: An International Blueprint', at the Royal United Services Institute conference, 17 June 2003, https://www.mi5.gov.uk/news/countering-terrorism-an-international-blueprint

[5] George W Bush: Address to a Joint Session of Congress and the American People, 20 September 2001, *White House archives,* https://georgewbush-whitehouse.archives.gov/news/releases/2001/09/20010920-8.html

[6] Dara Lind, 'Everyone's heard of the Patriot Act. Here's what it actually does'. *Vox,* 2 June 2015, https://www.vox.com/2015/6/2/8701499/patriot-act-explain

[7] Barack Obama address to the nation on the death of Osama Bin Laden, 2 May 2011, *White House archives,* https://obamawhitehouse.archives.gov/blog/2011/05/02/osama-bin-laden-dead

[8] BBC News website, 'Why is there a war in Afghanistan. The short, medium and long story', *bbc.co.uk/news*, 2 February 2020, https://www.bbc.co.uk/news/world-asia-49192495

[9] George W Bush: Remarks on the Iraqi threat at the Cincinnati Museum Center, 7 October 2002, *White House archives,* https://georgewbush-whitehouse.archives.gov/news/releases/ 2002/10/20021007-8.html

[10] Peter Bergen, David Sterman and Melissa Slayk-Virk, Terrorism in America 18 years after 9/11', *New America,* 18 September 2019, https://www.newamerica.org/international-security/reports/terrorism-america-18-years-after-911/

[11] Pew Research Center, "As Economic Concerns Recede, Environmental Protection Rises on the Public's Policy Agenda', 13 February 2020, www.people-press.org/2020/ 02/13/as-economic-concerns-recede-environmental-protection-rises-on-the-publics-policy-agenda/

[12] Erin M Kearns et al, 'Why do some Terrorist Attacks receive more media coverage than others', *Justice Quarterly 36:6,* 2019, https://www.tandfonline.com/doi/abs/10.1080/ 07418825.2018.1524507

[13] Jamie Grierson, 'Trump links UK crime rise to 'spread of Islamic terror'' *The Guardian*, 20 October 2017, https://www.theguardian.com/us-news/2017/oct/20/trump-mistakenly-links-uk-rise-with-spread-of-islamic-terror

[14] Erik Wemple, 'Fox News corrects, apologizes for 'no-go zone' remarks', *The Washington Post,* 18 January 2015, https://www.washingtonpost.com/blogs/erik-wemple/wp/2015/01/18/ fox-news-corrects-apologizes-for-no-go-zone-remarks/

[15] Agence France Presse report, 'Al Qaida leader calls for jihad on eve of US embassy moving to Jerusalem', *The Guardian,* 14 May 2018, https://www.theguardian.com/world/ 2018/may/14/al-qaida-leader-jihad-us-embassy-move-jerusalem

[16] Director of US National Intelligence, opening statement to Congress on the Annual Threat Assessment, 29 January 2019, https://www.dni.gov/files/documents/ Newsroom/Testimonies /2019-01-29-ATA-Opening-Statement_Final.pdf

[17] Nicholas Watt, 'UK deploys Tornado jets in Iraq to assist in Sinjar aid drops', *The Guardian,* 12 August 2014, https://www.theguardian.com/world/2014/aug/11/uk-to-deploy-tornado-jets-surveillance-after-iraq-aid-drop-fails

[18] BBC News website, '10 days in Iraq: Aid drops, air-strikes and 200,000 new refugees', 19 August 2014, https://www.bbc.co.uk/news/world-middle-east-28761383

[19] BBC News website, 'MPs support UK air strikes against IS in Iraq', 26 September 2014, https://www.bbc.co.uk/news/uk-politics-29385123

[20] Jessica Lewis McFate and Harleen Gambhir with Evan Sterling, 'ISIS Global Messaging Strategy Fact Sheet', *Institute for the Study of War,* December 2014, http://www.understandingwar.org/sites/default/files/GLOBAL%20ROLLUP%20Update.pdf

[21] James G Meek and Josh Margolin, 'NYC Ax Attacker was Consumed by Desire to Strike US Authority Figures, Police say', *ABC News,* 3 November 2014, https://abcnews.go.com/US/nyc-ax-attacker-consumed-desire-strike-us-authority/story?id=26664787

[22] BBC News website report, 'Islamic State: 'Baghdadi message' issued by jihadists', 13 November 2014, https://www.bbc.co.uk/news/world-middle-east-30041257

[23] Staff writers, 'Details of San Bernardino mass shooting emerge days after shooting', *The San Bernardino Sun,* 3 December 2015, https://www.sbsun.com/2015/12/03/details-of-san-bernardino-mass-shooting-emerge-days-after-shooting/

[24] Richard A Serrano, 'Tashfeen Malik messaged Facebook friends about her support for jihad', *The Los Angeles Times,* 14 December 2015, https://www.latimes.com/local/lanow/la-me-ln-malik-facebook-messages-jihad-20151214-story.html

[25] Ibid Director of US National Intelligence, statement to Congress, January 2019

[26] Andrew Shaver, 'You're more likely to be fatally crushed by furniture than killed by a terrorist', *The Washington Post,* 23 November 2015, https://www.washingtonpost.com/news/monkey-cage/wp/2015/11/23/youre-more-likely-to-be-fatally-crushed-by-furniture-than-killed-by-a-terrorist/

[27] Peter Bergen et al, 'Terrorism in America After 9/11, Part IV: What is the Threat to the United States Today?', *New America online,* accessed 12 May 2020, https://www.newamerica.org/in-depth/terrorism-in-america/what-threat-united-states-today/

[28] Peter Bergen et al, 'Terrorism in America After 9/11, Part II: Who are the Terrorists?', *New America online,* accessed 12 May 2020, https://www.newamerica.org/in-depth/terrorism-in-america/who-are-terrorists/

[29] US Department of Defense, National Defense Strategy 2018: Sharpening the American Military's Competitive Edge, https://dod.defense.gov/Portals/1/Documents/pubs/2018-National-Defense-Strategy-Summary.pdf

[30] Second Amendment to the US Constitution, *National Constitution Center,* https://constitutioncenter.org/interactive-constitution/amendment/amendment-ii

[31] Noah Shusterman, 'What the Second Amendment really meant to the Founders', *The Washington Post,* 22 February 2018, https://www.washingtonpost.com/news/made-by-history/wp/2018/02/22/what-the-second-amendment-really-meant-to-the-founders/

[32] Lucie Béraud-Sudreau, 'Global defence spending: the United States widens the gap', *The International Institute for Strategic Studies – iiss.org,* 14 February 2020, https://www.iiss.org /blogs/military-balance/2020/02/global-defence-spending

[33] Paul J Achter, 'McCarthyism', *Encyclopaedia Britannica,* 27 January 2020, https://www.britannica.com/topic/McCarthyism

[34] United States Senate, Historical Highlights: "Communists in Government service", McCarthy says, 9 February 1950, https://www.senate.gov/artandhistory/history/minute/Communists_In_Government_Service.htm

[35] History.com editors, 'HUAC', *A&E Television Networks*, 29 October 2009, updated 7 June 2019, https://www.history.com/topics/cold-war/huac

[36] Eudie Pak, 'Charlie Chaplin and 6 other Artists who were Blacklisted in Hollywood during the Red Scare', *biography.com,* 15 August 2019, https://www.biography.com/news/artists-blacklisted-hollywood-red-scare

[37] Biography.com editors, J Edgar Hoover biography, *A&E Television Networks*, 2 April 2014, updated 18 December 2019, https://www.biography.com/law-figure/j-edgar-hoover

[38] American Museum of Natural History website, 'McCarthy Era: Einstein the Radical', accessed 14 May 2020, https://www.amnh.org/exhibitions/einstein/global-citizen/mccarthy-era

[39] US Senate Historical Office, 'The Censure Case of Joseph McCarthy of Wisconsin (1954)', *senate.gov,* accessed 14 May 2020, https://www.senate.gov/artandhistory/history/common/censure_cases/133Joseph_McCarthy.htm

[40] John Swift, 'The Soviet-American Arms Race', *History Review, Issue 63 (March 2009),* https://www.historytoday.com/archive/soviet-american-arms-race

[41] Protect and Survive (1980), UK government booklet on what to do in the event of a nuclear attack, *Wilson Center Digital Archive,* https://digitalarchive.wilsoncenter.org/document/ 110193.pdf?v=c77f06e782d33a2ec8bf00d7c597ea10

[42] Ross Davies, 'Was Threads the scariest TV show ever made?', *BBC.com*, 26 September 2019, https://www.bbc.com/culture/article/20190925-was-threads-the-scariest-tv-show-ever-made?referer=https%3A%2F%2Fwww.google.com%2F

[43] Hank Stuever, 'Yes, 'The Day After' really was the profound TV moment 'The Americans' makes it out to be', *The Washington Post,* 12 May 2016, https://www.washingtonpost.com/news/arts-and-entertainment/wp/2016/05/11/yes-the-day-after-really-was-the-profound-tv-moment-the-americans-makes-it-out-to-be/

[44] BBC News website, 'Is there a crisis on the US-Mexico border?', *bbc.co.uk/news,* 11 July 2019, https://www.bbc.co.uk/news/world-us-canada-44319094

[45] Letter from James Madison to Thomas Jefferson, 13 May 1798, Founders Online, National Archives, https://founders.archives.gov/documents/Madison/01-17-02-0088

The Risks

[1] Abraham Lincoln, Address at Young Men's Lyceum of Springfield, Illinois, 27 January 1838, *Abraham Lincoln Online,* http://www.abrahamlincolnonline.org/ lincoln/speeches/lyceum.htm

Chapter Eleven: The Perils of Myth Blindness

[1] Tami Luhby, 'Many millennials are worse off than their parents – a first in American history', *CNN.com,* 11 January 2020, https://edition.cnn.com/2020/01/11/politics/millennials-income-stalled-upward-mobility-us/index.html

[2] Raj Chetty et al, 'The Fading American Dream: Trends in Absolute Income Mobility Since 1940', *Opportunity Insights,* December 2016, https://opportunityinsights.org/paper/the-fading-american-dream/

[3] Kim Parker, Rich Morin and Juliana Menasce Horowitz, 'Looking to the Future, Public Sees an America in Decline on Many Fronts', *Pew Research Center*, 21 March 2019, www.pewsocialtrends.org/2019/03/21/public-sees-an-america-in-decline-on-many-fronts/

[4] US Declaration of Independence, 4 July 1776, *US National Archives,* https://www.archives.gov/founding-docs/declaration-transcript

[5] J Bolt, M Timmer and J van Zanden, 'GDP per capita since 1820' in J van Zanden et al, "How Was Life? Global Well-being since 1820', OECD Publishing, 2014, https://doi.org/10.1787/9789264214262-7-en

[6] Ibid, US Declaration of Independence

The Solutions

[1] Lyndon B Johnson, Inaugural Address, 20 January 1965, *The American Presidency Project, UC Santa Barbara,* https://www.presidency.ucsb.edu/documents/the-presidents-inaugural-address

Chapter Twelve: A Path to American Renewal

[1] Cynthia Burress, 'Research Guides: The United States Constitution', *Dee J Kelly Law Library, Texas A&M University School of Law online*, http://law.tamu.libguides.com/usconstitution

[2] US Census Bureau: Historical Statistics of the US, Colonial Times to 1970, Bicentennial Edition, 1975, https://www.census.gov/history/pdf/histstats-colonial-1970.pdf

[3] US Census Bureau: U.S and World Population Clock, accessed 20 May 2020, https://www.census.gov/popclock/

[4] US Nation Archives website: Constitutional Amendment Process, accessed 20 May 2020, https://www.archives.gov/federal-register/constitution

[5] Adam Liptak, Supreme Court Invalidates Key Part of Voting Rights Act', *The New York Times,* 25 June 2013, https://www.nytimes.com/2013/06/26/us/supreme-court-ruling.html

[6] National Conference of State Legislatures website: Election Administration at State and Local Levels, 3 February 2020, https://www.ncsl.org/research/elections-and-campaigns/election-administration-at-state-and-local-levels.aspx

[7] Patricia Mazzei and Alan Blinder, 'What Happens When Politicians Who Oversee Elections Are Also the Candidates?', *The New York Times,* 14 November 2018, https://www. nytimes.com/2018/11/14/us/florida-georgia-scott-kemp.html

[8] Wikipedia online: Divided Government in the United States, 2 April 2020, accessed 22 May 2020, https://en.wikipedia.org/wiki/Divided_government_in_the_United_States

[9] Jay Shambaugh, Ryan Nunn, Audrey Breitwieser and Patrick Liu, 'The State of Competition and Dynamism: Facts about Concentration, Start Ups, and Related Policies', *The Hamilton Project,* 13 June 2018, https://www.hamiltonproject.org/assets/files/CompetitionFacts_20180611.pdf

[10] Karen Tumulty, 'The Great Society at 50', *The Washington Post',* 17 May 2014, https://www.washingtonpost.com/sf/national/2014/05/17/the-great-society-at-50/?utm_term=.89b4af755e00

[11] The National Commission on Terrorist Attacks upon the United States, Final Report, 22 July 2004, https://govinfo.library.unt.edu/911/report/index.htm

[12] James McBride, 'The State of U.S. Infrastructure', *Council on Foreign Relations,* 12 January 2018, https://www.cfr.org/backgrounder/state-us-infrastructure

[13] Tara Golshan, '4 Winners and 4 Losers from the Republican Tax Bill', *Vox.com,* 22 December 2017, https://www.vox.com/2017/12/20/16790040/gop-tax-bill-winners

[14] Drew Desilver, '5 Facts about Social Security', *Pew Research Center,* 18 August 2015, https://www.pewresearch.org/fact-tank/2015/08/18/5-facts-about-social-security/

[15] US Social Security Administration publication No. 13-11785: Fast Facts & Figures about Social Security 2019, released August 2019, https://www.ssa.gov/policy/docs/chartbooks/fast_facts/2019/fast_facts19.pdf

[16] Doug Criss, 'The one thing that determines how you feel about the police', *CNN.com,* 14 July 2017. https://edition.cnn.com/2017/07/14/health/police-confidence-gallup-polls-trnd/index.html

[17] Karl Evers-Hillstrom, 'Religious groups battle over Johnson Amendment as House Republicans eye last-minute repeal', *Center for Responsive Politics, 19* December 2018, https://www.opensecrets.org/news/2018/12/religious-groups-battle-over-johnson-amendment-repeal/

Epilogue: Can America Save itself and the West?

[1] Winston Churchill, Eulogy to Franklin Delano Roosevelt: The Greatest Champion of Freedom, House of Commons, London, 17 April 1945, *The Churchill Society,* http://www.churchill-society-london.org.uk/DthRovlt.html

[2] Pew Research Center report: 'The Partisan Divide on Political Values Grows Even Wider', October 2017, https://www.people-press.org/2017/10/05/the-partisan-divide-on-political-values-grows-even-wider/

[3] Pew Research Center: 'Partisan Antipathy: More Intense, More Personal', October 2019, https://www.people-press.org/2019/10/10/partisan-antipathy-more-intense-more-personal/

[4] Ibid Pew Research Center report: Partisan Antipathy: More Intense, More Personal

[5] Ibid de Tocqueville, Democracy in America

[6] The Bridge Alliance website: About pages, What we do, accessed 26 May 2020, https://www.bridgealliance.us/our_work

[7] Unite America website: Strategy page, accessed 26 May 2020, https://www.uniteamerica.org/strategy

[8] Braver Angels website: What We Do pages, accessed 26 May 2020, https://braverangels.org/what-we-do/

[9] Living Room Conversations website: About Us pages, accessed 26 May 2020, https://www.livingroomconversations.org/about-us/

[10] Pew Research Center report: 'The Public, the Political System and American Democracy', April 2018, https://www.people-press.org/2018/04/26/the-public-the-political-system-and-american-democracy/

Index

Made in the USA
Las Vegas, NV
18 September 2023

77754581R00177